21世纪高等院校经济管理类规划教材

外贸函电写作

□ 赵丹　李秋芹　徐艳甲　主编

人民邮电出版社
北京

图书在版编目（CIP）数据

外贸函电写作 / 赵丹，李秋芹，徐艳甲主编. -- 北京：人民邮电出版社，2014.7
21世纪高等院校经济管理类规划教材
ISBN 978-7-115-34966-8

Ⅰ. ①外… Ⅱ. ①赵… ②李… ③徐… Ⅲ. ①对外贸易－英语－电报信函－写作－高等学校－教材 Ⅳ. ①H315

中国版本图书馆CIP数据核字(2014)第080331号

内容提要

本书系统地阐述了商务书信写作的基本知识，包括商务书信的构成、格式、写作原则及措辞，并按照外贸业务磋商及执行过程中各个环节的顺序详尽介绍了外贸函电各类信函的写作内容及语言模式，包括确立贸易关系、询价及回复、报盘及还盘、订单、接受与回绝、支付方式、包装、装运、保险、申诉与索赔、代理等方面，每个单元由单元概要、信函示例、词汇注释套语、写作技法、信函模板和练习6个部分组成。

本书不仅适合普通高等院校使用，也可以满足高职高专院校教学的需要，同时可供业界人士参考使用。

◆ 主　　编　赵　丹　李秋芹　徐艳甲
责任编辑　梅　莹
责任印制　张佳莹　杨林杰
◆ 人民邮电出版社出版发行　　北京市丰台区成寿寺路 11 号
邮编　100164　　电子邮件　315@ptpress.com.cn
网址　http://www.ptpress.com.cn
北京隆昌伟业印刷有限公司印刷
◆ 开本：787×1092　1/16
印张：18.75　　2014 年 7 月第 1 版
字数：455 千字　　2014 年 7 月北京第 1 次印刷

定价：39.80 元

读者服务热线：(010)81055256　印装质量热线：(010)81055316
反盗版热线：(010)81055315
广告经营许可证：京崇工商广字第 0021 号

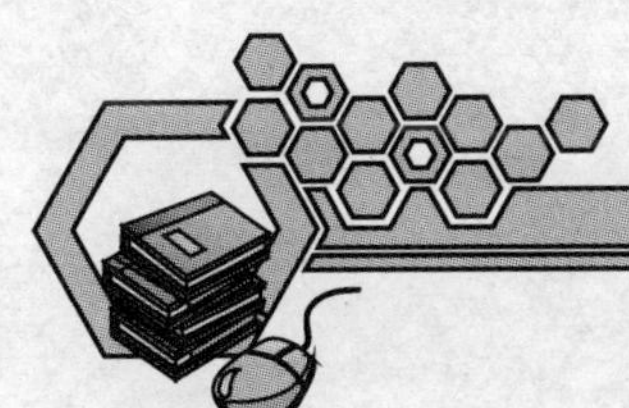

前言

我们所处的 21 世纪是一个高速发展的世纪，是一个催人奋进的时代。以信息技术为核心的新科技革命迅猛发展，经济全球化以及全球性产业结构调整步伐加快，国际竞争更加激烈。随着国内经济与国际经济的进一步融合以及市场经济的不断完善，迫切需要一大批熟悉国际贸易实务、市场营销技巧、熟练掌握商务英语的高级国际贸易人才。

在涉外经济活动中，外贸函电具有联络业务、沟通交流的作用，作为一种常用的英语应用文体，对于国际贸易商进一步开拓国际市场、发展对外贸易有着重要的促进作用，熟练应用外贸函电与客户沟通洽谈是国际贸易人才必备的重要技能之一。

外贸函电写作是国际贸易专业、国际商务专业和商务英语专业的一门主干专业课程。作者具备多年外贸教学经验和国际商务实践，在此基础上编写了这本突出实用性的《外贸函电写作》。本书系统地阐述了商务书信写作的基本知识，包括商务书信的构成、格式、写作原则及措辞，并按照外贸业务磋商及执行过程中各个环节的顺序详尽介绍了外贸函电各类信函的写作内容及语言模式，包括确立贸易关系、询价及回复、报盘及还盘、订单、接受和回绝、支付方式、包装、装运、保险、申诉与索赔、代理等方面，每个单元由单元概要、信函示例、词汇注释套语、写作技法、信函模板和练习 6 个部分组成。本书从商务英语的角度出发，由浅入深、由简入繁、循序渐近，共 13 章。

本书特点如下：

（1）突出专业技能，是一本更为实用的工具书。分单元逐一介绍外贸业务各环节所涉及的信函写作要领和写作技巧，并采取范文举例、案例分析和写作实践相结合的方式进行系统讲解，形式新颖、内容丰富生动、条理清晰。

（2）中英文对照，便于读者更好地理解和掌握外贸信函的写作特点；内容丰富，包括外贸业务往来信函的全过程，并有英文合同的写作原理、技巧及合同范本。

（3）大量的业务信息函范本和样信评述，帮助读者写出地道的外贸业务信函；配套习题丰富多样。

本书不仅适合普通高等院校，也适合高职高专院校教学的需要，推荐学时为 48~64 学时。本书可供业界人士参考使用，任何从事外贸业务的工作者都可以根据个人工作需要有针对性地选定相关信函类别，按照信函范文模式，更换具体内容，以最快捷有效的方式写出高质量的外贸业务信函。

本书主要由渤海大学赵丹、徐艳甲及河南工业贸易职业学院李秋芹等一线教师负责构思、编写、审阅、定稿等工作。其中，第 1 章由徐艳甲编写，第 2 章由郜珂编写，第 3 章和第 8 章由李秋芹编写，第 4 章和第 12 章由张喆编写，第 5 章由赵丹编写，第 6 章由贾辉编写，第 7 章由毕利编写，第 9 章由房圣贤编写，第 10 章由贾辉、郜珂编写，第 11 章由齐瑾编写，第 13 章由杨晶编写，全书由赵丹统稿。此外，我们还得到其他多方面人员的热心支持，对此表示由衷的感谢。在本书的编写过程中我们还参考了一些国内外资料，在此谨向有关作者致以衷心的感谢。

由于外贸行业发展变化较快，再加上编者水平有限，书中难免有不足之处，恳请广大读者批评指正。

编者

2014 年 1 月

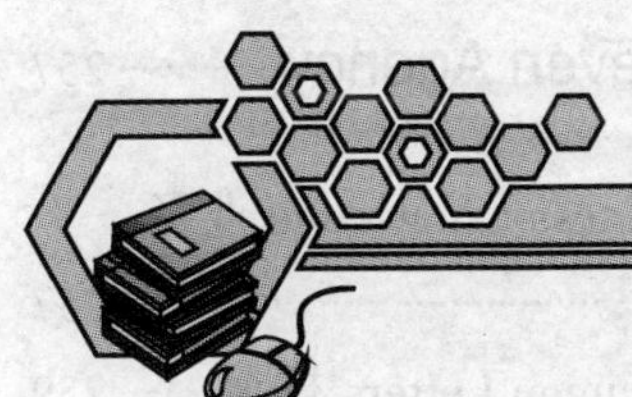

目录

Chapter 1

General Introduction

Section 1 Business Knowledge 业务知识

1.1 Structure and Layout of a Business Letter

1. Traditional letters

这里我们通过一封信函介绍英文商务信函的结构和格式要求。

① China National Cereals, Oils and Foodstuffs Imp & Exp Corp.

8 Jianguomen Nei Dajie

Beijing 10005, China

Telephone: 86-10-6526-8888

Fax: 86-10-6527-6028

E-mail: carl@cofco.com.cn

② Our Ref.

Your Ref.

Date: 15th November, 20××

③ Messrs H. Ronald & Co.

556 Eastcheap

London, E.C. 3, England

④ Attention: Import Dept.

⑤ Dear Sirs,

⑥ Aquatic Products

⑦ We thank you for your enquiry of 5 November.

In compliance with your request, we are sending you herewith a copy of our illustrated catalogue and a quotation sheet for your reference.

All prices are subject to our confirmation for our aquatic products have been selling well this season. Therefore, we would suggest that you advise us by a fax in case of interest.

We await your early favorable reply.

⑧ Yours truly,

⑨ China National Cereals, Oils and Foodstuffs Imp & Exp Corp.

Sig. ________________

(Manager)

⑩ QS/AN

⑪ Enclosures

⑫ cc our Shanghai Branch Office

⑬ P.S. We require payment by L/C for a total value not exceeding USD50,000.

（1）Heading 信头

信头就是指书信中发信人的地址和发信的日期等。

通常情况下，公司都会专门印制带有信头的信笺纸，包括发信人的姓名、地址、电话、传真等。当我们撰写传统信件时，可以直接使用这种信笺纸。

中英文有关公司、商号的名称、地址写法有所不同。中文：名称在上，地址在下，地址先大后小。英语：名称在上，地址在下，地址先小后大。

例如：Air Environmental Mechanical

Equipment Limited

2076 West Main Street

Devon, EX14 0RA

U.K

（2） Reference number and date 编号和日期

这部分内容是为了方便今后查询信件用的。

对于日期，英国人和美国人有不同的表达习惯。

美式：在信头和收信人名称地址之间

英式：通常在收信人名称地址之下

写法：均可以齐头，也可以靠右

美式：月—日—年

英式：日—月—年

- “月份”最好用文字，如：

① 2nd May, 20××

② 2 May, 20××

③ 2 May 20×× (Comma can be omitted)

④ September 21st, 20××

⑤ September 21, 20××

- 避免月份用数字，如：

11/12/2010

（3）Inside address 封内地址

这里指收信人的姓名和地址，一般写在信笺的左上方。收信人名称地址的格式和信头的格式相同，但必须把收信人的姓名一并写出。另外，如果不是完全公事化的书信往来，或者已经从公事的关系渐渐发展成为带有私人性质的友好信件往来，由于称呼这一栏的内容已经说明了收信人的身份，所以可以不必填写封内地址。

（4）Attention 经办人

经办人就是指收信方的具体收信人。其位置在收信人名称地址之下；齐头式靠左，缩格式居中；要加下画线。

该部分内容表示的是承办本信件的具体个人或部门，表示方法如下：

Attention: Mr. H. A. Donnan, Export Manager

Attention of Mr. Cave

To the attention of Mr. Liu Ming

（5）Salutation 称呼

指对收信人的一种称呼。较常使用的有 Dear Sirs, Dear Madam, Dear Mr. ××, Gentlemen，称呼后面的标点，一般使用逗号。称呼里的第一个字母要大写。

（6）Subject/caption 事由

事由也就是我们通常说的主题，可以直接写明信件的重点，让人不必读全信才了解到信的内容。所以事由要写得简明扼要，其位置在称呼和正文之间；齐头式靠左，缩格式居中；要加下画线。

事由表示方法有：

Re: Your Order No.463 for 1,000 Wide-screen TV Sets

SHEEP WOOL

（7）Contents of letter 信文

这是商务信函的主体，由开头语和正文组成。

开头语（opening sentence）没有统一的格式，但习惯上先用客套的语句把收到对方来信的日期、主题及简单内容加以综合叙述，使对方一目了然这是答复哪一封来信的。如果是第一次通信，也可以利用开头语做必要的自我介绍，并表明目的要求。开头语一般与正文分开，自成一节，要求简单明了。

正文（body）是商务书信的核心，阐述要沟通并将要办理的具体业务。一封信件的优劣，完全要看正文的好或坏。我们会在后面继续讨论写作商务信函的一些技巧和规则。

（8）Closing sentence 结尾语

结尾语一般用来总结文本所谈的事项，提示对收信人的要求，如“希望来信来函订货”，“答

复询问”等，另外也附加一些略带客套的语气。正文结束后，另起一段写结尾语。

（9）Complimentary closing and signature 结束语与签名

结束语即落款，是结束信函时的一种客套，也称结尾敬语，应该与前面的称呼相呼应。例如：“Sincerely,”、“Best Regards,”或“Yours Truly,”。结束语写在结尾语下隔一行，只有第一个字母大写，后面加逗号。

称呼与结尾敬语的对应关系

Salutation	Close	Occasion
Dear Sirs Dear Sir or Madam(Mmes)	Yours faithfully Faithfully yours	Standard and formal
Gentlemen Ladies/Gentlemen	Yours (very) truly Very truly yours	By American
Dear Mr. Malone	Yours sincerely/sincerely Best wishes(UK) Best regards/Regards(US)	Less formal and between persons known to each other

在结束语的下面，签上写信人的名字。如果是重要的信件，写信人最好亲笔签名，因为用印章的话，说明该信件并非本人亲自过目，只是通函而已，不为人重视。签名的下面，最好写上发信人的职位。

（10）Identification 主办人

这项内容主要是为了明确发信方信函责任的，与收信方没有关系。通常做法是把信件的主稿人和速记员的名字各部分首个字母打印出来，并用分号或冒号隔开。例如，HAP/DGS PAH:LP。

（11）Enclosure 附件

如果有附件随信发出，应在左下角注明 Encl. 或 Enc.。

例如：

Encls: 2 Invoices

Enc.: 1 B/Lading

（12）Carbon copy 抄送

如果函件要抄送其他有关单位，同时使对方也知道已抄送其他单位，可以在附件之下，靠左侧对齐表达抄送。

例如：

明抄：cc Marketing Department

暗抄：bcc Mr. Simpson

（13）Postscripts 再启/另启

信写完后，如果想起还有要紧的话需要补充，可以在信末加 P.S.引出补叙的内容，然后由发信人签署本人简笔签名（姓名每部分头一个字母，如 Park Davis，可以签成 P.D.）。另启表明写信人思考不够周密，一般应尽量避免出现这部分内容。

2. E-mail

众所周知，电子邮件（E-mail）是如今我们做电子商务使用最普遍的一种联系手段。电子邮件使用方便，信息传递迅速高效，且非常节省成本。但是电子邮件的撰写并不是一件很容易的事情。要知道，当一封电子邮件发送出去后，只要收信人在线，他可以几分钟内就收到。所以，在发送前，必须要检查一下所写的内容是否正确合适，因为一旦点击了发送键后，就再也无法将其收回了。

通常我们理解电子邮件的撰写风格可以比传统的信件、传真等稍随便一点。但是在这里还是要建议大家，即便是写电子邮件，由于是谈论公事，所以还需采用正式严肃的风格。尤其是第一次跟收信人联系，正式的商务信函能留给对方非常专业的印象。

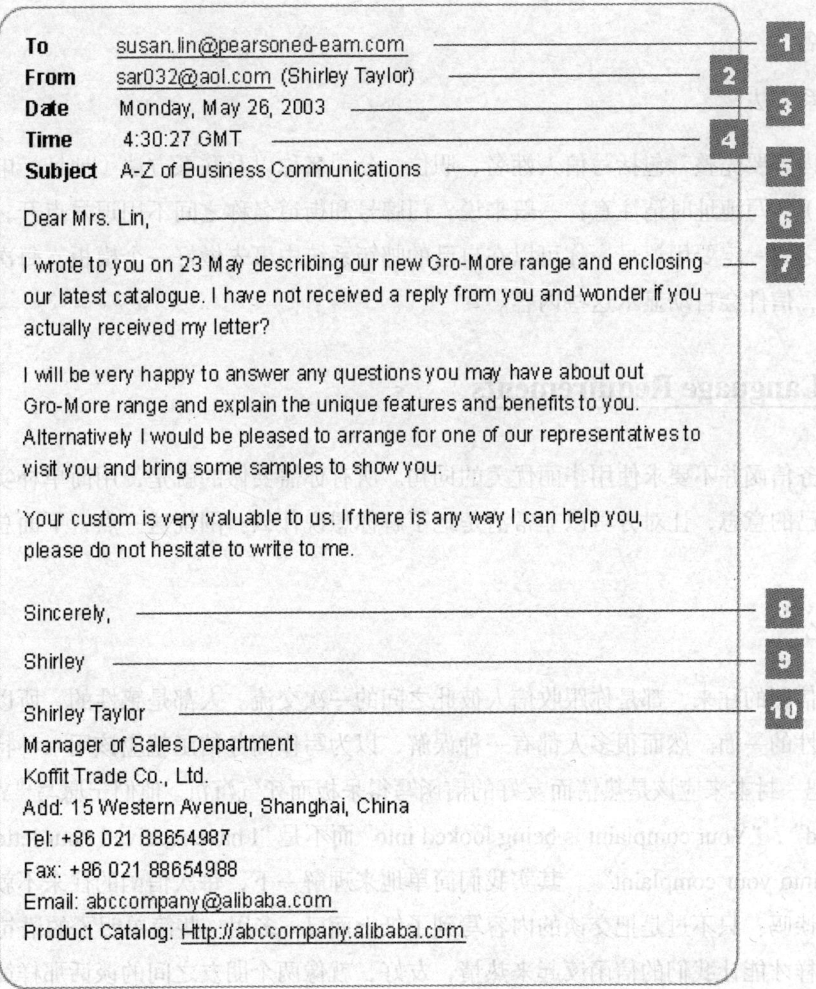

To susan.lin@pearsoned-eam.com 1
From sar032@aol.com (Shirley Taylor) 2
Date Monday, May 26, 2003 3
Time 4:30:27 GMT 4
Subject A-Z of Business Communications 5

Dear Mrs. Lin, 6

I wrote to you on 23 May describing our new Gro-More range and enclosing our latest catalogue. I have not received a reply from you and wonder if you actually received my letter? 7

I will be very happy to answer any questions you may have about out Gro-More range and explain the unique features and benefits to you. Alternatively I would be pleased to arrange for one of our representatives to visit you and bring some samples to show you.

Your custom is very valuable to us. If there is any way I can help you, please do not hesitate to write to me.

Sincerely, 8

Shirley 9

Shirley Taylor 10
Manager of Sales Department
Koffit Trade Co., Ltd.
Add: 15 Western Avenue, Shanghai, China
Tel: +86 021 88654987
Fax: +86 021 88654988
Email: abccompany@alibaba.com
Product Catalog: Http://abccompany.alibaba.com

1 收信人的邮箱地址

2 发信人的邮箱地址

3 写信日期

写日期时，请注意以下几点：

a. 年份要写完整，不能用03代替2003；

b. 月份要写英文名称，不能用数字来代替，如31/3/03 不能在正式的信件中出现。但是可以用英文缩写，如用Aug.代替August。

4 时间

5 主题

6 称呼

7 正文

8 结束语

9 签名

10 联系方法

这部分内容要完整，包括写信人姓名、职位、公司名称以及联系方法（地址、电话、传真、邮箱、网址）。写地址时请注意：一般来说，门牌号和街道名称之间不用逗号点开，但城市名称和国家名称之间一定要用逗号。你可以在自己的邮箱系统中事先做好一个模板。每次写信只要选择这个模板，信件会自动显示这些内容。

1.2 Language Requirements

写作商务信函并不要求使用华丽优美的词句。所有你需要做的就是，用简单朴实的语言，准确地表达自己的意思，让对方可以非常清楚地了解你想说什么。围绕这一点，下面总结了几方面的内容。

口语化

每一封信函的往来，都是你跟收信人彼此之间的一次交流。人都是感性的，所以你需要在信函里体现感性的一面。然而很多人都有一种误解，以为写作商务信函就应该用一种特殊的“生意腔”，于是把一封本来应该是热情而友好的信函写得呆板而死气沉沉。他们宁愿写“Your letter has been received”，“Your complaint is being looked into”而不是“I have received your letter”或者“We are looking into your complaint”。其实我们简单地来理解一下，每次信函的往来不就是跟对方进行了一次交谈吗？只不过是把交谈的内容写到了纸上而已。多用一些简单明了的语句，用我/我们做主语，这样才能让我们的信函读起来热情，友好，就像两个朋友之间的谈话那样简单、自然、人性化。

想象一下，如果由于无法准时交货而在电话上跟合作伙伴表示歉意时，你会怎么说？我想你会说“I am sorry we cannot deliver the goods today”。既然在电话中你会这样说，为什么在信件中要改成“It is regretted that goods cannot be delivered today”？放弃这种所谓的“生意腔”吧，让你的信也像谈话那样简单、自然、人性化。

语气语调

由于你写的信函都有其目的性，所以信函里所采用的语气、语调也应该符合该目的。在写之前先不妨仔细考虑一下，写这封信函是想达到一个什么样的目的？希望对收信人产生一种怎样的影响呢？是歉意的、劝说性的？还是坚决的、要求性的。这完全可以通过信函中的语气语调来表现。

真诚

不管是生活中的交往还是生意上的合作，真诚是最重要也是最基础的，所以你的信函也必须能够充分体现你的真诚。不管说什么，都要带着诚意去说。把写好的信函拿起来读一遍，确保如果此时对方正在电话中与你通话，他一定能够感受到你的自然和真诚。

直接

跟你一样，你的合作伙伴们每天都要阅读大量信函文件。所以，信函一定要写得简明扼要，短小精悍，切中要点。如果不符合主题或者对信函的目的不能产生利益的内容，请毫不留情地舍弃它们。因为这些内容不仅不能使交流通畅，反而会混淆视听，非但不能让读者感兴趣，反而会让他们产生反感。

礼貌

我们这里所说的礼貌，并不是简单用一些礼貌用语如 your kind inquiry、your esteemed order 等就可以的。而是要体现一种为他人考虑，多体谅对方心情和处境的态度。如果本着这样的态度去跟别人交流，那么就算你这次拒绝了对方的要求，也不会因此失去这个朋友，不会影响今后合作的机会。

特别要注意，当双方观点不统一时，我们首先要理解并尊重对方的观点。如果对方的建议不合理或者对你的指责不公平时，请表现一下你的高姿态，可以据理力争，说明你的观点，但注意要讲究礼节礼貌，避免用冒犯性的语言。

还要提醒一点，中国人有句话叫做“过犹不及”。任何事情，一旦过了头，效果反而不好。礼貌过了头，可能会变成阿谀奉承；真诚过了头，也会变成天真幼稚。所以最关键的还是要把握好“度”，才能达到预期的效果。

简洁

就像前面提到的，要用简洁朴实的语言来撰写信函，让你的信函读起来简单，清楚，容易理解。用常见的单词，避免生僻或者拼写复杂的单词。一个单词可以表达，就不要用词组。多用短句，因为短句更容易理解。少用“and”、“but”、“however”、“consequently”这些让句子变得冗长的连词。在同一封信函里，不要使用多个相同含义的单词。例如，前面写了“goods have been sent”，那后面再提到这件事时就不要再用其他单词如“forward”、“dispatch”等。因为这样写会误导读者无谓地去考虑这些词之间是否另有含义。

精确

当涉及数据或者具体的信息时，如时间、地点、价格、货号等，尽可能做到精确。这样会使交流的内容更加清楚，更有助于加快事务的进程。

针对性

请在邮件中写上对方公司的名称，或者在信头直接称呼收件人的名字。这样会让对方知道这封邮件是专门发给他的，而不是那种群发的通函，从而表示对此的重视。当然，如果无法确定收信人的名字，那就在称呼一栏里写"Dear Sirs"或"Dear Sir or Madam"。

语言朴实

前面我们说过，商务信函不需要用华丽的词句。根据西方的语言习惯，他们更愿意使用简练而朴实的语言。所以当我们跟西方人进行商务沟通时，也要尽量避免华丽复杂的词句。比如"We look forward to a bright and glorious future of cooperation"，就不如直接写成"We hope to have the opportunity to work together with you in the future."，这样才更加符合西方人的语言习惯。

回复迅速及时

给买家的回复，千万要迅速及时。因为买家通常只看最先收到的几封回复，从中去选择合适的供应商。如果你的回复不够及时，就可能因为抢不到先机而失去商机。

标题

这一点是特别针对写电子邮件的。也许很多人都没有意识到，事实上，电子邮件的标题是很重要的一个部分，你的邮件给对方的第一个印象就是通过标题来完成的。如果标题没有内容，看起来像群发的垃圾邮件的话，很多买家就会直接删除。如这样的标题"How are you?"，"Can we work together?"，建议改成"Proposal: Bright Ideas Imports—Zhejiang Textile's Partnership Opportunity"或者"Introduction: Our Product Offerings for Bright Ideas Imports."这样一来，邮件会显得更加专业。

校对

写完之后，一定要检查。最基本的是要确保拼写和语法正确，然后检查一下你所提供的事实，数据等是否有错。这是因为，即使在信函里有一个极小的失误，也可能会破坏你在沟通方面的可信度，并使人对你表达的其他信息投下怀疑的阴影。

1.3 Envelop Addressing

英文书信的信封写法要求写信人在上，收信人在下。根据收信人名称地址的写法分两种格式：

- 缩格式：收信人名称地址逐行右缩

MESSRS WILLIAM & SONS
76 Lancaster House
Manchester
England

Stamp

Mr Wang Qi-ming
CHINA NATIONAL TRANSPORT Co
121 Nanjing Road
Shanghai, China

Registered

- 齐头式：收信人名称地址左端对齐

CHINA NATIONAL CEARALS, OILS AND
FOODSTUFFS IMP. & EXP. CORP.
13th Floor，Jingxin Bldg, 2 A Dong san Huan BeiLu
Beijing, People's Republic of China

Stamp

EL MAR PACKING COMPANY
12 MAIN STREET, FRESNO
CALIFORNIA, USA

Confidential
Par Avion

信封左下角标注说明了信函的性质和邮寄方式，常用的表达如下。

邮寄方式

- Via Air Mail (By Airmail, or Par Avion) 航空信
- Registered 挂号
- Parcel Post 邮包
- Express 快递
- Samples Post 样品
- Private 私人信
- Personal 个人信
- Confidential 机密信
- Urgent 紧急信

当信件不是通过邮寄，而是托某人转交，即捎交，可在信封上做如下说明。

Mr. Charles Wood
Kindness of Mr. J. W. Smith

这表示信件由 Mr. J. W. Smith 捎交给 Mr. Charles Wood。托人转交信件还可以用 By Politeness of, Through the Courtesy of, Per/By Kindness of, Forwarded by, Per/By Favor of, Favored by, 在其后加上带信人的姓名即可。

如果信件通过邮局寄给第三者转交给收信人，则要在收信人姓名下面写清转交人姓名，并在前面加 c/o（care of 由……转交），例如：

Mr. Park Davis
c/o Mr. Harold Wood
316 Doswell Avenue
Fort Atkinson, Wisconsin
The United States of America

在学习了这么多理论知识后，我们来看一个例子。

Dear Sirs,

Your message has been received. Thank you.

It is difficult to understand your inquiry of 56mm×80mm waterproof speaker which can handle 102db, because through our vast experience, it is almost impossible in technology. Can you supply us with your sample? If so, it would be big help to this project.

Hope we could work together.

Yours faithfully,

很显然，这封邮件有很多缺点，首先语句呆板，严重的“生意腔”使邮件毫无生气。句子长而乱，含义模糊。没有提供足够的资料来支持自己的论点。更糟糕的是，措辞冒昧，极不礼貌。针对这些不足，我们再来看一下另一个版本。

Dear Mr. Jones,

Thank you for your inquiry dated April 9.

Regarding the product you are looking for, currently our factory doesn't have the exact specification as you mentioned. We would appreciate it if you could supply us more details about the product you need, such as usage, product structure, material, working condition and so on. That will help us to see if we are able to meet your specifications.

Please take a moment to review some similar products in the enclosed catalog. They are all of high quality and have been exported to many countries worldwide.

Thanks again and we are looking forward to establishing a business relationship with your company in the near future.

Any of your early comments will be highly appreciated.

Best regards,

Chen Rong
Director, International Marketing
Zhejiang Golden Textiles

现在觉得好多了吧！即使这次不能满足对方的需求，只要我们处理得当，还是可以保留住潜在合作的机会。有时候，信函的作用就是这么重要。

Section 2 Specimen Letters 样函

1.4 Block Style 平头式/齐头式

这种格式的特点是，打印上去的每一行字，包括日期、封内地址、事由和结尾落款，都是从左边的空白边缘对齐。

（1）

Johnson & Johnson
1 J&J Plaza New Brunswick,
NJ 089333 U.S.A.
Tel: 732-524-0400
Fax: 732-525-0622
E-mail: carrie@jnj.com

除信头外全部左对齐

Date: 22nd July, 20--

Soft Health Care Product Corp.
Room 2301 Yili BLD,
35 Nanjing Road,
Shanghai, China

Attention: Mr. Wang , Import Dept.

Dear Sir,

Re: SHAMPOO

We've received your letter of July 10th enquiring about our JOHNSON'S® Baby Shampoo With Natural Lavender, but unfortunately, the stock of this product is running low due to the heavy demand. But we will inform you as soon as the new supplies come up.

We sell a wide variety of Baby's Shampoo. All of them are made of the NO MORE TEARS formula. For your reference, we enclose an illustrated catalogue of our shampoos and we hope you will find it interesting.

We hope that we can close business to our mutual advantage in the future.

Yours faithfully,

Johnson & Johnson
Doris Fergoson
Doris Fergoson
(Manager)

（2）

GUANGZHOU ELECTRONICS PRODUCTS

IMPORT & EXPORT CORPORATION

13 Beijing Road, Guangzhou

People's Republic of China

Tel: 3456782

Fax: 3456782

June 23, 2009

Ocean Electronics Product Import Corp

131 Califford Street

LONDON W 1,

England

Dear sirs,

Re: Chinese Electronics Products

We have obtained your name and address from the London Chamber of Commerce, who has told us that you wish to import electronic goods manufactured in China.

We manufacture electronic appliance of the kind illustrated in enclosed catalogue, which we hope will be of interest to you. Also enclosed for your reference, is our latest pricelist.

Should you be interested in any of our products, please let us know and we will provide you with a quotation. In the meantime, should you require any further information about either our products or our corporation, please do not hesitate to let us know.

We look forward to hearing from you soon, and to the possibility of doing business with you in the future.

Yours faithfully,

(signature)

Liu Senyu

Sales Manager

1.5 Indented Style 缩进式/缩格式

这种格式的特点是，封内地址和其他需要分行的地方，后一行比前一行缩进二格或三格，当然也可以居左侧对齐。但信的正文，每一段的开始一行都缩进若干格（一般与称呼末一字母取齐）。

（1）

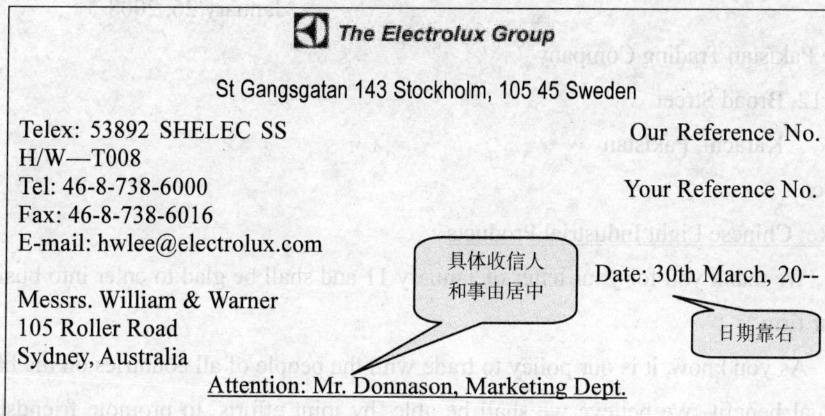

The Electrolux Group

St Gangsgatan 143 Stockholm, 105 45 Sweden

Telex: 53892 SHELEC SS
H/W—T008
Tel: 46-8-738-6000
Fax: 46-8-738-6016
E-mail: hwlee@electrolux.com

Our Reference No.

Your Reference No.

Date: 30th March, 20--

Messrs. William & Warner
105 Roller Road
Sydney, Australia

Attention: Mr. Donnason, Marketing Dept.

Dear Sir,

Re: Shipping Advice of Freezers

With reference to your order No. F256 of February 5 for 1,000 sets of Freezers, we're pleased to inform you that the goods have been loaded on board the s/s "Peace", which is sailing for your port on April 1st.

We've sent a telex to the above effect this morning. Please insure the goods as contracted and make preparation for taking the delivery. We are now making out the necessary documents for negotiation.

We assure you that our goods will be found satisfactory upon arrival at your port. We also hope that we can close more business with you in the future.

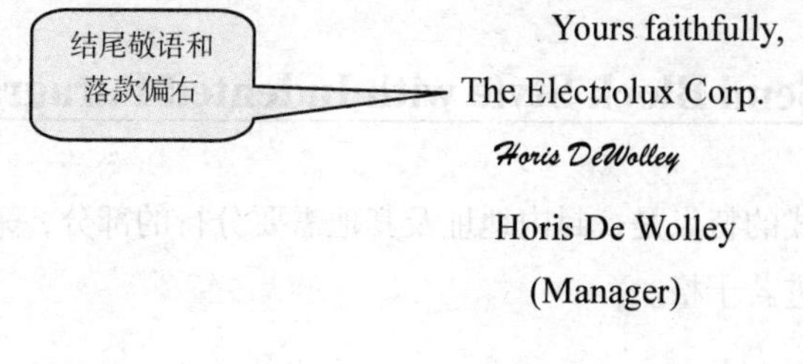

Yours faithfully,

The Electrolux Corp.

Horis DeWolley

Horis De Wolley

(Manager)

（2）

China National Light Industrial Products
Import & Export Corporation
83 Tian An Men Street
Beijing, China
Our Ref. No…
Your Ref. No…
January 26, 2008

The Pakistan Trading Company
12, Broad Street
Karachi, Pakistan

Gentlemen,

Re: Chinese Light Industrial Products

We thank you for your letter of January 11 and shall be glad to enter into business relations with your firm.

As you know, it is our policy to trade with the people of all countries on the bais of equality and mutual benefit. We believe we shall be able, by joint efforts, to promote friendship as well as business.

We are sending you 5 pamphlets and a pricelist covering part of our exports.

Please advise what articles you are interested in at present.

Your early reply will be highly appreciated

Yours faithfully,

CHINA NATIONAL LIGHT INDUSTRIAL
PRODUCTS IMPORT & EXPORT CORP.

(Signed)

Encl. as stated

1.6 Semi Block Style with Indented Paragraphs 混合式

这种格式的特点是，封内地址及其他需要分行的部分，采用平头式。在正文里，每一段的开始行向里缩进若干格。

（1）

M. D. Ewart Co., Ltd.
35 Tower Street
Toronto 4, Canada

August 23, 2010

Our Ref. No. SWF/119

Your Ref. No. 306/0038

China National Metals & Minerals

Import & Export Corporation

P.O. Box No.67

Beijing

People's Republic of China

Dear Sirs,

Re: Heating Supplies

We are wholesale distributors of plumbing and heating supllies and are interested in the products you show in the China Foreign Trade No. 2 of 2010.

We would like to here from you with reference to importing merchandise from China. If we can work together to our mutual benefit, arrangements can be made for one of our representatives to make the trip to China and contact your office in person.

We are herewith enclosing our latest catalogue showing the items we carry at the present time.

Please let us know whether you can manufacture items as per Canadian patterns.

Kindly send us your complete catalogue and pricelist quoting the best discount for quantity buying.

Thanking you for your kind attention to the matter and trusting to hear from you in the near future.

Yours truly,

(signature)

H. Smith

Manager

M. D. Eware & Co., Ltd.

Encl. as stated

(2)

GUANGZHOU ELECTRONICS PRODUCTS

IMPORT & EXPORT CORPORATION

13 Beijing Road, Guangzhou

People's Republic of China

Tel: 3456782

Fax: 3456782

June 27, 2009

Your Ref: TBL/xm

Our Ref: GED 9558

MR. JB. Lewis,

Superlus Electronics Ltd.

33 Bedford Square

UK

Dear Mr. Lewis,

Your letter of May 22 enquiring about the possibility of importing Chinese-made electronics goods into the United Kingdom, has been passed on to us by the Ministry of Commerce in Beijing.

We are a state-owned enterprise, and keen to expand our our foreign trade. As yet, we have no business contacts in the United Kingdom, and would be pleased to consider any business proposals you may have. We enclosed our latest illustrated catalogue together with our latest pricelists and terms and conditions of sales for your information, and shall be pleased to deal with any specific enquiries you may have concerning any of our products.

Should you require any further details about any of the above-mentioned points, please do not hesitate to contact us.

We look forward to hearing from you in the near future.

Yours sincerely,

(signature)

Wang Qian

Export Manager

Encls. As stated

1.7 Modified Block Style 改良齐头式

这种格式的信函，除日期、编号、结尾落款和签名部分外，其他部分每行开头都与左边空白边缘对齐。

(1)

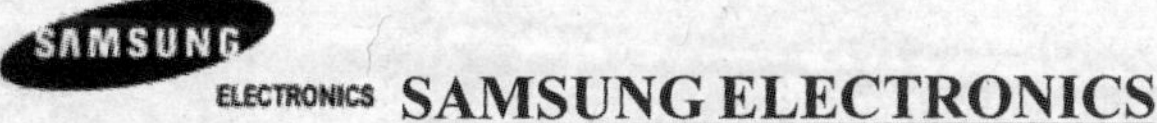

SAMSUNG ELECTRONICS

310 Taepyung-ro 2-ga, Chung-gu
Seoul, 100-102, Korea

Tel: 82-2-3706-1114
E-mail: qsl@samsungcorp.com

Our Reference No. ODL-11
Your Reference No.
Date: 23rd December, 20--

编号与日期偏右

Shandong Science & Technology Co. Ltd.
21/F Bright Plaza
138 Jinni Road, Jinan
Shandong, China

Attention: Mr. Zhou Jun, Import Dept.

Dear Sir,

Re: Our Offer for PDA Type III-H

Thank you for your interest in our latest Personal Digital Assistant Type III-H.

As requested, we offer you 500 sets of PDA at USD140 per set FOB Inchon for shipment in February, 20--. We require payment by L/C.

Because there is an increasing demand for this product, our price is non-negotiable. We look forward to your reply.

Yours truly,

落款与签名偏右

Samsung Electronics
Lavis Kim
Lavis Kim
(Manager)

(2)

Jameson & sons Ltd.
34 Madison Square
Melborne B. C. 3, Australia

Our Ref: …
Your Ref: …
20 January, 2008

China National Machinery Import & Export Corporation
P. O. Box 46
Beijing

People's Republic of China

Gentlemen,

Re: Compressors

We than you for your letter of 12th February acknowledging receipt of catalogues dealing with compressors manufactured by Messrs Peter Brotherhood Limited.

In accordance with the request containedin the last sentence of your letter, we are having the pleasure of sending to you under separate cover three copies of catalogue dealing with the compressors produced by Messrs Fullerton, Hodgart& Barday Limited.

We trust these will be of interest to you. Further compressor catalogues will be forwarded to you as soon as possible.

Yours faithfully,

(Signature)

S. F. Lover

Managing Director

JAMESON & SONS LTD.

Section 3 Supplements 知识补充

Useful Sentences

Opening Sentences and Closing Sentences

1．特此奉告。

a. We are pleased to inform you that…

b. We have pleasure in informing you that…

c. We have the pleasure of apprising you of …

d. We take the liberty of announcing to you that…

e. Please allow us to call your attention to…

2．专此奉告。

a. The purpose of this letter is to inform you that (of)…

b. The object of the letter is to tell you that (of)…

3．惠请告知。

a. Please inform me that (of)…

b. I will thank you for your informing me that (of)…

c. I should be glad if you would inform me that (of)…

4．兹确认我公司某月某日函。

a. We conform our letter of the …of this month…

b. We conform our last letter of the 10th June…

c. In conforming our telegram of this morning…

5．敬悉你公司某月某日来函。

a. We have pleasure in acknowledging receipt of your esteemed favour of the 3rd May…

b. We are in receipt of your letter of the 7th July…

c. We have duly received your favour of the 5th March…

d. We thank you for your letter of the 5th May…

6．敬复你公司某月某日函。

a. In reply to your letter of the 5th of May, I have to inform you that (of)…

b. We are in receipt of yours of the 15th May, in reply to which we are pleased to state that…

c. Replying to yours of the 8th of February regarding…, I would say that…

d. In reply, we would like to say…

7．本公司深感遗憾，必须奉告……

a. We regret to inform you that (of)…

b. We very much regret to announce you that…

c. It is most regrettable that we have to inform you (of)…

d. We are regretful that we have to inform you that (of)…

8．本公司深感遗憾，得悉……

a. We are very sorry to hear (know) that …

b. We very much regret to hear that…

c. We regret that we have been informed that (of)…

9．谢你公司某年某月的函询。

We thank you for your inquiry of the 10th May…

10．随函附上……，请查收……

a. Enclosed please find …

b. We enclose herewith…

c. We have pleasure in enclosing herewith…

d. We attached (hereto)…

11．遵照贵公司某月某日来函指示……

a. In accordance with the instructions given (contained) in your favor of the 10th May…

b. According to the instructions given in your letter under date of the 20th of last month…

c. In conformity with (to) your instructions of the 10th this month…

d. To conform to your instructions of the 10th this month…

e. In compliance with your instructions of the 10th this month…

f. To comply with your instructions of the 10th this month…

12．关于详情，将于下次奉告。

a. I will write you particulars in my next.

b. I will inform you more fully in my next.

c. I will inform you the details in my next.

13．盼你公司及早回复。

a. We hope to receive your favour at an early date.

b. We trust you will favour us with a prompt reply.

c. Your prompt reply would be greatly appreciated.

d. We look forward to your early reply.

e. We are looking forward to receiving your early reply.

14．我们将随时为你服务。

a. We assure you of our best services at all times.

b. We shall spare no efforts in endeavouring to be of service to you.

15．若有机会我公司也愿作类似的服务。

a. We shall be happy to have an opportunity of reciprocating to you on a similar occasion.

b. We wish to reciprocate the goodwill.

Exercises

Ⅰ. Arrange the following in proper form as they should be set out a letter.

1) Sender's name:China National Light Industrial Products Import & Export Corporation. Shanghai Branch

2) Sender's address: 128 Huchiu Road, Shanghai, China

3) Sender's cable address: INDUSTRY SHANGHAI

4) Sender's telex address: 33054 INDUS CN

5) Date: March 23, 20.

6) Receiver's name: H. G. Wilkinson Company, Limited

7) Receiver's address:245 Lombart Street, Lagos, Nigeria

8) Salutation used: Dear Sirs,

9) Subject-matter: Sewing Machines

10) The Message:

We thank you for your letter of May16 enquiring for the captioned goods.

The enclosed booklet contains details of all our Sewing Machines and will enable you to make a suitable selection.

11) Complimentary close: Yours faithfully,

Ⅱ. Please write a letter according to the following particulars.

你是上海轻工产品（light industry products）公司的经理王军。你的厂址是上海解放路 13 号，电话号码是 43725569。你收到太平洋贸易公司（Pacific Trading Inc.）的询函，其地址是美国纽约

百老汇街 83 号，邮编是 10407。

你的任务：

（1）设计你公司的信头；

（2）按照正式格式用英文写出对方地址；

（3）用英文写出下面的信文：感谢贵方对我公司纺织品的兴趣。按照您的要求，我们已寄出带有插图说明的目录和最新价格表各一份。期待早日得到您的回音。

注：要为此信加上日期和签名，说明有附件，格式用平头式。

Chapter 2

Establishing Business Relations

Section 1 Business Knowledge 业务知识

在国际商务活动中，商务信函是商家、厂家与客户之间联系业务、沟通商情、咨询答复的主要途径和工具。这类信函是对买卖双方权利、义务的规定，是双方解决争端的法律依据，因此商务信函尤其注重数字准确、文字正确、用词正式而又简洁易懂、格式规范。国际商务信函本质上是一种公函，构成了商务、外贸操作过程的根本内容。所谓“文字正确”，关键还是在于表达本意，帮助收信人充分地理解发信人的意图。

在不同的贸易环节上，商务信函会表现出一些不同的特点。一般的询问信和订货信往往写得比较简单，甚至简单到了格式化的地步；而索赔信和推销信以及其他负载着说服使命的信函，内容则可能会复杂一些，表述也会丰富一些。例如，撰写索赔信，写信人应当注意做到有理有据，以说服对方，从而达到索赔成功的目的；再如，在撰写以推销某些新产品为目的的促销信时，我们就有必要调动更多的文字技巧和修辞手段，去激发目标读者的购买欲。学习本课程时，我们应当注意掌握不同文书的特点，以便在写作时有意识地去体现它们各自的特点。

关于如何与对方建立起业务联系并开展业务活动，针对不同的目标读者或者客户，商务信函也会有不同的文字表现。为了吸引新客户，就可能比较详细地介绍情况，耐心地解释条款，附录更多的信息，目的在于通过信函建立业务关系；对于已经有所交往的老客户，则应当写得比较亲密甚至随便一些，严肃刻板了反而不好，业务内容上也可能会简单得多。

建立业务关系，实际上就是确定贸易对象，而贸易对象选择合适与否，决定了交易的成功与失败。因此，必须慎重对待。一般情况下，买卖双方通过毛遂自荐或第三者介绍，首先调查清楚贸易伙伴的资信状况、经营能力和业务范围等重要情况，再进行实质性的业务探讨。贸易双方只有在相互了解、彼此信任的基础上，才能进行积极的合作，顺利地开展双边的贸易活动。

我国的驻外商务机构、中国银行在国外的分支机构和老客户以及报刊杂志电视等媒体都是

有效了解贸易对象的渠道。交易会、博览会、商务代表团访问等也是直接摸清贸易伙伴的实力和意图的好机会。

在写作建立业务关系的信函时，应该遵循下列基本原则。

信的内容尽量简短，以不超过一页纸为好。Write short letter no more than one page.

语言要礼貌，态度要谦虚、诚恳。In polite language, with courteous and sincere attitude.

第一段就奔向主题。Direct to the point at the very beginning paragraph.

对自己公司有合理的高度评价。Say something high about your company reasonably.

如有知名客户，可列举一二。List some well-known customers, if any.

明确表达你公司的合作愿望。Express clearly your desire of cooperation.

Section 2 Specimen Letters 样函

(1)

Dear Mr. Lewis,

We have learned[1] your name and address from the advertisement of *China Foreign Trade* (Volume 2, 2009) . We are a state enterprise[2], and are keen[3] to expand our foreign trade. As yet[4], we have no business contacts in the South Africa, and would be pleased to consider any business proposals you may have. Enclosed please find[5] our latest illustrated catalogue[6], together with our latest price list and terms and conditions of sales for your information[7], and shall be leased to deal with any specific enquiries you may have concerning[8] any of our products.

Should you require any further details about our company, please do not hesitate to contact us.

We look forward to hearing from you in the near future.

Words, Expressions & Notes

1. have learned …from… 从何处获悉、了解到

2. state enterprise 国有企业，表示“国企”的说法还有 state-run enterprise, state-owned enterprise, state-operated enterprise

3. keen 渴望的，热衷的。在与其他词汇搭配时，还有很多其他含义，如：

keen smell 刺鼻的气味，keen competition 激烈的竞争，keen price 有竞争力的价格，即低价。

句子示例：Competition is very keen.竞争很激烈。

They are rather keen on trying out a sample shipment.他们很想买一批样货试销。

Please quote keen price. 请报低价。

4. as yet，到现在为止，义同 to date，until now，so far

习惯用语 So far, so good. 到目前一切良好、顺利。

5. enclosed please find 随函寄去，请查收。类似的表达还有，enclose (herewith)

Enclosed you will find…

We are enclosing…

Please refer to the enclosed...

We are sending you herewith…

We are sending you under cover…

attach (hereto)

6. illustrated catalogue 带有插图的产品目录

7. for your information 供你方参考

8. concerning 关于，义同 regarding， with respect to， respecting

（2）

Dear Sirs,

We have been informed by Mr. Chen Hua, the Chinese Commercia Counselor[1] in Singapore, that your corporation specializes[2] in the export of various electrical appliances, and that you are keen to extend your overseas trade. We are, therefore, contacting you with a view to introducing some of your products into our market.

We have been in the import and export business for over thirty years and have extensive contacts throughout Sri Lanka. It appears that demand for electrical appliances is now increasing and we are sure that your corporation can do considerable[3] business in our market.

At the present, we are now particularly interested in electrical sewing machine, and we would be appreciated[4] if you could send us your latest catalogues for the items and the sales conditions as well.

We are awaiting your early reply, and looking forward to[5] hearing good news from you.

Yours sincerely,

Words, Expressions & Notes

1. commercial counselor 商务参赞

2. specialize 专门从事，专营

3. considerable 相当规模的，很可观的

4. appreciate 感激。注意其形容词用法：

appreciable *adj.* 可估量到的，能了解到的，如下面这句：

There is no appreciable difference between the two.

这两个之间没有多大的区别。

appreciative *adj.* 备受感激的，如下面这句：

We are extremely appreciative of your friendly advice.

对你方的友好建议，我们万分感激。

5. look forward to 盼望、期盼，后接名称，或动词分词 ing

forward looking 远见

myopic/unforesightful thinking 短见 marketing myopia 市场短见

Marketing hyperopia 营销远视症

(3)

Dear Sirs,

Electric Sewing Machines

We were much impressed by the captioned goods[1] displayed at the Chinese Economic and Trade Exhibition held in Saudi Arabic last July, and we have been told that you export these products.

One of our potential customers[2] intends to purchase a number of electrical sewing machines, we would be therefore grateful should you send us a proforma invoice[3] for 400 Sewing Machines with three drawers[4] quoting your rock-bottom price[5] including our commission. On replying, please state the earliest possible date of delivery.

We look forward to hearing from you as soon as possible.

Yours sincerely,

Words, Expressions & Notes

1. captioned goods 标题商品
2. potential customer 有潜力的客户，有潜力的买家
3. proforma invoice 形式发票

形式发票是一种非正式发票，是卖方对潜在的买方报价的一种形式。买方常常需要形式发票，以作为申请进口和批准外汇之用。“Proforma”是拉丁文，它的意思是“纯为形式的”，所以单从字面来理解，Proforma Invoice 是指纯形式的，无实际意义的发票。这种发票本来是卖方在推销货物时，为了供买方估计进口成本，假定交易已经成立所签发的一种发票。实际上，并没有发出货物的事实，正因为如此，在日本这种发票也被称之为“试算发票”。

4. drawer 这里指抽屉
5. rock-bottom price 最低价格

(4)

Dear Sirs,

We have come to know[1] the name of your firm from the advertisement in “Foreign Trade” and have the pleasure of addressing this letter to you[2] in the hope of establishing business relations with you.

We specialize in the export of Chinese light industrial products[3] that have enjoyed great popularity[4] in the world markets. Enclosed please find a copy of our catalogue for your reference and hope that you would contact us if any item is of interest[5] to you.

Yours faithfully,

Words, Expressions & Notes

1. have come to know 得知
2. address this letter to you 向你方去函
3. light industrial products 轻工业产品，对应的有 heavy industrial product 重工业产品
4. popularity 这里指产品享有盛名，很有知名度
5. interest 兴趣，感兴趣的事物。作为动词时指引起兴趣。此外，还有其他用法，如：

annual interest 年利息 compound interest 复利

credit interest 存息 interest bill 计息票据

equity interest 股东权益，股权

to promote one's own interests 牟取私利

interested=related *adj.*有关的

the interested parties 有关当事方，义同 the parties concerned

pique sb's interest 吊某人胃口

shipping interests 航运界

banking interests 银行界

（5）

Dear Sirs,

We have obtained you name and address from the Colombo Chamber of Commerce[1], who has informed us that you wish to import light industrial goods manufactured in China.

We manufactured the light industrial products of the kind illustrated in the enclosed catalogue. We hope they will be of interest to you. Also enclosed is our latest price list for your reference[2].

Should you be interested in any of our products, please let us know and we will provide you with a quotation[3]. In the meantime, should you require any further information about either our products or our corporation, please do not hesitate to let us know.

We look forward to hearing from you soon, and to the possibility of doing business with you in the future.

Yours sincerely,

Words, Expressions & Notes

1. chamber of commerce 商会

其他团体组织的说法：

association 协会

guild 行会

trade union 工会

2. for your reference 供你方参考
3. quotation 报价

(6)

Dear Sirs,

Your name and address have be highly recommended[1] to us by ABC company as being interested in establishing business relations with an exporter of cotton piece goods[2]. This happens to fall in our line[3].

We have been the leading manufacturer of the same for 50 years, our products are of various designs and patterns[4], and they have proven very successful in the Asia markets.

We address this letter to you in order to enter into direct relations with you. We are enclosing the details and prices of the full range of[5] our products for your information. We wish to draw your attention to the fact that we offer a commission of 5 % on all orders.

We are confident that a mutually beneficial business will be built up with our cooperation.

We are looking forward to hearing from you on the above at an early date.

Yours sincerely,

Words, Expressions & Notes

1. recommend 举荐、推荐
2. cotton piece goods 棉布匹、棉布
3. fall in our line 由我方经营、是我方经营范围。此外，line（s）可表示（轮船、航空、航运等）公司。如：

Atlantic Container Line 大西洋集装箱海运公司

Hawaiian Air Lines 夏威夷航空公司

4. designs and patterns 款式与样式
5. full range of 全系列的、全套的

(7)

Dear Sirs,

We have received an order for us $57,500 worth of goods from Atlantic Electronic Co. Ltd., USA. They have given us your bank as a reference[1]. We wish to know if they are good[2] for this amount and in every way trustworthy and reliable. We shall be most grateful for any information you give us.

We should of course treat as strictly confidential[3] any advice you tell us and be only too pleased to[4] perform a similar service for you should the opportunity ever arise. We enclose a stamped and addressed envelope for your reply.

Yours faithfully,

Words, Expressions & Notes

1. reference 这里是指资信证明人。此外还有参考、参考文献的意思

2. good 此处意指信誉好

3. confidential 保密、机密

4. only too pleased to… 特别乐于、愿意去做……

注意：be only/all/but/ready too glad/pleased to *=be very much glad=be very much pleased=to be more than pleased to ...*

too+*adj.*(apt, ready, eager, easy, inclined, willing, happy) +to + infinitive 很，非常，十分

He will *be but too glad to* have an opportunity of thanking one who has saved his only child.

他十分想找个机会感谢救他唯一孩子的人。

If there is a special song that you would like us to play *we would be only too pleased to* oblige。

如果有那首曲子你想让我们演奏，我们很愿意效劳。

He *is too ready to* suspect.

他太多疑了。

The shopkeeper *was too willing to* serve the customers like you.

店员特别愿意向你这样的顾客服务。

Beginners *are too apt to* make mistakes.

新手很容易犯错误。

The guide *was too eager to* show the tourists to some bargains shops（便宜货商店）, and this made them suspicious.

导游特别急于引导游客去便宜货商店购物，这引起了游客的疑虑。

（8）

Dear Sirs,

We are pleased to state that the company you referred to[1] in your letter of November 13, 2009 is a small but well-known company and has enjoyed high reputation[2] that has been in this line[3] in our city for nearly forty years.

We have been doing business with the company for many years and have found that they are very reliable and their financial status[4] is sound. Although they have not as a rule[5] taken advantage of our cash discounts[6], they have always paid their accounts promptly on the net dates. The credit[7] we often allow has been well above the amount you mention in your letter.

Though the information is given to the best of our knowledge[8], we hope it will be helpful and trust you will treat it as confidential.

Yours faithfully,

Words, Expressions & Notes

1. refer to 提到的，所指的

2. enjoy high reputation 信誉良好

3. line 这里指行业
4. financial status 财务状况
5. as a rule 惯例
6. cash discount 现金折扣
7. credit 信用，此处实为赊销 credit sales
8. to the best of our knowledge 就我们所能了解到的

（9）

Dear Sirs,

We have completed our investigations about the company mentioned in your letter of November 13 and regret that we must advise you to regard their request for credit with caution.

About two years ago the company has experienced a serous difficulty in finance and an action[1] was brought against it by one of its suppliers for recovery of sum due[2], thought payment was later recovered in full.

Our investigations reveal nothing but[3] to suggest that the company's difficulty was due to bad management, particularly overtrading[4]. Consequently, most of the company's suppliers either give only very short credit[5] for limited sums, or make deliveries on a cash basis[6].

We trust that the information we give is of course supplied in the strictest confidence and we won't hold any responsibility on our part.

Yours faithfully,

Words, Expressions & Notes

1. action 这里指投诉
2. sum due 到期的货款
3. nothing but 只是、只不过
4. overtrading 过多的交易、盘子太大
5. short credit 短期信贷
6. on a cash basis 现金结账

（10）

Dear Sirs,

We will be obliged[1] if you will kindly give us the information about credit standing[2] of the Waston & Jones Newcastle International Trade Co., Ltd. in your city. We understand that you have regular transactions with the firm. So we take the liberty[3] to ask you to give your views concerning the actual position of the firm in order that we may take steps to avoid getting into trouble.

Any information you give will be highly appreciated and kept in strict confidence. We shall be pleased to reciprocate[4] if you should need our services at this end[5].

We are awaiting your early reply.

Yours faithfully,

Words, Expressions & Notes

1. oblige 此处表示感谢、感激
2. credit standing 信誉状况
3. take the liberty 冒昧地做
4. reciprocate 此处意为提供对等的服务
5. at this end 在这一方面

end 的几种用法：

to the end 到最后、最终

in the end 结果

at the end of...在……的结尾、末端

（11）

Dear Sirs,

We are pleased to announce that we intend to intensify our activities in your country. It is our serious and keen interest to realize such a development for our mutual benefit.

We are a trading company involved in[1] import and export business throughout the world. We belong to a group of companies established during the turn of 21st century[2]. The attached statement[3] will give you some more information which will surely be helpful to open business relations between us.

Within the activities of the company we have recently established a new department under the management of Mr. Smith who has long experience in the Far East Trade since 1994. this department is mainly interested in the import of products from your country especially in:

Native produce and animal by-products[4] for the foodstuffs and chemical industry[5]

Raw materials and semi-finished products[6]

Chemicals and pharmaceutical[7] raw materials

Minerals and essential oils[8]

However, we will be also active in export of chemicals and we invite your inquiries[9].

We seriously hope that a voluminous[10] and continuous business might be established and please rest assured[11] that we are always doing our utmost to realize a good business relationship with you

We would be very pleased to be of service to you and hope to submit to you our inquiries soon.

Yours faithfully,

Words, Expressions & Notes

1. involved in 从事 parties involved 当事人、当事各方

2. turn of 21st century 世纪之交

3. attached statement 随函寄去的财务报告书

4. by-product 副产品 by- 表示次要的、副、附带的，如：

by-law 附则

by-work 业余工作

5. industry 工业、行业、产业

small-scale industry 小型产业

cottage industry 家庭手工业

tourist industry 旅游业

arms industry 军需产业

entertainment/leisure industry 娱乐产业

building industry 建筑工业

tertiary industry 第三产业

注意两个不同形式的形容词

industrial 工业的；industrious 勤劳的，勤奋的

例句：He is an industrious worker.

他是一个勤劳的工人。

An industrial worker is one who is engaged in industry.

产业工人是从事工业的人。

6. semi-finished product 半成品

7. pharmaceutical 药品、药物的、药学的

8. essential oils 精油，香料油

9. inquiry 同 enquiry，表示询问，询盘，要货、调查。动词为 enquire

例句：we will make inquiries about the business possibilities of this new product.

我们将调查一下这种新产品的销售可能性。

We thank you for your enquiry for basketball.

我们感谢你方对篮球的询盘。

There are large enquiries for steel from the Mid-east countries.

中东国家拟购大量钢材。

10. voluminous 很多的，广泛的

11. please rest assured 请放心，确信无疑

有关公司的各种说法

除 company 外，表示公司的词汇还有很多如：firm，house， business， partnership， complex， group，consortium（国际财团），establishment， venture， conglomerate， multinational，transnational，Conglomerate（集团公司）等。

1．Line（s）：（轮船、航空、航运等）公司

e.g.

Atlantic Container Line

大西洋集装箱海运公司

Hawaiian Air Lines，夏威夷航空公司

2．Agency：公司、代理行

e.g.

Austin Advertising Agency

奥斯汀广告公司

China Ocean Shipping Agency

中国外轮代理公司

3．Associates （联合）公司

e.g.

British Nuclear Associates

英国核子联合公司

Subsea Equipment Associates Ltd.

海底设备联合有限公司（英、法、美合办）

4．Office 公司

多与 head，home, branch 等同连用。

e.g.

3M China Limited Guangzhou Branch Office

3M 中国有限公司广州分公司

China Books Import and Export Corporation （Head Office）

中国图书进出口总公司

5．Service（s）（服务）公司

e.g.

Africa-New Zealand Service

非洲—新西兰服务公司

Tropic Air Services

特罗皮克航空公司

此外，exchange，center 等词在特定的上下文中也可转义表示"公司"。

e.g.

American Manufacturers Foreign Credit Insurance Exchange

美国制造商出口信用保险公司

Binks（Shanghai）engineering Exhibition Center, Ltd.

宾克斯（上海）涂装工程设备展示有限公司

Industry"实业公司"

太平洋实业公司 Pacific Industries

华广轻工实业公司 Hua Guang Light Industrial Corporation

广联实业有限公司 The Guanglian Industrial Commerce Corporation

珠海特区发展实业公司 Zhuhai SEZ Developing Enterprises Corporation

广东省外贸实业公司 Guangdong Foreign Trade Industry Enterprise Corporation

Property Development Company 房地产开发公司

PLC/Plc Public Limited Company 股份上市公司

(Am.E) Inc.=Incorporated

an incorporated company 股份有限公司

(Br.E) Ltd.= Limited liabilities 有限责任公司

ABC Co.,Ltd.

（12）

Dear Sirs,

We owe your name and address to[1] the Commercial Counselor's Office of the Swedish Embassy in Beijing who have informed us that you are in the market[2] for textiles.

We avail ourselves of [3] this opportunity to approach[4] you for the establishment of trade relations with you.

We are a state-operated corporation[5], handling[6] both the import and export[7] of textiles. In order to acquaint[8] you with our business lines[9]; we enclose a copy of our Export List covering[10] the main items suppliable at present.

Should any of the items be of interest to you, please let us know. We shall be glad to give you our lowest quotations upon receipt of you detailed requirements.

In our trade[11] with merchants of various countries, we always adhere to[12] the principle of equality and mutual benefit[13]. It is our hope to promote, by joint efforts[14], both trade and friendship to our mutual advantage.

We look forward to receiving your enquiries soon.

Yours faithfully,

Words, Expressions & Notes

1. owe your name and address to… 承蒙…告知你公司的名称和地址。owe 的基本含义及用法有以下几种：

（1）owe: to be indebted or obliged for: 感恩于，应归功于，例如：

They owed their riches to oil.

有了石油才有他们的财富。

She owes her good health to diet and exercise .

她的健康归功于饮食和锻炼。

（2）owe:to have a moral obligation to render or offer 应尽…的道义：负有道德义务来归还或提供，例如：

I owe them an apology.

我应向他们道歉。

（3）owe:to be in debt to: 负债，如：

I owe you a favor.

我欠你一个人情。

Write out an IOU (I Owe You)　打欠条

There is still a balance of US$ 1000 owing to us.

仍欠我方 1000 美元的余额。

2. in the market for 此处理解成拟购买，想要买进。若用于卖方表示欲销售、想卖出

market 市场，动词意为推销、销售。各种市场的表达有，

auction market 拍卖市场　　bond market 债券市场

exchange market 外汇市场　　financial market 金融市场

futures market 期货市场　　niche market 利基市场

secondhand market 旧货市场　　security market 证券市场

service market 劳务市场

注意：marketer 市场营销人员 marketing 市场营销、营销学

marketable 可卖的，适合在市场销售的

marketability 可销性，适销性

习惯搭配：corner market 囤积市场　　hit the market 投入市场

come to/into market 上市　　find a market 找销路

good market 畅销　　poor/no market 滞销、没销路

例句：We are in the market for wool.

我们想买羊毛。

We will contact you as soon as the new crop comes to the market.

一旦新谷物上市，我们将和你方联系。

We are trying to find a market for this toy.

我们正在努力为这种玩具找销路。

There is a good market for these articles.

这些商品是畅销的。

We will try to market this product at our end if you allow us a 5% commission.

若你方提供 5%的佣金，我方愿在本地设法推销这件产品。

3. avail oneself of …利用

例句：We avail ourselves of this opportunity to express our thanks to you for you close cooperation.

我们借此机会对你方的密切合作表示感谢。

4. approach 此处意为同……联系、接洽

此外还有靠近、临近的意思。

名词表示方法、途径

例句：We shall approach the department concerned on this matter.

我们将同有关部门联系此事。

As the manufacture of your order is approaching completion, you are requested to open your L/C without any further delay.

你方订货即将制造完毕，请立即开立信用证。

5. state-operated corporation 国营公司

各类所有制公司、企业的表达有：

state-owned/run corporation 国营公司

state-designated second grade enterprise 国家认定二级企业

collective-owned enterprise 集体企业

individual-owned enterprise 个体企业

private-owned enterprise 私营企业

merchandizing enterprise 商业企业

small and medium enterprises (SMEs) 中小企业

township/rural enterprise 乡镇企业

enterprise for joint venture, for cooperative and with sole foreign capital/investment 三资企业，即中外合资企业、中外合作企业、外商独资企业

6. handling 此处指经营

此外还有处理、装卸、搬运的意思。

例句：We understand your corporation handles foodstuffs for export.

我们了解你公司经营食品出口的业务。

Fragile goods must be handled carefully.

易碎物品一定要小心装卸。

No complication will arise if the matter is handled properly.

如果此事处理妥善，将不会引起麻烦。

7. import and export 进出口

关于 import 和 export 的常见短语有：

amount of export 出口额	amount of import 进口额
export control 出口管制	import control 进口管制
export declaration 出口申报单	import declaration 进口申报单
export drawback 出口退税	export dumping 出口倾销
export document 出口单据	import document 进口单据
export entry 出口报关	import entry 进口报关
export license 出口许可证	import license 进口许可证
export-oriented economy 出口导向型经济	
export quota 出口限额	import quota 进口限额
export subsidy 出口补贴	

8. acquaint 使熟悉、认识、了解

惯用搭配，acquaint sb with/of sth… be/get acquainted with…

例句：You will have to acquaint us with the details.

你们必须让我方了解详情。

We are well acquainted with the market condition in China.

我们对中国市场行情很了解。

9. line 此处指业务领域、业务范围

此外还有其他意思，如：

写出的短函、诗句、通知，As soon as you reach a decision, please drop us a line.

一旦你们做出决定，请告知我方。

产品的货色、成色，This is a good line of metal hardware.

这是金属器皿中的好货。

习惯搭配：along/on this line 关于这件事　　fall in line with 同意，符合

in line 相合　　out of line 不相合

in line with 按照　　on sound lines 用正确的方法

on the wrong lines 用错误的方法　　line up 安排

line with 做衬里

例句：We may be able to line up 50 tons goods for you in a few days.

几天后我们可能给你方安排 50 吨货。

Please line the cases with wax paper.

箱内请用蜡纸做衬里。

We believe we are handling the matter on sound lines.

我们相信正用正确的方法处理此事。

In line with cables exchanged, we confirmed having sold you the following.

按照往来电报，我方确认售给你方以下产品。

Your price is entirely out of line with the market.

你们的价格与市场价完全不符。

We do not think we can fall in line with your views.

我们认为无法同意你方的意见。

We will write to you along these lines.

关于这些事情，我们将来再向你方去函。

10. covering 有关的，涉及……的，如：

Please let us have your price list covering your computers.

请寄来有关你方计算机的价目表。

11. trade 贸易、行业。动词表示做生意，经营，如：

We do not want to trade with them.

我们不想和他们做生意。

They trade mainly in textile product.

他们主要经营纺织品。

常见短语：barter trade 易货贸易　　barriers to trade 贸易壁垒

bilateral trade 双边贸易　　compensation trade 补偿贸易

frontier trade 边境贸易　　processing trade 加工贸易

multilateral trade 多边贸易　　transit trade 转口贸易、过境贸易

trade friction 贸易摩擦　　trade gap 贸易失衡

trade practice 贸易惯例　　trade procurator 商务代理人

trade terms 贸易条件、贸易术语

12. adhere 忠于，坚持，如：

We always adhere to our commitments.

我们一贯忠实履行义务。

13. equality and mutual benefit 平等互利

14. by joint efforts 通过共同努力

（13）

Dear Sirs,

Through the courtesy of[1] our Commercial Counselor's Office in London，we notice that you are in interested in doing business with us.

Our lines are mainly textiles. We wish to establish business relations by the commencement[2] of some practical transactions. To give you a general idea[3] of the various kinds of textiles now available[4] for export, we are enclosing herewith a catalogue[5] and a pricelist for your examination[6]. We would appreciate receiving your specific enquiries.

We look forward to receiving from you good news.

Yours faithfully,

Words, Expressions & Notes

1. through the courtesy of 感谢某人的推荐、介绍

相关短语，by courtesy of ，蒙…许可；由于…的好意；经由…的途径

2. commencement 开始、开端

动词形式是 commence，用法有两种：

commence doing sth；commence to do sth

注意：begin，start，commence 都表示开始的意思。但从修辞角度看，begin 是中性词；start 口语色彩浓；commence 主要用于正式场合。这三个词语所对应的反义词是：

begin—end

start—stop

commence—conclude

例句：Now that you are all back, we'd better start the work right away.

既然你们都回来了，我们最好马上开始工作。

Returning office, he began drawing up the contract.

回到办公室后，他开始草拟合同。

The opening ceremony of the fair will commence at 9 a. m. tomorrow.

交易会开幕典礼将于明日上午九时开始。

3. general idea 大致的了解，大体的认识

4. available 可利用的，可供应的

例句：We will ship by the first steamer available next month.

我方将于下月用第一条可订到的船转运。

This is the only stock available.

这是唯一可供应的货。

Our terms are L/C available by draft at sight.

我方条款是凭即期汇票支付的信用证。

The book you need is not available in this library.

你需要的书在这家图书馆找不到。（本图书馆没有你需要的藏书）

5. catalogue 产品目录、目录册。几种惯用的表达，

classified catalogue 分类目录

descriptive catalogue 带有说明的目录

illustrated catalogue 带有插图的目录

此外，用于促销、宣传目的的产品文字介绍资料还有，产品使用手册（handbook），介绍产品的小册子（pamphlet），产品小册子（booklet，brochure）

6. for your examination 供你方参考，供你方查询

义同 for your reference，for your information

类似的表达方式还有：

for your study, for your perusal, for your consideration

（14）

Dear Sirs,

The Foreign Department of the Bank of China here has recommended[1] your corporation as being interested in establishing business relations with Chinese corporation for the purpose[2] of selling light industrial products of your country.

We invite you to send us details and prices of your products, and we shall gladly study the sales possibilities[3] in our market.

We shall always be very happy to hear from you and will carefully consider any proposals[4] likely to lead to business between us.

Yours truly,

Words, Expressions & Notes

1. recommend 推荐，介绍

在这里详细阐述一下 recommend 的用法。

可以有双宾语，如：

They request you to recommend them some products that suits African market.

他们请你方推荐一些适合非洲市场的商品。

可直接接名词作为宾语，如：

We strongly recommend concentration of offer.

我方极力建议集中报盘。

接动名词，如：We recommend buying a small quantity for trial.

我们力劝购买少量商品试用。

接 that 从句，如：

We recommend that you try the African market.

我们建议你方尝试一下非洲市场。

注意，recommend 不可直接接动词不定式。

recommend 接从句时，名词从句中的谓语用虚拟形式：should + 动词原形，should 可以省略。从句要用虚拟语气的其他标志词还有很多，包括 ask、advise、beg、command、demand、decide、deserve、desire、determine、insist、move（提议）、order、prefer、propose、require、request、suggest、urge 等。

习惯搭配，recommend sb for a post 推荐某人担任某职务

2. for the purpose of 为了…的目的、意图

作动词时表示打算、企图。

惯用搭配，to do sth. on purpose 故意做某事。answer/serve purpose of...符合…的要求，符合…的目的。

例句：The goods needed are for medical purpose.

所需之货是供医药使用的。

The quality does not suit the purpose.

这种质量不符合要求。

We note that your Mr. Brown purpose taking a trip to our city.

我们得知你方布朗先生打算来我市访问。

3. possibility 可能性

后接介词 of 再接动名词或名词或 that 从句。其复数形式 possibilities 意指前途、展望。

例句：Is there any possibility of your placing additional quantities?

你方是否有继续订货的可能？

The possibility of a fall in price is rather remote.

降价的可能性是很渺茫的。

Please assess the possibilities and let us know.

请对业务展望进行评估，并告知为盼。

4. proposals 提议，计划，建议

（15）

Dear Sirs,

Your communication[1] of the 28th May addressed to our sister corporation in Shanghai has been passed on to us for attention and reply[2] as the export of enamelware[3] falls within the scope of our business activities.

However, we very much regret that we are not in a position[4] to supply you with enamelware direct, as we are already represented[5] by Messrs, Freemen and Brothers Co., Ltd., 267 Broad Street, for the sales[6] of this commodity in your district[7]. We would advise you to get in touch with[8] them for your requirements.

In case[9] you are interested in other items, kindly let us know and we shall be only too please to make you offers directly.

Yours faithfully,

Words, Expressions & Notes

1. communication 通信，传达，通讯

动词 communicate，习惯搭配：communicate with sb.和某人联系。communicate…to sb.把某事告知某人。

例句：All communications are to be addressed to Shipping Department.

所有的函件请寄交运输部门。

If you are interested, please communicate with us.

如果有兴趣，请和我方联系。

Please communicate this matter to your buyers.

请将此事通知你方买主。

2. attention and reply 进行处理并回复

3. enamelware 搪瓷器

4. position 情况、状况。此外，还有交易、期货、头寸的意思。

习惯搭配：financial position 财务状况

cash position 现金头寸

easy position 头寸宽裕

to cover position 轧平头寸

long/bull position 多头交易，买空交易

short/bear position 空头交易，卖空交易

例句：Please advise position of our order No.139.

请告知我方第 139 号订单的执行情况。

After dipping briefly, prices rallied to close near the highs of the day with the March position at ￡1982 a tonne.

在短暂下降后， 价格又回升，收盘时接近当天的 3 月份期货最高价，即每吨 1982 英镑。

5. represent 代理，代表

6. sale 出售，卖，销货，交易，销路。惯用搭配：

clearance sale 清仓削价销售，清仓甩卖

on sale 上市，廉价出售

rummage sale /jumble sale 二手货（second hand goods）大拍卖

white sale 床上用品大甩卖

Sales Confirmation 销售确认书

Sales Contract 销售合同

Sales allowance 销售折让

Sales promotion 促销

Sales tax 销售税

Salesman（saleswoman）营业员

sales gimmick 销售噱头

例句：Bicycles command a ready sale in the US market.

自行车在美国市场畅销。

Large sales are reported to have been made.

据说大笔交易已经做成。

The pretty girl on the cover of the pictorial is just *a sales gimmick*.

画报的封面上印上美女不过是吸引顾客的一种销售噱头。

7. in your district 在你方地区

类似的说法还有：

in your place，on your side，at your end

8. get in touch with 与……联系

touch 作动词时、有达到、涉及、停靠、引起等意思，例句：The development touched off an alteration of working plan.

这一发展引起了工作计划的改变。

This steamer touches at Dalian.

该船在大连停靠。

In your letter of April 4, you did not touch the point at issue.

你方 4 月 4 日信件未涉及问题的要点。

It is generally felt that the price has touched peak(bottom).

一般认为价格已达到最高（低）点。

When we are again in apposition of supply, we shall not fail to get in touch with you.

当我们能再行供应此货时，一定与你方联系。

9. in case 如果，以备万一

惯用搭配：in any case 无论如何

in case of 假若，如果，万一

in no case 决不

in the case of 就……而言，至于

in this case 即使这样，既然这样

such being the case 情况既然如此

例句：Such being the case, we regret being unable to make you an offer at present.

情况既然如此，抱歉我方目前无法报盘。

In this case, we will not fail to cable you an offer.

如果是这样，一定去电给你方报盘。

In the case of payment terms, we are unable to accept D/P at 60 days' sight.

至于付款条件，我方无法接受远期（见票后 60 天付款的）付款交单。

You may be rest assured that in no case will the L/C be delayed.

请你方放心，信用证绝对不会迟开。

In case of offer, please quote your best price.

如能报盘，请开最低价。

In any case we are unable to effect shipment in this month.

无论如何，这个月我们不能装运、发货。

We would suggest you placing an order at present in case new crop may fail.

我们建议你方现在订货，以防新谷物欠收。

Section 3 Supplements 知识补充

Useful Sentences on Establishing Business Relations

1. Your firm has been kindly recommended to us by Messrs. J. Smith & Co., Inc., in New York, as large importers of furniture.

纽约史密斯公司向我们介绍，贵公司是主要的家具进口商。

2. We have obtained your name and address through the Commercial Counselor's Office of the Embassy of the People's Republic of China in your country and understood that you would like to establish business relations with us.

我们从驻贵国的中国大使馆商参处得到贵公司的行名和地址，并获悉贵公司愿同我们建立业务关系。

3. Through the courtesy of…we have learned that you are one of the representative importers of …

承……的介绍，获悉你们是……有代表性的进口商之一。

4. Your name and address has been given to us by Messrs. J. Smith & Co., Inc., in New York, who have informed us that you …

据纽约史密斯公司所告，得悉你公司名称和地址，并得知你们……

5. We take the liberty of writing to you with a view to building up business relations with your firm.

我们冒昧通信，以期与你公司建立业务关系。

6. We are given to understand that you are potential buyers of Chinese…, which comes within the frame of our business activities.

据了解，你们是中国……（商品）有潜力的买主，而该商品正属我们的业务经营范围。

7. We have the pleasure of introducing ourselves to you with the hope that we may have an opportunity of cooperating with you in your business extension.

我们有幸自荐，盼望能有机会与你们合作，扩大业务。

8. We are glad to send you this introductory letter, hoping that it will be the prelude to mutually beneficial relations between us.

我们欣然寄发这些自荐信，希望是互利关系的前奏。

9. We are a state-operated corporation handing light industrial products.

我们是经营轻工业产品的国有公司。

10. The purpose of this letter is to explore the possibilities of developing trade with you.

本信目的是探索与你们发展贸易的可能性。

11. We are exporters of long standing and high reputation, engaged in exportation of following articles.

我们是声誉卓著的出口商，长期经营下列商品的出口业务。

12. Being specialized in the export of Chinese Arts and Crafts goods, we express our desire to trade

with you in this line.

我们专门出口中国工艺品，愿与贵方开展这方面业务。

13. Please let us know by return what your experience has been in your dealings with them.

请尽快把贵公司同他们的交往经验告诉我们。

14. Messrs Smith & Co., have given us your name as a reference. We should be obliged if you would advise us whether they are of good repute.

史密斯公司提供贵公司为其咨询人，请告该公司的信誉是否良好。

15. The above information is given confidentially and without responsibility on our part.

对以上情况请保守秘密，我方对此不负责任。

Exercises

Ⅰ. Translate the following phrases and then make sentences.

be of interest to

enquire for

inquire about

keep sb. informed of

be in the market for

acquaint sb. with

be in line with

enclosed pleased find

get in touch with

meet one's requirements

trade in

adhere to

look forward to

for one's examination

in one's place

take the liberty of

be in a position to

in case

Ⅱ. Complete the following sentences in English.

1. We are given to understand that___________.

a. 你公司是经营化工产品的国有公司

b. 你公司有意在平等互利的基础上与我公司建立业务关系

2. We are desirous of___________.

a. 获得你方最近供应出口的商品目录

b．把你的新产品介绍给我方的客户

3. Please do not hesitate to write us_____________.

a．关于推销中国水果和干果的任何建议

b．当你方需要订购中国缝纫机的时候

4. As you know, _____________.

a．许多外国商人渴望和我们进行贸易

b．我们是信誉良好的照相机进口商，希望与你们建立商务关系

5. On the basis of equality, mutual benefit and exchange of needed goods，我们已经和世界上 100 多个国家商号建立了贸易关系。

6. We are appreciative of__________________.

a．你方有和我公司建立贸易关系的意图

b．你公司愿望到广交会来谈判业务

7. We hope you can provide us with__________________as soon as possible.

a．由中国商家雕刻的照片 2 张

b．中国天津制造的足球 20 个

8. We are glad that in the past few years，我们之间通过双方努力在业务上和友谊上都有很大的增进。

9. Upon receipt of your specific enquiries，我们即将办理一切必要的事宜。

Ⅲ．Translate the following Sentences into English.

1．我们从驻伦敦的商务参赞处得知，你公司有兴趣与我们进行交易。

2. 为了使你们对我们可供出口的各类纺织品有一个总的概念，随信寄上样品和价格表各一份，供你们查阅。

3．经本地的中国银行国外分部推荐，得知你公司有意与一家中国公司建立贸易关系，以推销你们的轻工业产品。

4．搪瓷器皿出口业务属于我公司经营范围。

5．我们希望你方尽最大努力既促进业务又增进友谊。

6．我们的一个客户想要购买中国红茶。

7．我们了解到你公司是中国手工艺品的出口商，因此冒昧地写信给你。

8．由于希望与你公司建立业务关系，我们向你们自我介绍，我公司是法国南部各式男女衬衫的进口商。

9．你方 2 月 15 日函悉，并已转交了上海分公司。他们会直接答复你们，因为你所询问的商品是由他们经营的。

10．我们是一家在全世界范围内进行进出口业务的贸易公司。

Ⅳ．Translate the following Sentences into Chinese.

1. We look forward to your favorable and prompt reply.

2. We are state-owned corporation specializing in the export of table-cloth.

3. We are convinced that with joint efforts business between us will be developed to our mutual benefit.

4. It will be greatly appreciated if you will give us your cooperation.

5. As requested, we are airmailing to you, under separate cover, a sample each of Art. No. 1253 and 1267 for your reference.

6. We can assure you that all your orders will receive our immediate attention.

7. This type of letter is an outgoing letter and may be called a "First Inquiry".

8. We are the largest food trading company in Japan, and have offices or representatives in all major cities and towns in Japan.

9. Your letter of November addressed to our sister corporation in Shanghai has been transferred to us for attention.

10. As the items falls within the scope of our business activities, we shall be pleased to enter into direct business relations with you.

Ⅴ. Write a letter to a foreign company for establishing business relations covering the following contents:

1. the source of your information
2. your intention
3. your business scope
4. the reference as to your firm's financial stangding
5.your expectation

Ⅵ. Translate the following into Chinese.

ABC Toy was established in 1993. Our office and factory are located in … .

We started business as a manufacturer of plastic toys. Our main products are plastic vehicles for kids such as tricycle; bicycle, baby walker, baby rocker and accessory for toys i.e. wheel. Our products are very popular and distributed nationwide.

With over 15 years experience, we develop more than 60 designs each to satisfy customers' want. Each year we introduce a lot of new toys and our products have remained consistently popular in the market. We dedicated our efforts to make toys that bring smile to children's face and also stimulate the physical and intellectual development.

For more information, please contact us at…

Chapter 3

Enquiries 询盘

Section 1 Business Knowledge 业务知识

询盘，也叫询价，是买方对所要购买的商品向卖方做出的探询。其内容并不仅限于价格，还可以兼问商品的规格、性能、包装和交货期等。询问的目的主要是从卖方即出口商获得具有竞争性的价格，然后从几家报价中选择最佳者。因此对同一商品的询盘，往往不只向一家公司发出，而是向不同的国家的，在经营某种商品有名气的，而且是相互竞争的若干家公司同时发出，外贸行业有句口头禅“货比三家”就是这个意思。

询盘常常是交易洽商的第一步，我国《合同法》称之为洽商邀请或要约邀请（invitation to treat）。询盘可分为口头和书面两种形式。询盘信比较好写，一般不会出什么问题。因为询盘一般情况下是没有任何约束力的，也就是说询盘的一方没有任何义务非要买被询盘一方的货物，因此就算问得不妥，也不会或不容易造成经济损失。另外，一般情况下，卖方会比买方对达成交易更加积极，所以，即使买方在询盘信中没有详细询问的一些情况，有经验的卖方也会主动告知有关事宜以利于早日成交。虽然询盘信比较好写，但我们在写询盘信时却不能抱有马虎从事的心理，因为询盘信质量的高低往往反映写信人的业务素质和可靠程度，从而影响到被询盘人对交易条件的各种考虑，而且，如果询盘信丢三落四，该问的没问，问了的又没问清楚，就有可能耽误时间，错过时机，造成无形的损失。

询价依其性质和意图可分为以下两种：

1．一般询价 general inquiry

这种询价并不一定立即接触具体交易，一般属于摸底性质。其内容包括：（1）请寄某种商品的样品，目录及/或价格表；（2）探询某种商品的品质、价格、数量、交货期等。

2．具体询价 specific inquiry

所谓具体询价实际上就是请求对方报盘，也就是说，买方已经准备购买某种商品，或已有

现成买主，请卖方就这一商品报价。

由买方发出的询盘属于邀请发价（invitation to make an offer），其目的是促使对方向自己报盘，提出产品的出售条件。例如：

PLEASE OFFER NANSHAN PONGEE 33 × 48，1000kg，5/6 SHIPMENT FOB DALIAN

这句电文的含义是，请报南山府绸（炼）33 × 48，1000 千克，5/6 月份装运，FOB 大连。

另外，在买方市场情况下，卖方也可以主动发出询盘，即为出售某种货物，向买方探询其购买条件。卖方询盘被称为邀请递价（invitation to make a bid），目的是促使对方向自己递上购买条件。例如：

CAN SUPPLY NORTHEAST (CHINA) SOYABEAN PLEASE BID

这句电文的含义是，可供中国东北大豆，请递价。

询价信函的写作原则主要有下述 6 个方面。

第一，应该告知对方你从什么渠道获悉人家的名称、产品和地址。To tell where you learned the company and its products.

第二，阐述具体要求，但不承诺购买意向。To describe your specific needs but with no promise of booking the proposed products.

第三，强调你需要的信息的重要性，尽量取悦对方以获取更多信息。To stress the importance of your needed information and try to flatter the reader for getting more information.

第四，如有疑问，应请对方明确回复。If any questions, ask the reader to give you a definite reply.

第五，如不熟悉对方，也尽量把信文写出老朋友间的叙谈。If you write to an unfamiliar reader, try to personalize your letter like the one between friends.

第六，使用礼貌谦和的字眼。Use courtesy words.

在回复贸易伙伴的询盘时，应遵循下面几项原则。

第一，如果能满足对方信文中的所有要求，尽快回复。If you can meet all the requirements of the addresser, let him know as soon as possible.

第二，若只能满足部分要求，首先告知对方你能做到多少，然后解释你不能做的。If you can only meet part of the requirements, tell the addresser first what you can do for him and then explain those that you fail to do.

第三，如果完全不能满足人家的要求，首先要向对方的询盘表示感谢，然后抱歉自己无法做到的。要让对方感到自己的真诚和良好愿望。If you can't meet any of the requirements, first, express your thanks for the enquiry and then your regret. Try to make your reader feel the sincerity and heart-felt desire.

第四，在回函中可以附寄宣传单，多介绍一下自己公司和产品的情况。When reply enquiry, you can enclose some literatures to introduce more about your company and your products.

第五，尽最大努力为潜在的顾客提供满意的服务。Try your best to please your potential customer by offering satisfactory services.

Section 2 Specimen Letters 样函

（1）

Dear Sirs,

We are in the market[1] for Melon Seeds[2] of the first and second grade[3] and should be appreciated if you let us have your offers with some representative samples[4] by airmail[5]. When offering the seeds, please state the earliest possible time of shipment and quantities available.

Yours faithfully,

Words, Expressions and Notes

1. in the market 此处是指拟购买
2. Melon Seeds 西瓜子
3. first and second grade 甲级和乙级，或一等与二等
4. representative samples 具有代表性的样品
5. by airmail 以航寄的方式

（2）

Dear Sirs,

We are pleased to tell you that we are interested in hand-made gloves[1] in a variety of genuine leather[2]. Recently there is a growing demand[3] here for gloves of high quality at our end[4]. Although sales are not particularly high, good price can be obtained.

We wish you would send us a copy of your illustrated catalogue of the gloves we wish to buy, together with details of your price and terms of payment[5]. We should find it most helpful if you could also send us samples of the various leather, of which the gloves are made.

Yours faithfully,

Words, Expressions and Notes

1. hand-made gloves 手工制作的手套
2. genuine leather 真皮
3. growing demand 日益增长的需求
4. at our end 在我方市场，在我处
5. terms of payment 支付条件

(3)

Dear Sirs,

Thank you for your letter of May 5th and your interest in our products. A copy of our illustrated catalogue has been sent to you today, in which you will find samples of some skins we regularly[1] use in our manufactures.

Unfortunately, we can not send you immediately a full range of samples[2], but you may agree, after checking them, which such skins as chamois and doeskin[3], not represented in the parcel, are of the same high quality.

Mr. Li, our sales representative[4], will be in Tehran early next month and will be pleased to call[5] on you. He has brought with him a wide range of our manufacturers and, when you see them, we think you will agree that the quality of the materials used and the high standard of craftsmanship[6] will appeal to the most selective buyers[7].

We also manufacture a wide range of hand-made leather handbags[8] in which we hope you may be interested. They are fully illustrated in the catalogue and are of the same high quality as our gloves. Mr. Li will show you the samples when he calls on you.

We look forward very much to the pleasure of receiving an order from you.

Yours sincerely,

Words, Expressions and Notes

1. regularly 经常地、惯常地
2. a full range of samples 全套的样品
3. chamois and doeskin 羚羊皮和鹿皮
4. sales representative 销售代表、售货代理
5. call on 拜访某人。call at 用于到某地拜访
6. standard of craftsmanship 工艺标准
7. the most selective buyers 最为挑剔的买主
8. handbags （女用）手提包

(4)

Dear Ms. Barnes:

Many of my customers have been asking recently about books on tape[1], and I know almost nothing about this relatively new product. I have an idea, though, that taped books may be a splendid[2] item for my store.

I will be grateful if you would send me literature[3] concerning this exciting new (for me) market. I'd like not only to know which books are available on tape, but also want to inquire about tape-playback equipment[4] that either you carry[5] or know about.

Cordially[6] yours,

Words, Expressions and Notes

1. book on tape, a book that is read out loud, usually by an actor or a famous person, and recorded on a cassette tape or CD 录音书
2. splendid 极好的，很棒的
3. literature 这里指产品资料、商业资料
4. tape-playback equipment 录音播放设备
5. carry 此处意为经营
6. cordially 用作信件落款处，指谨上

（5）

Dear …:

I am delighted to[1] have your letter in which you ask about books on tape.

Today I am sending you a special brochures[2] that we've just had printed[3], "Books on Tape", which contains an up-to-date[4] listing and description of all our taped books. The sales number of taped book is expanding at an accelerating pace and the market increases daily. I'll see to it[5] that you are kept up-to-date on new arrivals.

I am sorry I am out of stock on the booklet[6] describing the play-back equipment, but I'll get a copy to you right away[7] next week for sure.

Sincerely yours,

Words, Expressions and Notes

1. be delighted to 乐于去做，高兴去做
2. brochures 小册子
3. print 印刷
4. up-to-date 最新的，时髦的
5. see to it 保证、务必、注意。后常接 that 从句
6. booklet 产品小册子
7. right away 立刻、马上

（6）

Gentlemen:

I am so intrigued[1] by the announcement of your new 4 ½ -inch television set that I'd like six copies of your color brochures, one for me and one for each of our regional manager[2] whose names and addresses are attached[3].

Thank you!

Yours faithfully,

Words, Expressions and Notes

1. intrigued 好奇的，被迷住了
2. regional manager 地区业务经理
3. attached 随附此函

（7）

Dear …:

Here are six copies of our color brochure on our new 4 ½ -inch TV set as featured in… . I am especially pleased that you want a copy for each of your regional managers.

The brochure "tells it all[1]", so I do not need to expand[2] on the TV's features in this letter. I do want you do know, however, that the brand is being purchased in large quantities by retailers[3] everywhere, and they predict[4] that this is only the beginning. It is especially popular with the younger crowd for home, dorm[5], and travel use.

The price to retailers is $… and the suggested retail price[6] is $… . Please let me know if there is other information your need.

Sincerely yours,

Words, Expressions and Notes

1. tells it all 全面描述
2. expand 补充、追加
3. retailers 零售商
4. predict 预计、预测
5. dorm 宿舍
6. suggested retail price 建议零售价

（8）

Dear Sirs,

Messrs Johns &Smith of New York inform us that you are exporters of all cotton bed-sheets and pillowcases[1]. We would like you to send us details of your various ranges[2], including size, colors and prices, and also samples of the different qualities of material used.

We are large dealers[3] in textiles and believe there is a promising[4] market in our area for moderately priced[5] goods of this kind mentioned.

When quoting, please state your terms[6] of payment and discount[7] you would allow on purchase of quantities[8] of not less than 100 dozen[9] ndividual items. Price quoted should include insurance and freight to Liverpool.

Yours faithfully

Words, Expressions and Notes

1. bed-sheets and pillowcases 床单和枕套

与此相关的表达：

bedspread 床单

bedcover 床罩

color-checked bed sheets 彩格床单（被单）

color-checked printed bed sheets 彩格印花床单

color- stripped bed sheets 彩条床单

color stripped bath towels 彩条浴巾

colors tripped face towels 彩条毛巾

horizontal stripes 横条纹

vertical stripes 竖条纹

2. various ranges 各个方面的

range 作为名词意为系列、种类、差距、范围，如，a full range of samples 一整套样品；a full range of documents 一整套单据

作动词时表示从……到……，涉及

例句：We can supply carpets in a wide range of designs.

我们可供应花样繁多的地毯。

There is only a narrow range of prices.

价格仅有很小的差距。

This article falls within the range of our business activities.

这种商品属于我公司经营范围。

In regard to woolen serge, stock is available in various shade of blue, prices range from RMB¥30 to 50 per yard.

关于蓝毛哔叽，蓝色深浅不同的产品有货可供，每码价格自 30 元人民币至 50 元不等。

3. dealers 商人、商号

几种习惯表达：

dealer in toilet articles 盥洗用品商

licensed dealer 有许可执照的商人

petty/small dealer 小商贩

dealership 经销权

4. promising 这里指有前景的、前途看好、有希望的

5. price 这里是动词，表示定价、作价

如：Please price your offer as keen as possible。请尽可能报低价。The new product is moderately priced。这项新产品定价适度。各类价格的表示方法：

wholesale price 批发价

retail price 零售价

unit price 单价

half price 半价

gross price 毛价、总价

total price 总价，同 lump-sum price

basic price 基价

average price 平均价格

actual price 实际价格

"under the hammer" price 拍卖价格，同 auction price

top price 最高价，同 peak price，outside price，highest price，ceiling price

floor price 最低价，同 bottom price，bedrock price

tender price 投标价格

target price 目标价格

cost price 成本价格、生产价格

tape price （证券）牌价

stock price 股票价格、交易所价格

special price 特价，同 exceptional price

selling price 销售价格

buying price 购买价格

purchasing price 收购价格，同 procurement price

security price 证券价格

ruling price 市价、时价

revised price 修正后的价格

price gouging 价格欺骗

prevailing price 现行价格，同 present price，current price

piece price 计件价格

price support 价格补贴

pay heavy price 付高价

opening price 开盘价

closing price 收盘价

fixed price 固定价格，同 firm price

official fixed price 官定价格

offered price 卖方的开价

bid price 买方出价、标价

nominal price 名义价格

market price 市价

legal price 法定价格

keen price 低价

illegal price hike 乱涨价

ideal price 理想价格

fresh price 最新价格

forward price 期货价格，同 future price

favorable price 优惠价格

fair price 合理价格

external price 对外价格、国外价格

exalted price 高昂的价格

discount price 折扣价格

competitive price 竞争价格、公开招标价格

black market price 黑市价格

6. terms 条件，此外，term 还有时间和专有名词的意思。

例句：It is not our practice to accept term L/C.

接受远期信用证不是我们的习惯做法。

This is a technical term.

这是技术上的一个专有名词。

7. discount 折扣。此外还有贴现、减价、没销路、不受欢迎的意思。动词表示打折、贴现、不完全相信。

例句：The highest discount we can allow on this article is 10%.

我们对这件商品最多只能打九折。

The rate of discount in London is now 5%.

现在伦敦的贴现率是 5%。

Many articles are reported to be selling at a discount.

据报道，有许多商品按低于正常价格出售。

Off-grade qualities are now at a discount.

等外货现在没有销路。

Your design being outdated, your product is at a discount in this district.

因为款样过时，你方产品在此地不受欢迎。

Bills can be easily discounted in New York.

汇票在纽约贴现不算麻烦。

We discount the information, which seems to be somewhat exaggerated.

我方不完全相信这一消息，它似乎有些夸大。

注意，discount 是卖方给予买方的优惠或折让。

commission 表示佣金，是给予中间商或代理商的报酬。

8. quantity 数量，复数 quantities 表示多批、大批、大量

例句：We are prepared to purchase a shipment quantity of this material.

我们准备购买数量够一次装运的这种商品。

Quantities of black tea have been exported.

曾有大批红茶对外出口。

If you can not arrange entire quantity, please offer us at least half.

如果你方办不到全数，请至少报给我方半数。

在交易中，各类产品数量的表达方法：

additional quantity 追加数量

average quantity 平均数量

considerable quantity 大数量，同 large quantity，substantial quantity

corresponding quantity 相应的数量

enormous quantity 巨大的数量，同 huge quantity

entire quantity 整个数量

equal quantity 同等数量

estimated quantity 估计数量

exact quantity 准确数量

further quantity 额外数量

liberal quantity 充足的数量

limited quantity 有限的数量

maximum quantity 最大数量

minimum quantity 最小数量

moderate quantity 中等数量

reasonable quantity 相当数量

shipment quantity 够装运的数量

sizable quantity 可观的数量

small quantity 小数量

sufficient quantity 足够的数量

total quantity 总数量

9. dozen 一打=12 个 score=20 gross=144 个/12 dozen

（9）

Dear Sirs,

We are very pleased to receive your enquiry of January 15th and enclose our illustrated catalogue and price list giving the details you ask for. Also by separate post[1] we are sending you some sample[2] and feel confident that when you have examined[3] them you will agree the goods are both excellent in quality and reasonable in price.

Our regular purchases[4] in quantities of not less than 100 dozen of individual items we would allow you a discount of 2%. Payment is to be made by irrevocable L/C at sight[5].

Because of their softness and durability[6], our all cotton bed sheets and pillowcases are rapidly becoming popular and after studying our prices you will not be surprised to learn that we find it difficult to meet the demand[7]. But if you place your order[8] not later than the end of this month, we would ensure prompt shipment[9].

We invite your attention to[10] our other products such as tablecloth and table napkins[11], details of which you will find in the catalogue, and look forward to receiving your first order.

Yours faithfully,

Words, Expressions and Notes

1. by separate post 另外邮寄，同 under separate cover，by separate mail

注意，under cover 是随函寄去的意思。

例句：We are sending you catalogues under separate cover/by separate mail.

我方将把目录册另行寄出。

We have received, under cover, photographs of the offered goods.

我们已随函收到所报产品的照片。

2. sample 样品，动词表示取样、取样检验

例句：The sample is for reference only.

样品仅供参考。

We are advised by the users that they have sampled the goods and found the quality answer the purpose very well.

用户告诉我们他们曾取样检验，认为质量完全符合要求。

与样品有关的习惯表达：

counter sample 反样、对等样品

outturn sample 到货样品

as per sample 按照样品

equal to sample 和样品相同

free sample 免费样品，同 sample free of charge，sample of no charge

on the basis of sample 根据样品

up to sample 与样品相符

random sample 随机取样

representative sample 有代表性样品

sample book 样品册

sample pad 样品簿

sample of no value 无价样品

sample for reference 参考样品

3. examine 检验、审查

注意相关词汇的用法：

examine 指严密调查，以确定质量、效力、真实性或功能

inspect 指认真搜查可能出现的错误、缺陷

scrutinize 指密切观察微小细节

audit 指认真检查账目、审计账目

check 认真仔细检查以便一切都正确无误

例句：You'd better send your accountant to check the statement.

你最好派会计去查对一下报表。

Each bank is audited annually by a certified public accountant.

每年各家银行的账目都要由注册会计师进行审计。

The jeweler scrutinized the diamond of flaws.

珠宝商仔细查看钻石有无瑕疵。

On close inspection, it was found to be a forgery.

仔细检查，才发现它是伪造物。

4. regular purchases 经常性购买，长期购买

注意：buy 是一般性购买，而 purchase 强调较正式或规模较大的购买。

Procurement 正式大规模采购，如，Agreement on Government Procurement 政府采购协定

5. irrevocable L/C at sight 不可撤销即期信用证

at sight，即期；after sight，远期

6. softness and durability 指产品的柔软和耐用性

7. meet the demand 满足需求

8. place your order 你方订货。order 既是名词也是动词，表示订货、订单、订购短语 Place an order with…for…向……订购某种产品

例句：We thank you for your order of 100 tons Bitter Apricot Kernels.

感谢你方从我们这里订购 100 吨苦杏仁。

We are glad to place an order with you for 50 tons Dried Potato Slices.

我们很高兴向你方订购 50 吨干薯片。

Please do not send any remittance until the order is confirmed.

在未确认订单之前，请勿将款项汇来。

If you order immediately, we can probably arrange 5000 cases.

如果你方立即订货，我们可能安排 5000 箱。

We note that you contemplate ordering 2000 volleyballs at the same price as last.

我们注意到你方打算照上次价格订购 2000 个排球。

关于 order 的常见短语：

accept an order 接受订单

article made to order 订制品

bank money order/banker's order 银行汇票

be on order 已订货（尚未发货）

back order 尚未交货的订单

cancel an order 取消订单，同 cut an order，rescind an order，revoke an order

carry out an order 执行订单，同 execute an order，fulfill an order

confirm an order 确认、接受订货

decline an order 谢绝订货，同 refuse an order，turn down an order

hold up an order 暂停执行订单，同 suspend an order

mail order 邮购

letter order 信函订货

pending order 未完成的订单

repeat order 再次订货

trial order 试购订单

withdraw an order 撤回、取消订单

9. prompt shipment 即期装运，即刻发货

10. invite your attention to 提请某人注意。类似用法还有，call one's attention to, draw one's attention to, direct one's attention to

短语，bring sth to one's attention，提出某事请某人注意

receive one's attention 得到注意，予以办理

例句：We wish to call your attention to the shipment of our Order No.41.

我们提请你方注意办理装运我方 41 号订单的货物。

Your letter has received our careful attention.

来信已引起我们密切关注。

11. table napkins 餐巾

（10）

Dear Sirs,

We welcome[1] your enquiry of 5th January and thank you for your interest in our embroidered linen products[2].

As you may be well aware[3], we are a state-operated corporation handling this line of business for many years. So we are in a good position to serve our customers with the most reliable quality[4] of the line you suggested.

We can make products according to the given designs[5] and produce the designed goods in large quantities.

We are enclosing our illustrated catalogue giving the details you ask for. Also, under separate cover, we are sending you a full range of samples and, when you have a chance to examine them, we feel confident that you will agree that the quality of material used and the high standard of workmanship[6] will appeal[7] to the most selective[8]buyers.

We hope the catalogue and samples will reach you in good time[9] and look forward to your order.

Yours very truly,

Words, Expressions and Notes

1. welcome 欢迎。形容词表示受欢迎的，可以随便使用

例句：You are welcome.

欢迎，别客气，不用谢。

You are welcome to (use) any care here.

你可以随意使用这里的车。

Welcome in the new year.

欢喜迎新年。

2. embroidered linen products 刺绣亚麻产品

3. aware 知道的，后接 of 或 that 从句

当接 how，what，where，why 引起的名称从句时，介词 of 常常省略。在表示知道了解的很详细、充分时，习惯用 well，fully。

例句：We are well/fully aware of its importance.

我们充分认识到它的重要性。

We are not aware why you have not opened the L/C.

我们不知道你方为何还没有开出信用证。

We are aware of the change in the market.

我们看到了市场的变化。

We are not aware what has taken place.

我们不知发生了什么。

4. reliable quality 可靠的质量

形容词表示高质量的

例句：The goods are available in various qualities.

有各种不同质量的这种货物可以供应。

This is a quality product.

这是一种高质量的产品。

与 quality 有关的习惯短语：

average quality 平均质量

bad quality 劣等质量

above the average quality 一般水平以上的质量

below the average quality 一般水平以下的质量

best quality 最好的质量

choice quality 精选的质量，同 selective quality

common quality 一般质量

excellent quality 优良质量

fair quality 尚好的质量

fair average quality （F.A.Q）大路货

first-rate quality 头等质量

high quality 高质量

good merchantable quality（G.M.Q）尚好可销质量

inferior quality 次质量

low quality 低质量

popular quality 受欢迎的质量，大众化质量

prime quality 第一流质量，同 tip-top quality

sound quality 完好的质量

standard quality 标准质量

top quality 上等质量，同 top-notch quality

usual quality 通常质量

5. given designs 给定款式，既定样式

design 意为图样、图案、设计

6. high standard of workmanship 高水平的工艺标准

workmanship 表示手艺、工艺、做工，与 craftsman 相似。Standard，标准，习惯短语有：

up to standard 合格，达到标准

above standard 超过标准，高于标准

below standard 不达标，低于标准

standard job cost hour 标准人工小时

accounting standard 会计标准

financial standard 财务标准

product standard 产品标准

7. appeal 引起兴趣，另外还有呼吁、号召的意思

例句：We trust this new product of ours will appeal to your market.

相信我们的新产品将引起你方市场的兴趣。

They appealed to the public to help the distressed children.

他们呼吁公众帮助受难儿童。

8. selective 挑剔的

select， elect，pick，choose 都有选择、挑选的意思。但用法有所区别：

select 指大范围的挑选、精选，在选择中需要对价值有鉴别力。

pick 根据个人意愿仔细挑选。

choose 指采用确定下来的事物，含有判断的行为。

elect 常指选举

例句：This is a selected quality.

这是精选的质量。

The chairman of the board of directors was elected by ballot.

董事会主席是从不记名投票中选出的。

I don't know which of the three dresses to pick, I like them all.

我不知道这三件衣服选哪一个，这三件我都喜欢。

These samples are for you to choose from.

这些样品是供您选择的。

9. in good time 及时的，按时到

同 in due time，at the right and proper time

例句：We have received your letter of credit in good time.

我们已及时收到贵方信用证。

We expect to receive your shipping advice in due time.

我们盼望早日收到你方的装船通知。

（11）

Dear Sirs,

Thank you for the beautiful catalogue you sent us.

We are very interested in purchasing samples of various items. But we need to know the prices of your table and bed linens[1] so that we can decide which pieces to buy for use as sample. Would it be possible for you to give us the prices to the items you pictured in the catalogue? Then we can decide which items we want to buy.

We have contacted US Customs[2] and waiting to hear from the tariff[3] expert. He will give us a binding[4] rule as to which tariff rate applies to these products. He will also let us know about quota regulations[5].

Thank you for your cooperation in these matters. We look forward to hearing from you again soon.

Very truly yours,

Words, Expressions and Notes

1. table and bed linens 床单与桌布
2. customs 复数指海关、关税

此外，还有习惯、光顾的意思；形容词意为定制的、定做的，如：custom car 定制车；custom shoes 定做的鞋

例句：They say it is their custom to do so

他们说这样办是他们的惯例。

We look forward to your continued custom.

我们期待你不断光顾。

相关短语：

custom of merchant 商业习惯

custom of trade 贸易惯例、行业习惯

customs auction 海关拍卖

customs authorities 海关当局

customs area 海关境界（关境）

customs barrier 关税壁垒

customs broker 海关经纪人，报关行

customs bond 海关保税

customs clearance 出口结关

customs charges 海关收费

customs cover 关封

customs detention 海关扣留

customs duties 关税

customs declaration 报关单

customs entry 进口报关

customs examination 验关

customs formalities 海关手续

customs invoice 海关发票

customs officer 海关人员

customs seal 海关加封

customs tariff 关税税则

customs union 关税同盟

3. tariff 关税，也有收费、费用表的意思

习惯短语：freight tariff 运费费率表

tariff barrier 关税壁垒

non-tariff barrier 非关税壁垒

railway tariff 铁路运费表

tariff bargaining 关税协商

tariff ceiling 关税最高额

tariff preference 关税特惠

tariff free 免税

tariff free zone 自由关税区

tariff rate 关税税率

注意，duty，tariff 和 tax 的用法。

duty 主要表示进口税；tariff 既表示进口税，也表示出口税；tax 是指由政府机关强制征收、并用于政府开支的税款。

4. binding 有约束力的，例如，

The decision made by the arbitration organization shall be taken as final and binding both parties.

仲裁机构的裁决是终局的，对双方均有约束力。

5. quota regulations 配额规定

关于配额的习惯短语：

absolute quota 绝对配额　annual quota 年度配额

bilateral quota 协定配额　customs quota 海关配额、关税配额

exchange quota system 外汇限额制度

export quota 出口限额　export retention quota 出口外汇保留额

import quota system 进口配额　quota administered 配额管理

quota allocation 配额分配

例句：The quota is to be allocated on pro-rata basis.

配额将按照比例分配。

regulation，规章、条例、规则。相关短语：

currency regulations 外汇条例

detailed regulation 细则，同 minor regulation

economic regulation 经济调整

price regulation 定价法则

trade regulation 贸易条例

例句：The regulations shall, subject to the approval of the Ministry of Finance of the People's Republic of China, become effective as from August 1, 2009.

本规章经中华人民共和国财政部批准，自 2009 年 8 月 1 日起执行。

（12）

Dear Sirs,

Many reports have been received from our selling agents[1] in Hong Kong, that there are very heavy demands[2] for the captioned garments[3].

From Taiwan Export Directory[4], we are pleased to know that your mill[5] is the most well known producer of this item in Taiwan. We, therefore, are writing to you for quotations for Acrylic Sweaters[6] for men and women of all three sizes: large, medium, and small. As expected, the quantity of our orders to be placed will be very large, and it is anticipated[7] that the prices you are going to quote would be very competitive. Moreover, since the season[8] is coming soon, early deliveries[9] are absolutely necessary.

Please be assured that should your prices be competitive, we will place our orders with you and open L/C in your favor[10] in time.

Your prompt reply to this inquiry will be appreciated.

Faithfully yours,

Words, Expressions and Notes

1. agent 代理人

agency 表示代理处、代理权；机构部门如厅、署、局、社

相关短语：agent middleman 代理中间人

agent service 代理业务

buying agent 采购代理人，同 purchasing agent

chartering agent 租船代理人

forwarding agent 货运代理人、运输代理人

press agency 新闻社

advertising agency 广告公司

agency agreement 代理协议

agency commission 代理手续费，代理佣金

a government agency 政府机构

law enforcement agency 执法当局

exclusive agent 独家代理，同 sole agent

selling agent 销售代理人

ship's agent 船舶代理人

the delcredere agent 信用担保代理人

the agent carrying stock 储货代理人

the agent of necessary 可观需要时代理人

例句：We have decided to entrust you with the sole agency for our embroideries in US for a period of one year.

我方已决定委托你公司为我方刺绣产品在美国的独家代理，期限一年。

2. heavy demands 很大的需求

demand 既可用作名词，也可用作动词

常见短语：active demand 畅销

actual demand 实际需要

articles in great demand 畅销货

consumer demand 消费需求

demand draft 即期汇票

demand deposit 活期存款

demand loan 活期贷款

latent demand 潜伏需求

overfull demand 过多需求

payable on demand 见票即付

total demand 总需求

3. garments 服装、衣服

4. Export Directory 出口指南

5. mill 公司、工厂

各类工厂的习惯表达：

flour mill 面粉厂　paper mill 造纸厂

printing and dyeing mill 印染厂　timber mill 木材厂

wool-spinning mill 毛纺厂，同 woolen mill

tobacco factory 香烟厂　cloth factory 制衣工厂

garmenting/clothing factory 服装厂

cosmetics factory 化妆品厂　furniture factory 家具厂

canning factory 罐头厂　pharmaceutical factory 制药厂

grain processing factory 粮食加工厂

non-staple food processing factory 副食品加工厂

water pump factory 水泵厂

aeroplane factory/works 飞机制造厂

chemical factory/plant/works 化工厂

ship-building plant/yard 造船厂

diesel engine plant 柴油机厂

automobile plant/works 汽车制造厂

power plant 发电厂　electric machinery plant 电机厂

heat and power plant 热电厂　crane factory 起重机厂

feed processing plant 饲料加工厂

wrist watch plant 手表厂　munition works 军工厂

gun- power woks 火药厂　brick works 砖厂

petrochemical works 石油化工厂　cement works 水泥厂

iron works 炼铁厂

6. Acrylic Sweaters 人造纤维毛绒衫，acrylic 丙烯酸纤维、树脂、颜料

7. anticipated 盼望、预计、期望

另外，还有提前的意思。anticipation 是名词。

例句：We anticipate your acceptance.

盼你方接受。

We anticipate that fresh supplies will arrive next month.

我们预计新货将于下月到货。

We can not anticipate shipment by any length of time.

我们无法提前装运期。

We thank you in anticipation.

先此致谢。

Buyers are holding off in anticipation of lower prices.

买主预计价格下跌而停止买进。

8. season 季节（商业等）当令期、生产年度

习惯搭配：be in season 正合时令

be out of season 不合时令

be off/dull/slack season 淡季

be busy/rush/peak season 旺季

例句：It is off (dull, slack) season for walnuts.

这是核桃的淡季

The goods are out of season now.

此货现在不合时令。

It is reported that in an effort to make up for its smaller domestic production this season, China had imported large quantities of coconut oil.

据报道，为了弥补本生产年度国内生产的不足，中国已进口大量椰子油。

We wish you the Compliments of the Season!

祝节日好！恭贺佳节！

9. deliveries 交货。远洋贸易中表示交货期时 deliver 与 shipment 可互用。

关于 delivery 的习惯短语有：

take delivery 提货　　make delivery 交货

actual/physical delivery 实际交货

forward delivery 远期交货

near delivery 近期交货

partial delivery 分批交货

short delivery 交货不足，短交

例句：We will take delivery of the goods as soon as they are released from the Customs.

一旦海关放行我们就把货物提出。

When we made delivery to the buyers, they refused it on seeing the damaged condition.

当我们向买方交货时，他们见到残损情况拒绝收货。

注：FOB（free on board）俗称离岸价，CIF（cost insurance and freight）被称作到岸价。它们都是典型的贸易术语，用来描述国际贸易中买卖双方权利、责任和风险的划分，以及商品价格的构成。

自 1936 年起，国际商会就制定了《国际贸术语解释通则》来指导进出口贸易各方当事人的商业行为。同时为适应环境变化和科技进步，平均每 10 年就对“通则”修订一次。其中，《2010 年国际贸易术语解释通则》（International Rules for the Interpretation of Trade Terms 2010，缩写 Incoterms® 2010）是国际商会根据国际货物贸易的发展，对《2000 年国际贸易术语解释通则》的修订，2010 年 9 月 27 日公布，于 2011 年 1 月 1 日实施。

《2010 年国际贸易术语解释通则》删去了《2000 年国际贸易术语解释通则》4 个术语：DAF（Delivered at Frontier）边境交货、DES（Delivered Ex Ship）目的港船上交货、DEQ（Delivered Ex Quay）目的港码头交货、DDU（Delivered Duty Unpaid）未完税交货，新增了两个术语：DAT（delivered at terminal）在指定目的地或目的港的集散站交货、DAP（delivered at place）在指定目的地交货。即用 DAP 取代了 DAF、DES 和 DDU 三个术语，DAT 取代了 DEQ，且扩展至适用于一切运输方式。

修订后的《2010 年国际贸易术语解释通则》取消了“船舷”的概念，卖方承担货物装上船为止的一切风险，买方承担货物自装运港装上船后的一切风险。在 FAS，FOB，CFR 和 CIF 等术语中加入了货物在运输期间被多次买卖（连环贸易）的责任义务的划分。考虑到对于一些大的区域贸易集团内部贸易的特点，Incoterms® 2010 不仅适用于国际销售合同，也适用于国内销售合同。

《2010 年国际贸易术语解释通则》共有 11 种贸易术语，按照所适用的运输方式划分为两大类：

第一组：适用于任何运输方式的术语 7 种：EXW、FCA、CPT、CIP、DAT、DAP 和 DDP

EXW（ex works）	工厂交货
FCA（free carrier）	货交承运人
CPT（carriage paid to）	运费付至目的地
CIP（carriage and insurance paid to）	运费/保险费付至目的地
DAT（delivered at terminal）	目的地或目的港的集散站交货
DAP（delivered at place）	目的地交货
DDP（delivered duty paid）	完税后交货

第二组：适用于水上运输方式的术语 4 种：FAS、FOB、CFR、CIF

FAS（free alongside ship）	装运港船边交货
FOB（free on board）	装运港船上交货
CFR（cost and freight）	成本加运费
CIF（cost insurance and freight）	成本、保险费加运费

10. in your favor 以你方为受益人，即有权依据信用证开出汇票索取信用证金额的当事人。favor 作为名词有欢迎、赞许的意思；作为动词意为赞成、支持、有利于

例句：Chinese commodities have enjoyed rowing favor among buyers abroad.

中国商品在国外受到越来越多买家的欢迎。

The opportunity does not favor our making a binding arrangement.

这一机会不利于我们做出一项有约束性的安排。

He said he favored the development of permanent trade relations with China.

他说他赞成与中国发展永久性的贸易关系。

The letter of credit has been opened in your favor.

信用证已开给你方名下（以你方为受益人）。

(13)

Re: SWC Sugar

Dear Sirs,

We have just received an enquiry from one of our Japan Clients who needs 10000 metric tons of the captioned sugar and shall appreciate your quoting us your best price at the earlier date[1].

For your information[2], the quality required should be superior white crystal sugar packed in new gunny bags[3] of 100 kgs each. Meanwhile, the goods should be surveyed[4] by an independent surveyor as to[5] their quality and weight before shipment. For this enquiry, the buyers will arrange shipping and insurance, therefore the price to be quoted by you should be on a FAS Dalian basis.

As there is a critical shortage[6] of sugar in Japan, the goods should be ready for shipment as early as possible. Please be assured that if your price is acceptable, we will place order with you right away.

Your early reply to this enquiry is requested[7].

Faithfully yours,

Words, Expressions and Notes

1. date 日期，约会，动词意为约定、注明日期

习惯搭配：up to date 时髦、新颖　　out of date 过时、陈旧

Chinese date 红枣　　dating agency 婚姻介绍所

at an early date 不久，在最近期间

例句：We confirm your fax of even date.

我们确认收到你方当天的传真。

We have sold you a total of 100 tons to date.

我们迄今为止卖给你方共 100 吨货。

The design is out of date.

这个图案过时了。

The letter was dated February 5 from Hong Kong.

这封信是 2 月 5 日写于香港。

Dating agency shouldn't be the first choice for those graduates.

婚姻介绍所不应成为大学毕业生的首要选项。

Chinese date is becoming very popular on Japanese market.

红枣在日本市场非常受欢迎。

2. for your information 顺便告知你方

3. gunny bags 麻袋

4. survey 检查，鉴定，调查。动词意为现场调查

惯用短语：customs surveyor 海关调查人员

engineer surveyor 工程检验员

insurance surveyor 保险检验员

marine surveyor 海事鉴定人

survey report 鉴定报告

surveyor's report 检验行报告，鉴定行报告

project survey 工程勘察、测量

例句：Please survey the business possibilities and advise your findings.

请调查交易可能性并告知结果。

Please survey the situation closely and keep us informed of developments.

请密切观察形势并将发展情况随时告知我们。

5. as to 至于，关于，根据

6. critical shortage 严重短少

shortage 作为名词表示不足，数量不够

例句：Please do your utmost to ship shortage by the next available steamer.

请尽力把短交数目由下次船运来。

There is a shortage of 200 lbs.

货物短少 200 磅。

7. request 请求、恳求

习惯短语：request sb. to do sth. 请求某人做某事

at the request of (at one's request) 应某人的请求

on request 一经要求就做

by request 依照请求

in request 需要

例句：Visitors are requested not to touch the exhibits.

来宾请勿触碰展品。

It is requested that the two orders be shipped in one lot.

两笔订货请一次发运。

At your request, we give you an estimate of approximate requirements for this year.

应你们的要求，我们给你方今年需求量的大概估计数。

We gave your representative, by request, a list of our current availabilities.

如有要求，我们会给你方代表一份本公司现在可供给的货单。

Catalogues will be sent on request.

目录承索即寄。

This commodity is now in enormous request.

需要此货的客户很多。

Section 3 Supplements 知识补充

Useful Sentences On Enquiries

1. We are interested in the desk lamps you advertised in the May issue of *Good Housekeeping*.
你们在 5 月期《好管家》刊登的台灯广告，我们很感兴趣。

2. Please let us know their prices for the bamboo toys as advertised in yesterday's *New York Times*, and the earliest possible date of delivery.

请告昨日《纽约时报》所刊登广告介绍的竹制玩具价格及最早交货期。

3. We specialize in supplying small stores in rural areas. Over 3 000 of these stores virtually depend on us, and this assured sales outlet enables us to dispose of fairly large quantities.

我们专向乡镇小商店供货。3000 家以上的这种商店全都依靠我们。这些有保证的销路足使我们能大量推销。

4. We regularly buy…and would like to know what you have to offer.

我们定期购买……并且想知道贵公司的报价如何。

5. We would like very much to continue to do business with you and are now awaiting your offer.

我公司很乐意跟你公司继续有业务往来，且正在等待你公司的报盘。

6. As the brochures you sent us were badly damaged in the mail, we would like you to mail us some more.

你公司寄来的产品简介小册子在邮寄途中已完全损坏，希望你公司能再多寄一些来。

7. Please tell us how long this price list is valid.

请告诉我们这个价目单的有效期有多长。

8. Please inform us whether you guarantee your products.

请通知我们，贵公司是否愿意对商品加以保证。

9. What quantities of the specified item can you regularly deliver on short notice?

请通告我们在短期内你公司能定期运送多少数量的上述这些产品？

10. Your samples should give us an idea of the colors and quality of the products.

你公司寄来的样品，使我们对你公司产品的色彩与品质有所了解。

11. Please send us three copies of you latest catalogue at your earliest convenience.

请尽早寄最新目录 3 份。

12. We would appreciate your sending us a catalogue of your Rubber Boots together with terms of payment and the largest discount you can allow us.

请寄橡胶靴目录，并注明你方付款条件及能给予的最大折扣。

13. Please send us your latest catalogue with your best CIF Pairs prices. We will also appreciate your telling us the approximate weight of each article.

请寄附有最优惠的成本加保险费、运费到巴黎价的最新商品目录，并请告知每件货物的大约重量。

14. We have the pleasure of sending you under separate cover, a new catalogue which lists the complete line of our sporting goods. For your information, we checked the items which we hope especially interest you.

现另邮寄我们全部体育用品的新目录一本。为供你方参考，我们核对了那些我们认为你们会特别感兴趣的项目。

15. We cannot trim (take) anything off the price.

此价不能再降。

16. Heavy enquiries witness the quality of our products.
大量询盘证明我方产品质量过硬。

17. As soon as the price picks up, enquiries will revive.
一旦价格回升，询盘将恢复活跃。

18. Enquiries are dwindling.
询盘正在减少。

19. Generally speaking, inquiries are made by the buyers.
一般来说，询盘由买方发出。

20. We regret that the goods you inquire about are not available.
很遗憾，你们所询购的货物现在无货。

21. We can not take care of your enquiry at present.
我们现在无力顾及你方的询盘。

22. Your enquiry is too vague to enable us to reply you.
你方询盘不明确，我们无法答复。

23. China National Silk Corporation received the inquiry sheet sent by a American company.
中国丝绸公司收到了一份美国公司的询价单。

24. May I have an idea of your prices?
可以了解一下你们的价格吗？

25. If your prices are favorable, I can place the order right away.
如果你方价格优惠，我们可以马上订货。

26. When can I have your firm CIF prices, Mr. Li?
李先生，什么时候能得到你们到岸价的实盘？

27. We would rather have you quote us FOB prices.
我们希望你方报离岸价。

28. He inquired about the varieties, specifications and price, and so on.
他询问了品种、规格和价格等情况。

29. Your ad in today's *China Daily* interests us and we will be glad to receive samples with your prices.
你们刊登在今天《中国日报》上的广告，我们很感兴趣。如能寄来样品并附上价格，不胜欣慰。

30. Please quote your lowest price CIF Seattle for each of the following items, including our 5% commission.

请就下列每项货物向我方报最低到岸价，运费、保险费付至西雅图，其中包括我方5%的佣金。

Terms Used in Making Enquirres

discount	折扣
reduction	降价

allowance 折扣
rebate 回扣
cash discount 现金折扣
quantity discount 数量折扣
special discount 特别折扣
credit 信用
credit analysis 信用分析
credit information 信用情报
credit limit 信用限额，贷款限额
credit line 信用透支
credit rating 信用评级
credit reference 信用参考
credit standing 信用状况
do business on a credit basis 凭信用交易
enjoy credit 享有信誉
impair one's credit 危害信誉
make credit purchase 凭信用采购
spoil one's credit 损害信誉
price 价格
advance 上涨
boost 上涨
decline 下降
dip 下降
drop 跌落
fall 下降
gain 上涨
go down 下降
increase 上涨
jump 上涨
raise 提高

Exercises

Ⅰ. Use the following words and phrases in the sentences of your own.

in advance
up to sample
direct one's attention to
appeal to

state-operated

in large quantities

under separate cover

first-rate quality

fair average quality

in due time

customs entry

tariff rate

ruling price

by request

on sale

trade regulation

be in receipt of

at a discount

out of season

forwarding agent

sole agent

articles in great demand

ceiling price

exceptional price

take delivery

make delivery

for your information

packing list

on request

Documents against Acceptance

Ⅱ. Translate the following sentences into English.

1. 承蒙伊斯威尔的布朗公司告知你公司地址，现我们想了解。
2. 从 ABC 公司处得知你公司现能供应的水果和干果。
3. 你们在本月《中国对外贸易》上所刊登的广告，我们很感兴趣，现请告该商品的详细情况。
4. 我们有意获得你方刺绣亚麻品的商品目录及价目单。
5. 这笔交易不是根据样品成交的。
6. 正如你们所知，我们是经营此类商品已有多年的国有公司。
7. 易碎物品需小心装卸。
8. 如果你们第一笔运来的货令人满意，随后将有大批续订。
9. 你们的价格与当前这里的市场价一致。

10. 买主要求卖方在一周内装运 1 万吨的磷酸岩。
11. 我们已收到日本一客户的询价，他需要 13 吨的标题糖。
12. 一旦收到你方具体询盘，我们将立即给你们报最优惠的拉格斯到岸价。
13. 关于支付条件，我们需要不可撤销的凭即期汇票支付的信用证。
14. 我们过去通常由美国进口自行车，但现在转向其他国家购买。
15. 随函附上根据你方第 15 号询价单所开的报价单，期待你方确认。

Ⅲ. Translate the following letters into English or Chinese.

1

承蒙英国驻北京大使馆商赞处得知你公司地址。该处已告知我们，你公司要购买化工产品。为此今特与你公司联系，希望与你公司建立互利的贸易关系。

我公司是国有公司，独家经营化工产品进出口业务。现随函附寄我公司目前可以供应的主要出口商品表一份。如你公司需要该表所列项目以外的任何商品，我公司一旦接到你方详细货单，将尽力为你方提供所需商品。

兹并奉告，我们在同欧洲国家的客户进行贸易时，一贯坚持平等互利，互通有无的原则，以便通过双方共同努力，促进业务和友谊，共同受益。

盼早日接到你公司的询盘。

2

Dear Sirs,

We learn from the Chamber of Commerce of Tokyo, Japan that you are producing for export shoes and handbags in a variety of natural leathers. There is a steady demand here for leather products of high quality and although sales are not particularly high, good prices are obtained.

Will you please send me a copy of your catalogue, with details of your prices and terms of payment? I should find it most helpful if you could also supply samples of the various skins in which the shoes and handbags are supplied.

Yours sincerely,

Ⅳ. Draw a letter of a general enquiry asking for all the information you need.

Chapter 4

Offers

Section 1 Business Knowledge 业务知识

报盘，又叫发盘、发价，在法律上叫“要约”，即一项定约的建议。在中文里以上几种叫法都可以，但在英文里只有一种叫法——offer。

报盘按报盘人的身份可分为买方报盘和卖方报盘。习惯上常由卖方报盘，若买方接受，就依照卖方条件成交。买方报盘（bid 或 buying-offer），是由买方向卖方报出交易条件，卖方如接受，买方就可以依据这些条件订货。

如果从报盘形势来分，又可以分为口头和书面两种。口头一般是通过电话洽谈发出的报盘。书面报盘又有信件报盘和传真报盘之分。信件报盘是各种报盘的基础，如果不掌握好信件报盘的写作，无论是口头还是传真都不可能做好。

报盘按先后顺序可分为主动报盘（volunteer offer）和对询盘信的答复（reply to inquiry）。这两种报盘内容相似，只不过主动报盘的内容多一些宣传、劝说型的色彩；而对询盘信的答复则多半是针对来信的内容。

报盘从法律责任来分，又可分为有约束力的报盘（offer with engagement）和无约束力的报盘（offer without engagement）。有约束力的报盘也叫正式发盘（formal offer）或有效发盘（effective offer）；无约束力的报盘也叫自由发盘（free offer）。

有约束力的报盘属于实盘（firm offer），无约束力的报盘属于虚盘（non-firm offer）。在日常的外贸业务中，我们主要就用这两种说法。分清实盘和虚盘，掌握两者的关键性区别，是本单元学习的重点。

实盘对报盘的人有约束力，在发盘规定的有效期内不得更改或撤销已发出的报盘。反之，虚盘则没有约束力，可以更改、撤销已发出的报盘。下面着重介绍一下实盘的业务知识。

实盘，也即有效发盘，根据有关国际公约，它的成立需满足如下条件。

（1）向一个或一个以上特定的人提出（Offer is aimed at an specific person or persons.）

特定的人是指在发盘中指明个人姓名或企业名称的受盘人，这一点是区别普通广告的重要特征。大众商业广告通常没有指出特定的接受者，所以并没有普遍的约束力。

（2）表明订约意旨（Indicate sincere intention of reaching agreement or concluding a contract

作为发盘人（offerer）在受盘人（offeree）同意其发盘内容时，要有与对方缔结合同的诚意。若发盘文中含有“仅供参考”（FOR REFERENCE），“须以发盘人的最后确认为准”（SUBJECT TO OUR FINAL CONFIRMATION）等类似用语，则表明发盘人不受约束，发盘也就不是实盘了。

（3）内容必须十分确定（Contents of an offer should be sufficiently definite.）

发盘内容十分确定要具备以下 3 个基本要素：标明货物的名称，明示或默示地规定货物的数量或规定数量的方法，明示或默示地规定货物的价格或规定价格的方法。所以这里讲的十分确定其实是对发盘内容的最低要求。为了提高效率、利用成交，发盘的内容不应以此为限。

（4）送达受盘人（Offer should reach the offeree.）

送达受盘人是发盘在时间上的生效起点。送达的标志是发盘到达受盘人的营业地点或惯常居住地，或送抵受盘人特定的接收系统。在此之前，即便受盘人从其他渠道获悉了发盘内容，也不能对在传递途中的发盘表示接受。

关于发盘的约束力，各地区的习惯做法并不相同。

英美法系的国家认为发盘原则上对发盘人没有约束力。发盘人在受盘人对发盘表示接受之前的任何时候，都可以撤回发盘或变更其内容。发盘的撤回（withdraw）是指发盘人将尚未被受盘人收到的发盘予以取消的行为。

大陆法系的国家普遍认为发盘对发盘人有约束力。

一项发盘在特定情况下，其效力会终止（termination）。这意味着发盘人不再受发盘的约束；同时受盘人失去了接受该发盘的权利。发盘失效的情形主要有以下 4 方面的原因。

（1）在有效期内未被接受而过期

发盘规定的有效期（valid period）是给受盘人考虑交易条件、决定是否接受的时间限制。这期限究竟多长，并无定则。一般来说，发盘有效期的长短取决于商品的种类、市场情况和交易额等因素。因为世界各地之间有明显的时差，规定有效期最好将时差因素考虑进来。若到期，受盘人尚未接受发盘内容。发盘将失去约束力，发盘人可以变更交易条件。

（2）发盘被受盘人拒绝或还盘

如果拒绝通知或还盘（counter-offer）经由受盘人做出，则表明他已经拒绝了发盘提出的交易条件，此时发盘亦将失去效力。

（3）发盘人有效撤销发盘

发盘撤销（revocation）是指发盘已送达受盘人的情况下，发盘人将其取消的行为。按公约规定：已为受盘人收到的发盘，如果撤销的通知在受盘人发出接受通知之前送达受盘人，可予以撤销。但是，下列两种情况不能撤销：发盘规定有效期或以其他方式表明是不可撤销的；受盘人有理由信赖这项发盘是不可撤销的，并已本着这种信赖采取了行动。

（4）不可抗力

某些特定的不可抗力（force majeure），如严重的自然灾害会导致发盘人丧失行为能力，无法

按发盘中的条件来履行义务。这种情况下，应解除发盘对发盘人的约束力。

至于发盘信函的写作，需要遵循以下 4 个主要原则。

（1）明确、准确的答复对方的询盘。（To reply to enquiry of your trade partner definitely and accurately.）

（2）在报盘中最好包含全部交易条件。（You had better comprise all the trade terms in the offer.）

（3）如是实盘，需要注明有效期。（If it is firm offer, write clearly the validity.）

（4）在报盘时对商品值得炫耀的地方多加渲染。（To stress the part of the commodity worth saying high.）

Section 2 Specimen Letters 样函

（1）

Dear Sirs,

We have recently received a number of enquiries for your light-weight raincoats[1] and have good reasons to believe[2] that we could place regular orders with[3] you if your prices are competitive.

From the description in your catalogue we learn that your "D.D." range is the one most suitable for these clients[4] and should be glad if you would send us your quotation for men's and women's raincoat, in both small and medium sizes[5], delivered on CIF Kuwait basis. If your prices are reasonable, we should place a first order for 400 raincoats, namely 100 raincoats each of the four qualities. Shipment would be required within four weeks of order[6].

We would particularly stress the importance of price since the principal market here is for mass-produced[7] goods at popular prices[8].

Yours sincerely,

Words, Expressions and Notes

1. light-weight raincoats 轻便雨衣
2. have good reasons to believe 有充分的理由相信
3. place regular orders with 向某人长期订货
4. clients 客户，常客
5. small and medium sizes 小号和中号
6. within four weeks of order 签订单后 4 周内
7. mass-produced 大量生产的
8. popular prices 大众化价格

（2）

Dear Sirs,

Thank you for your letter of May 6th. We are glad to learn of the inquiries you have had from your customers for our raincoats. Our "D.D" range is particularly suitable for warm climates[1], and

during the past years we have supplied this range to dealers in several tropical countries[2], from many of whom we have already had repeated orders[3]. This range is popular not only because it is light in weight, but also because the material used has been specially treated[4] to prevent excessive condensation[5] on the inside surface.

For the quantities you mentioned we are pleased to quote as follows:

"D.D" Raincoats

100 men's medium @ US$ 14.50 US$ 1,450

100 men's small @ US$ 14.0 US$ 1,400

100 women's medium @ US$ 13.2 US$ 1,320

100 women's small @ US$ 12.7 US$ 1.270

Total US$ 5,440

Payment: by irrevocable L/C at sight[6]

Shipment: will be effected within three or four weeks after receiving the L/C.

This offer is subject to[7] our final confirmation. We feel you may be interested in our other products and enclose some pamphlets for your reference.

We are awaiting your early orders.

Yours sincerely,

Words, Expressions and Notes

1. warm climate 暖热气候
2. tropical countries 热带国家
3. repeated orders 重复订货
4. specially treated 经特殊处理的
5. excessive condensation 过多的水汽、冷凝液
6. irrevocable L/C at sight 不可撤销的即期信用证
7. be subject to 以……为准，须经……才有效

（3）

Dear Sirs,

We thank you for your inquiry of July 11th for Eiderdown Pillows[1].

The item you inquired is handled by China National Animal By-products[2] Import and Export Corporation, Guangdong Branch[3]. We have accordingly[4] passed on your inquiry to[5] them and they will get in touch with you directly.

We trust your inquiry will get the careful and prompt attention[6] by our sister corporation[7].

Yours faithfully,

Words, Expressions and Notes

1. Eiderdown Pillows 羽绒枕，eiderdown 的意思是鸭绒、鸭绒被

2. Animal By-products 畜产品
3. Branch 这里指分公司
4. accordingly 相应地，因此
5. passed on…to 把某物转交给……
6. careful and prompt attention 认真即时地处理、对待
7. sister corporation 指兄弟公司

（4）

Dear Sirs,

Thank you for your letter of June 25th, 2008 and we are pleased to offer you as follows:

Commodity: Green Bean[1]

Hebei Origin[2], 2007 Crop[3]

Quantity: 200 metric tons[4]

Price: ￡240 per metric ton CFR Antwerp[5]

Packing: in ordinary second-hand gunny bags[6]

Shipment: in September 2008

Payment: by irrevocable L/C, payable by draft at sight

This offer is subject to our confirmation. If you find it acceptable, please let us have your reply as soon as possible.

Yours faithfully,

Words, Expressions and Notes

1. Green Bean 青豆，嫩菜豆
2. Hebei Origin 产地在河北省
3. 2007 Crop 2007 年的收成、产量
4. metric tons 度量衡为公制单位时的重量单位，意为吨
5. ￡240 per metric ton CFR Antwerp 每吨 240 英镑，成本加运费，目的港为安特里普
6. second-hand gunny bags 旧麻袋

（5）

Dear Sirs,

Re: Copper

We thank you for your letter of March 10th, and confirm having faxed you today in reply, as per confirmation copy enclosed[1]. You will note from our fax that we are in a position to[2] offer you 50 tons of copper at the attractive price of Stg.[3] 500 per ton CFR Shanghai for delivery within one month after you placing an order with us. Payment of the purchase is to be effected by an irrevocable L/C in our favor, payable by draft at sight in Pounds Sterling[4] in London.

This offer is firm subject to your immediate reply that should reach us not later than the end of this month[5]. There is little likelihood of the goods remaining unsold once this particular offer has lapsed[6].

Yours faithfully,

Words, Expressions and Notes

1. as per confirmation copy enclosed 如所附抄件
2. be in a position to do 可以做……
3. Stg. 英镑的缩写
4. Pounds Sterling 英制货币单位，英镑
5. not later than the end of this month 不晚于本月底

此句表示发盘的有效期（validity）。发盘有效期多种规定如下。

规定最迟接受期限

This offer is subject to your reply reaching us before 18th.

此发盘限 18 日复到我方。

规定一段接受时期

The offer is effective for 7 days.

该项发盘有效期为 7 天。

不明确规定有效期

一般情况下，没有明确有效期的发盘，其效力应保持在一段合理时间（reasonable time），“合理时间”究竟有多长，各国并没有明确规定或解释。一般说来，“合理时间”要考虑到双方当事人的利益，既不能让发盘人等待太久，又要给受盘人足够的考虑及准备时间，还要适当考虑到交易的情况及行业惯例和习惯做法供受盘人考虑交易条件，决定是否接受。

口头发盘的有效期

对口头发盘，立即接受才能视为有效或者另行规定有效期。

6. lapse 过期，失效

（6）

Dear Sirs,

Thank You for your enquiry of October 13th for Flax Waste[1], admixture[2] not exceeding 15%. In reply, we make you an offer for 30 tons for January 2010 shipment at USD 224 per metric ton CIF Hamburg. We trust you will find our offer profitable[3]. If so, please telex[4] us your acceptance before its expiry[5] on November 15.

As regards[6] Flax Waste 2nd grade, admixture 20% ~ 30%, the price remains unchanged at the level last quoted[7].

We await your further news.

Yours faithfully,

Words, Expressions and Notes

1. Flax Waste 废亚麻
2. admixture 杂质
3. profitable 可获利的，有利可图的
4. telex 电传

在交易磋商中，常用的电讯方式有

Telegraph /cable 电报

Facsimile /Fax 传真

e-mail 电子邮件

SWIFT （Society for Worldwide Interbank Financial Telecommunication）环球同业银行金融电讯协会

5. expiry 届满，到期。此处指发盘有效期终止
6. As regards 关于
7. unchanged at the level last quoted 与上次报价一样

（7）

Dear Sirs,

We thank you for your inquiry of August 1st. As requested[1], we are airmailing you, under separate cover, one catalogue and sample books[2] for our Shanghai printed pure silk fabrics[3]. We hope they will reach you in due course and will help you in making your selection. In order to start a concrete transaction between us, we take pleasure in making you a special offer, subject to our final confirmation, as follows:

Article: No. 8002 Shanghai Printed Pure Silk Fabrics

Design: No. 46829-2 A

Specification: 30×35

Minimum[4]: 20,000 yards

Packing: in bales[5] or in wooden cases, at seller's option

Price: US$ 54 per yard CIF Lisbon

Shipment: to be made in three equal monthly installments[6], beginning from November, 2009

Payment: by confirmed, irrevocable L/C payable by draft at sight to be opened 30 days before the time of shipment.

We trust the above offer will be acceptable to you and await with keen interest your trial order.

Yours faithfully,

Words, Expressions and Notes

1. As requested 根据要求
2. sample book 样品册
3. printed pure silk fabrics 印花纯丝细布
4. Minimum 这里指对外贸易中的最小购买量、启购量
5. bales 包，打成包，捆装
6. in three equal monthly installments 分 3 次按月平均装运

(8)

Dear Sirs,

We confirm your fax of 2nd July asking us to make you a firm offer for Dried Plum[1].

We would inform you that few parcels[2] we have at present are under offer elsewhere[3]. However, if you should make us an acceptable bid[4], there is the possibility of your obtaining them.

As you know, there has been a large demand for dried plum lately, and such a growing demand can only result in increased prices. However you may avail yourselves of the advantage of this strengthening market[5] if you will send us an immediately reply.

Yours faithfully,

Words, Expressions and Notes

1. Dried Plum 干李子、干梅
2. parcels 此处指产品、货物
3. under offer elsewhere 向其他人报盘
4. an acceptable bid 可以接受的递价，指买方提出购买条件
5. strengthening market 坚挺的市场，行市上涨

类似的表达如下。

The market is advance.

The market rises.

The market stiffens.

The market hardens.

flat 与此相反，表示冷清、平淡，如：

The market has been flat this year. 今年市场上生意一直冷清。

(9)

Dear Sirs,

We thank you for your telex enquiry for both Groundnut and Walnutmeat[1] CFR Copenhagen dated Sept.25.

In reply[2], we offer[3] firm, subject[4] to your reply reaching us on or before Sept.30th for 250 metric tons[5] of Groundnuts, Handpicked, Shelled and Ungraded[6] at RMB¥2000 net per metric ton CFR Copenhagen[7] and any other European Main Ports[8], Shipment to be made within two months after receipt of your order, payment by L/C payable by sight draft.

Please note that we have quoted our most favorable price[9] and are unable to entertain[10] any counteroffer.

As you are aware that there has been lately a large demand for the above commodities, such growing demand has doubtlessly resulted in[11] increased prices. However you may avail yourselves of the strengthening market if you will send us an immediate reply.

Yours faithfully,

Words，Expressions and Notes

1. Groundnut and Walnutmeat 花生与核桃仁

常见坚果的单词如下。

apricot kernel 杏仁

cashew kernel 腰果

chestnut 栗子

groundnut in shell 带壳的花生

hazelnut 榛子

groundnut shelled 去壳花生

Hawaiian nut 夏威夷坚果

macadamia nut 澳洲坚果

peanut/ monkey nut 花生、落花生

pecan 美洲山核桃；碧根果

pine nut 松子

pistachios 开心果

water chestnut 菱角、荸荠

短语：the nuts and bolts 基本要点

a hard/tough nut to tackle 很棘手、难解决的问题

nut house 疯人院

be nuts about/on 热恋、迷恋于

off the nut 发疯的

do one's nut 非常气愤

2. reply 答复、回复（接介词 to）

固定搭配 in reply，此复；in reply to，为答复…，意思同 in answer to。

例句：In reply, we would like to observe that we can not do business on your condition.

我们不能按你方条件进行交易，此复。

We anxiously await your reply to our enquiry.

我们急切等待你方对我们询盘的回复。

In reply to your letter of 23rd August, we are sending you today a copy of price list.

兹答复你方 8 月 23 日函，我方今天寄出价目表一份。

3. offer 发盘、报盘

既是名词，也是动词。quote 与 offer 有所不同，前者意为报价，只涉及价格，offer 可以包括各种交易条件。

关于 offer 的常见短语：

to accept offer 接受报盘

to conform offer 确认报盘

to decline offer 拒绝报盘

to entertain offer 考虑报盘

to extend offer 延长报盘

to withdraw offer 撤回报盘

to revoke offer 撤销报盘
to cancel offer 取消报盘
to renew offer 恢复报盘
to reinstate offer 恢复报盘（恢复过期较长如十天前的报盘）
combined offer 搭配报盘
lump offer 综合报盘，复合报盘
package offer 一揽子报盘
firm offer 实盘
non-firm offer 虚盘

例句：Please make us an offer CIF London for/on 30 metric tons ground nut.

请给我们 30 吨花生伦敦到岸价的报盘。

The offer is firm (valid, good, open, effective, enforced) for two weeks.

此报盘两周内有效。

We are working on your offer of 300 kilos green tea.

你方 300 千克绿茶的报盘，我们正在执行。

At present, we can not offer more than 500 short tons.

目前，我们的报盘不能多于 500 短吨。

We offer you firm subject to reply by 7 p. m. our time, Wednesday, 3rd Oct.

兹报实盘，以我方时间 10 月 3 日下午 7 时前答复为准。

We offer you firm subject to your reply here within one week from today.

兹报实盘，以自本日起一周内你方复到有效。

We make you an offer subject to the goods being unsold.

我们向你方报盘，以货物未售出为准。

We submit you this offer subject to change without notice.

我们向你方报盘，此报盘如有变化不另行通知。

The new crop is quoted on the cotton Exchange at £25 per ton.

棉花交易所的新货报价为每吨 25 英镑。

4. subject 常与介词 to 连用，表示以……为条件

此外，还表示易遭受……的。

例句：The above prices are subject to fluctuations of the market.

上述价格得随行就市。

Perishable goods are subject to damage in transit.

易腐烂货物在运输途中容易损坏。

We offer 100 m/tons Bitter Apricot Kernels at RMB ¥300 CIF, prompt shipment, subject to our cable confirmation.

兹报盘即期装运 100 吨苦杏仁，每吨到岸价人民币 300 元，以我方电报确认视为有效。

Subject to your agreement, we will proceed.

如你方同意，我们就进行下去。

5. metric tons 吨，公制单位，1 吨相当于 1000 千克。此外，

美制单位下，重量吨称 short ton，短吨，1 吨合 907 千克

英制单位下，重量吨称 long ton，长吨，1 吨合 1016 千克

6. Handpicked, Shelled and Ungraded 手捡、去壳且未分等级

7. RMB ¥2000 net per metric ton CFR Copenhagen 每吨 2000 元人民币，成本加运费，目的港为哥本哈根

net 一词强调所报价格是净价，不含佣金或折扣。

8. European Main Ports 欧洲主要港口

9. most favorable price 最为优惠的价格

10. entertain 此处表示加以考虑。此外，还有接受、招待、娱乐的意思

例句：

We are too heavily committed to be able to entertain fresh orders.
我们承担的任务太多，不能再接受新订货。

We shall be glad to entertain any constructive suggestion you make.
我们乐于考虑你方提出的任何建设性意见。

We should do our utmost to entertain guests coming afar.
我们应尽全力招待远方来的客人。

The affair in entertainment circle is very complicated.
娱乐圈的事情太复杂。

11. resulted in 导致某种结果

result from 表示结果因……而产生

例句：

We confirm the sale to you of 18 metric tons Licorice resulting from faxes exchanged.
经双方传真往来，我们确认售给你方 18 吨甘草。

We confirm telexes exchanged resulting in the sale to you 500 footballs.
经确认双方电传往来，卖给你方 500 个足球。

（10）

Dear Sirs,

We thank you for your letter dated April 8 inquiring for leather handbags. As requested, we take pleasure[1] in offering you, subject to our final confirmation, 300 dozen deerskin[2] handbags style No. MA 190 at $124.00 per dozen CIF Hamburg. Shipment will be effected[3] within 25 days after receipt[4] of the relevant L/C issued by your first class bank[5] in our favor upon signing Sales Contract.

We are manufacturing various kinds of leather purses and waist belts[6] for exportation, and under separate cover, a brochure of products has been sent to you by airmail today. We hope some of them would meet your customers' taste and need[7].

If we can be of any further help, please feel free to[8] let us know. Customers' inquiries always meet with our careful attention.

Yours truly,

Words，Expressions and Notes

1. pleasure 愉快、高兴、满意

pleasure 的常见短语如下。

take/have pleasure in doing (to do) sth.乐于做某事，同 take/have the pleasure of doing(to do) sth.

at one's pleasure 听便，同 at will/at discretion

with pleasure 愉快地接受、同意

pleasure ground 游乐场

例句：

"May I borrow your car?" "Yes, with pleasure."

"我可以借用你的车吗？" "可以，很愿意借给你。"

You may go or stay at your pleasure.

去留随你。

We take the pleasure of making you a firm offer as follows:

兹乐于向你方报实盘如下：

2. deerskin 鹿皮，鹿皮制作的衣服

3. effect 实现，完成，达到（目的）

名词表示效果、作用，生效，意义

习惯短语如下。

come/go into effect 开始生效，开始实行

take effect 生效

in effect 有效，在实施中

to the effect that… 大意是……，以便

bring/carry/put sth. into effect 实施、实行某事

例句：

Insurance is to be effected by the buyer.

由买方投保。

We hope you will effect improvement in your packing.

我们希望你方对包装加以改进。

This agreement will come into effect as soon as it is signed.

本协议一经签字立即生效。

These import regulations are still in effect.

这些进口规章仍然有效。

This regulation will take effect beginning from Oct 1st.

本条例自 10 月 1 日起开始生效。

We have received from our buyer a letter to the effect that he is still waiting for the import licence.

收到买主来信，信中大意说他仍在等待进口许可证。

We are enclosing our proforma invoice in triplicate to the effect that you may apply for the import quota.

随函附送我方形式发票一式三份，以便你方申请进口配额。

4. receipt 收到、接到，收据、收条

复数 receipts 表示收进的款项或物品

常用短语如下。

cargo receipt（陆运）货运收据

deposit receipt 存单、存款凭证、存放凭证

freight receipt 运费收据

mate's receipt 大副收据、收货单

parcel post receipt 邮包收据

例句：

The goods will be sent upon receipt of your remittance.

收到你方汇款后即发货。

We are in receipt of your letter of Sep 4th offering us 60 metric tons of captioned goods at RMB ¥2140 per metric ton on the usual terms.

我们收到你方 9 月 4 日函，获悉向我方供应 60 吨标题货物，按惯常条款，每吨 2140 元人民币。

This month's receipts are estimated to be in the region of US$30,000.

本月进款估计在 3 万美元左右。

5. first class bank 一等银行（主要指信用等级）

6. leather purses and waist belts 皮制钱包和皮带

7. meet your customers' taste and need 满足你方客户的品味和需要

8. please feel free to do sth 请随时做，别客气

（11）

Dear Sirs,

We are in receipt of your letter of July 15th, 2004 asking us to offer 10,000 metric tons of White Crystal Sugar[1] for shipment to Japan and appreciate very much your interest in our product.

To comply[2] with your request, we are offering you as follows:

1. Commodity: Dalian superior[3] White Crystal Sugar.

2. Packing: To be packed in new gunny bag of 100 kgs. each[4].

3. Quantity: Ten thousand (10000) metric tons.

4. Price: US dollars one hundred and five (US $105.00) per metric ton, FAS Dalian[5]

5. Payment: 100% by irrevocable and confirmed[6] letter of credit to be opened in our favor through A1 bank[7] in Dalian and to be drawn at sight[8].

6. Shipment: Three or four weeks after receipt of credit by the first available boat sailing to Yokohama direct.

Your attention is drawn to the fact that we have not much ready stock[9] on hand[10]. Therefore, it is imperative[11] that, in order to enable us to effect early shipment, your letter of credit should be opened in time if our price meets with your approval[12].

We are awaiting your immediate reply.

Yours faithfully,

Words, Expressions and Notes

1. White Crystal Sugar 白砂糖

2. comply 依从、遵照，后接介词 with

例句：

Buyers must comply with the terms of contract.

买方必须按照合同条款办理。

The offer does not comply with our requirement.

这个报盘不符合我们的需要。

We hope you will be able to comply with our request.

我们希望你能按我方要求办。

3. superior 此处指优质、上等质量

4. in new gunny bag of 100 kgs. each 新麻袋包装，每包重 100 千克

关于 pack 的习惯搭配如下。

packed in bulk 散装

packed in bundle 捆装

packed in coils 卷装

nude packing 裸装

packed in bales of 50 kgs. net 打成包，每包净重 50 千克

packed in cases of 200 lbs. 箱装，每箱重 200 磅

Packing, in galvanized iron drums of 175 kgs.net.

包装，镀锌铁桶，每桶净重 175 千克。

Packing, in case of 25 Ibs.net. Each containing 50 tins.

包装，一箱净重 25 磅，每箱内装 50 听。

Packing, in new single jute bags, each containing 100 kilos net, tare weight not less than 1 kilo.

包装，新制单层麻袋，每袋净重 100 千克，麻袋皮重不低于 1 千克。

5. FAS Dalian，即 Free Alongside Ship，在装运港大连船边交货。此术语的含义是：卖方必须在装运港将货物交至买方指定船舶的船边，办理出口清关，并负担货物交到船边为止的一切费用和风险。买方自该时起负担货物以后发生的各项费用和一切风险。该术语下若轮船靠不上码头，卖方需要自出费用租用驳船将货物驳运到货轮船边。

6. confirmed 此处指加保兑的信用证。confirm 作为动词，指确认、证实，常用在外贸书信的开头，表示证实自己的去信（电）或收到对方的来函（电）。

例句：

We confirm your letter of 5th regarding Dried Egg Products.

我们证实你方 6 日关于干蛋品的信件。

This credit should be confirmed by the bank acceptable to us.

此信用证应由我们能接受的银行加以保兑。

7. A1 bank 一等信用的银行

8. to be drawn at sight 这里指开立即期汇票

关于开汇票的习惯说法如下。

We can not agree to draw at 30 days D/A.

我们不同意开立 30 天的承兑交单汇票。

We would like to draw at 60 days D/P.

我方愿意开出 60 天期限的付款交单汇票。

此外，draw 还可以表示抽取、提取、招致，（船）吃水等。

例句：

We have drawn a clean draft on you for the balance of ￡100.

我们已向你方开出光票索取 100 英镑的余额。

As agreed, we will draw on you at sight against your purchase of a sample lot.

对你方所买的一批样品，按照商定办法，我们将开出即期汇票向你方索款。

Samples were drawn from the bales at random.

样品系从货包中随意抽取的。

The U.S will draw $3bn from its entitlement at the International Monetary Fund.

美国将从国际货币基金组织应得款项中提取 30 亿美元。

We would draw your attention to the fact that the date of shipment is approaching, but your L/C has not reached us so far.

装运期日益临近，而你方信用证至今未到，特此提请你方注意此事。

How much does your ship draw?

你的船吃水多少?

9. ready stock 现成的存货，充足库存

stock 的常用短语如下。

in stock 库存，现货

from stock(ex stock) 可供现货，自库存中供应

out of stock 缺货，无货

stock up 进货，使（商店）储足货物

stock assets 存量资产

stock budget 库存预算

stock adjustment 库存量调整

stock book 库存簿

stock balance 库存余额

stock turnover 库存周转率

stock bonus 股份红利

stock breeding 畜牧业

例句：

Spot stocks are insufficient to meet demand.

现货不足以满足需求。

Our stocks are running short.

我们存货日渐减少。

At the moment, we have only a limited stock of linen goods.

目前，我们只有有限的亚麻制品存货。

We have at present 80 metric tons of walnutmeat in stock.

我们目前有 80 吨核桃仁现货。

Only Type 9 is in stock. Type 8 is out of stock.

仅第 9 型号有货，第 8 型号没货。

We have run out of stock.

我们的存货已卖完。

We can supply this quantity ex stock.

我们可以从现货中供应此数量。

We are well stocked with men's shirts of different sizes.

我方备有充足的各种尺码的男式衬衫。

10. on hand 手头上（现有），在场、到场，即将发生

与 hand 有关的常用短语如下。

at hand 在附近，近在手边，即将到来

by hand 用手，由专人做

in hand 手头上，在进行中，控制住

例句：

As we still have a great number of back orders on hand we regret being unable to accept any fresh orders.

由于我们手头上尚有大量未交货的订单，很抱歉我们无法接受任何新订单。

We invite your agent to be on hand at the time of inspection.

我公司请你方代理人检验时到场。

The company you mentioned is located at hand.

你提到的公司就在附近。

The question can be further discussed at Guangzhou as the autumn fair is at hand.

由于秋季交易会即将举行，这个问题可在广州进一步商谈。

The table cloth is embroidered by hand.

这种台布是用手工刺绣的。

We will send the draft agreement to your hotel by hand.

我们会派专人把协议草稿送到您的酒店。

Stock in hand is running low.

手中存货越来越少。

The work is in hand and can be completed in a few days.

工作正在进行中，不日即可完成。

They have had the situation well in hand.

他们已完全控制了局势。

11. imperative 必要的，它比 necessary 的语气重，后面常接 that 引起的虚拟从句，例如：It is imperative that you fax your reply immediately.

你方必须立即传真回复。

12. meet with your approval 得到你方的认同

meet 作动词有遇见（后接 with），满足，支付（汇票）的意思

例句：

We believe you will meet with no difficulty is selling this article.

我们相信，销售这种商品你方不会有困难。

The ship met with an accident.

这条船发生了一次事故。

We might say our products have met with warm reception everywhere.

我们可以说我方产品到处都受到热烈欢迎。

We hope you will be able to meet our requirements.

希望你能满足我们的要求。

We are sure they will meet the draft on presentation.

我们肯定他们在汇票被提示时付款。

approval 作名词表示批准，赞成，同意，认可

例句：

We believe that quality will meet with your approval.

我们相信这种质量会得到你方赞许。

The goods were bought subject to "approval of sample''.

此货是凭“认可样品”购买的。

Your suggestion has our approval.

我们同意你方的建议。

Without government approval, this project was suspended.

由于没有政府审批，这项工程被搁浅了。

（12）

Dear Sirs,

We have for acknowledgement your letter of 23rd. April and take pleasure in making you the following offer subject to your reply reaching us by the end of this month:

Commodity:　Iron Nails

Specifications[1]:　"1—4"

Quantity:　50 metric tons

Packing:　16 packets[2] of 4kgs, to a carton[3], 6 cartons to a wooden case

Price:　Average US $　× × ×　per metric ton CFR Osaka

Shipment:　Within two months after receipt of your L/C.

Payment:　By confirmed, irrevocable L/C payable by draft at sight in our favor for the full invoice value[4].

Wit regard to Electric Wire JB—1598, it is very regrettable that the goods are out of stock now. We will revert[5] to this matter with you as soon as the supply position improves[6].

Yours truly,

Words，Expressions and Notes

1. specification 规格

产品质量的一种最为常用的表示方法。商品的规格是指足以反映商品品质特征的主要指标，如化学成分（chemistry composition）、含量（content）、纯度（purity）、性能（performance）、容量（capacity）、长短（length）、大小（size）等。以规格表示商品的品质比较简便、准确，还可以根据商品用途的不同选择相应的指标限制品质变化。

specify 作动词，表示指定、规定

specific 作形容词，表示具体的，确切的。名词表示详细方面，特效药。

2. packets 小盒，小包装

3. carton 纸板箱

4. the full invoice value 发票全额

invoice 名词指发票，动词表示开发票

例句：

Please send us four additional copies of invoice.

请多寄给我方发票副本 4 份。

You may invoice the goods at contract price less commission.

你方可按合同价格除去佣金来开发票。

The shipment was over-invoice (under invoice, short-invoiced) by US$ 500.

这批货的发票多（少）开了 500 美元。

5. revert 重新考虑、重提，再回到某个问题上

6. supply position improves 供给情况有所改善

（13）

Dear Sirs,

We are in receipt of your letter dated March 22th and, as requested, are airmailing you, under separate cover, one catalogue and two sample books for our Printed Shirting[1]. We hope they will reach you in due course [2]and will help you in asking your selection.

In order to start a concrete transaction[3] between us, we take pleasure in making you a special offer, subject to our final confirmation, as follows[4];

Art. No. 8100 Printed Shirting

Design No.72435—2 A

Specifications: 30×35

Quantity: 18000 yards

Packing: In bales or in wooden cases, at sellers' option[5]

Price: US dollar×××per yard CIF Lagos.

Shipment: To be made in three equal monthly installments[6], beginning from June, 2006

Payment: By confirmed, irrevocable L/C payable by draft at sight to be opened 30 days before the time of shipment.

We trust the above will be acceptable to you and await with keen interest your trial order[7].

Faithfully yours,

Words, Expressions and Notes

1. Printed Shirting 印花细布

2. in due course 及时、按时，在适当的时候

例句：We trust the shipment will reach you in due course.

我们相信此货将如期到达你处。

We look forward to having your Sales Confirmation in due course.

我们盼望及时收到你方的售货确认书。

习惯搭配： golf course 高尔夫球场。其他运动场所的表达如下。

bowling alley 保龄球馆

billiard room 台球厅

cricket field 板球场

diamond ballpark 棒球场

shooting range 射击场

sumo stable 相扑道馆

tennis court 网球场

3. concrete transaction 实质、具体的交易

4. as follows 如下，同 as what follows

The fax read as follows: 传真内容如下：

The items are as follows: 项目例举如下：

We state as follows: 兹陈述如下：

following 的意思是下面，下述的，随后

例句：

We have sold you the following:

我们已售给你方的货物如下：

The following is the points suggested.

下面是建议的要点。

Please advise the position of the following orders.

请告知下列订单的执行情况。

Following the talks, a contract was signed.

谈判后随即签署了合同。

5. option 这里的意思是由卖方选择

例句：

The destination on the B/L is to be written "London option Hamburg".

提单上目的港一栏写成："伦敦或汉堡任选"。

You have the option of accepting all or part of the quantity.

这个数量全部接受或部分接受，由你方任选。

We have no option but to do so.

我们除了这么做以外，别无选择。

6. installments 分若干批次

此句的意思是，从 2006 年 6 月起，货物分 3 次按月平均装运。

例句： We did not buy the goods on installment basis. We want the goods shipped in one lot.

此货不是按分批装运买进的，我们要一次性装运。

Payment by installments is allowed since the products under negotiation involve big sum of money.

因为所磋商的产品涉及金额很大，所以允许分期付款。

7. trial order 试订货

trial 的意思是试验，实验性的。

例句：

We will buy a small lot of your ball-bearings and put them to trial.

我们将买一小批你们的轴承试用。

We suggest you placing a trial order to see how it goes.

我们建议你方试订一批货，看看情况怎样。

Section 3 Supplements 知识补充

Useful Sentences On Offers

1. Their fine quality, attractive designs and the reasonable prices at which we offer them will convince you that these materials are really of good value.

它们的良好品质、富有吸引力的花样以及我们所报的合理价格将会使你方相信，这些料子是货真价实。

2. We trust that you will be able to accept our offer, which shall be kept open against reply by cable.

我们确信，你公司将接受我们所提供的价格。此报盘至回电为止都有效。

3. It is our desire to have the pleasure of serving you.

本公司乐于为你效劳。

4. We were very pleased to receive your enquiry of 2nd July and now confirm our cable offer of this morning, as follows:

谢谢 7 月 2 日来函。兹确认今天早晨的电报报价如下：

5. We must stress that this offer is firm for three days only because of the heavy demand for the limited supplies of this velvet in stock.

本公司必须强调，此报价仅有效 3 天。此乃因为天鹅绒的存货有限，而需求却很大。

6. Confirming our telephone conversation this morning, we can offer you the rice of 400 lbs, at the special low price of $ 80 per lb., CIF Keelung.

确认我今天早上的电话交谈如下。本公司提供给贵公司 400 磅稻米，特别低廉价，每磅 80 美元，CIF 基隆价。

7. We will keep this offer open up to the end of this month.

我方保留该报盘有效至本月底。

8. We can offer as follows, subject to your reply received here by four o'clock p.m. , our time, September 25th.

现报盘如下，以我方时间 9 月 25 日下午 4 时前复到有效。

9. This offer must be withdrawn if not accepted within five days.

此盘 5 天内不接受，就作撤销论。

10. On condition that you take more than 2000 sets, we are prepared to offer this special price of $ 9.10 per set, a 5% discount.

如订购 2000 台以上，准备特价报盘，每台 9.10 美元，即给 5%的折扣。

11. Unless otherwise stated or agreed upon all prices are without any discount.

除非另有说明或约定，价格一律没有折扣。

12. Only 0.3% is to be deducted from the CIF price, if buyers like to trade with us on CFR basis and insure the goods themselves.

如买方愿意做成本加运费价，自动投保，则从成本加保险费，运费从中减去 0.3%。

13. We shall be pleased to make delivery in January if our manufacturers accept your terms.

如我们厂方接受你方条款，我们将乐于在 1 月份交货。

14. We can effect shipment within one month after your order has been confirmed.

在确认你方订单后 1 个月内可装运。

15. Please note that goods supplied on approval must be returned, carriage paid, within 7 days if not required.

请注意，试销货物，如不需要必须在 7 天内退回，运费先付。

16. we have the offer ready for you.

我们已经为你方准备好报盘了。

17. I come to here about your offer for fertilizers.

我来听听你们有关化肥的报盘。

18. Please make us a cable offer.

请来电报盘。

19. We are in a position to offer tea from stock.

我们现在可以对茶叶现货报盘。

20. We will let you have the official offer next Monday.

下周一就给您正式报盘。

21. Please make us a cable offer for 8 metric tons of walnutmeat.

请电报 8 吨核桃仁。

22. Our offer is RMB ¥300 per set of tape-recorder, FOB Tianjin.

我方报价是每台录音机 300 元人民币，天津离岸价。

23. We are not interested unless your price is reduced to a level in line with the market price.

除非你们把价格降到与市场价相符，否则我们不感兴趣。

24. Sellers decide to wait no matter when the price picks up.

不管价格何时回升，卖方决定再等一等。

25. Our prices are highly competitive when you consider quality.
如果你们考虑一下质量，我们的价格是很有竞争力的。

26. Our price is net without commission.
我方价格是净价，不含佣金。

27. I'm awfully sorry. This is our floor price. If you find it unworkable, we may as well call the deal off.
这是我方的底价。如果你们觉得价格不可行，很遗憾，我们只好取消这笔交易。

28. I have to consult my home office before I can give you a definite answer on the price terms.
在答复你方有关价格条件之前，我得先跟我方国内公司联系一下。

29. My offer was based on reasonable profit, not on wild speculations.
我方报价以合理利润为依据，不是漫天要价。

30. We can't accept your offer unless the price is reduced by 5%.
除非你方降价 5%，否则我们无法接受报盘。

31. We'll give you the preference of our offer.
我们将优先向你方报盘。

32. You'll see that our offer compares favorably with the quotations you can get elsewhere.
你方会发现我们的报价比别处要便宜。

33. Our offers are for 3 days.
我们的报盘三天有效。

34. We have extended the offer as per your request.
我们已按你方要求将报盘延期。

35. The offer holds good until 5 o'clock p.m. 22nd June, 2010, Beijing time.
报盘有效期截止到北京时间 2010 年 6 月 22 日下午 5 时。

36. Please quote us lowest price CIF Los Angeles inclusive of our 5% commission, stating the earliest date of shipment.
请报洛杉矶最低到岸价，含我方 5%佣金，并告知最早装船日期。

37. It's really impossible for us to make any concession by allowing you any commission.
在给你方佣金问题上，我们真的不能做出任何让步。

Terms Used in Making Offers

market area	市场区域
market condition	市场状况
market fluctuation	市场波动
market information	市场信息
market price	市场价格
market report	市场报告
market research	市场研究
market risk	市场风险
market survey	市场调查
domestic market	国内市场

foreign market	国外市场
forward market	远期市场
futures market	期货市场
overseas market	国外市场
money market	货币市场
product market	产品市场
spot market	即期市场
stock market	股票市场
market glut	市场饱和
market quotation	市场行情
market structure	市场结构
market shortfall	市场供应不足
market transaction	市场交易
marketing blitz	营销战
market value	市（场）价（格），市值
put sth. on the market	把……投放到市场
take market sharing	抢占市场份额
open up new market	开拓新市场
active	活跃的
advancing	旺盛的
animated	有生气的
bearish	下跌的
brisk	兴旺的
bullish	兴旺的
declining	衰退的
depressed	不景气的
dull	退缓的，呆滞的
easy	轻松的
excited	活跃的
feverish	波动的
firm	稳定的
flat	平稳的
inactive	不活跃的
overstocked	存货过多的
quiet	平静的
panicky	惊慌的，恐慌的
sluggish	滞缓的，萧条的
steady	稳定的
weak	疲软的

Exercises

Ⅰ. Translate the following phrases and then make sentences.

call one's attention to
in reply
firm offer
non-firm offer
extend offer
result in
avail oneself of…
take pleasure in
in one's favour
out of stock
be in receipt of
as follows
with regard to
on or before
to comply with
effect shipment
meet with
approval of sample
in compliance with
upon receipt of
brisk demand
be subject to
draw on
in due course
trial order
draw up

Ⅱ. Complete the following sentences.

1. We have offered the goods at ₤ 1000 per metric ton 这是目前最好的价格。
2. We have quoted you our lowest price 按此价我们已与其他客户做了许多交易。
3. Please reply as soon as possible 说明最早装船期和付款条件。
4. If you are interested, pleased cable us 说明所需数量。
5. We cabled you yesterday 报你 5000 千克核桃仁，3 月船期。
6. Please reply as soon as possible 告知我们必要的详细情况。
7. We cabled you today 向你订购 2000 吨当年产的黄豆。
8. We make you this offer 以 5 天内复到为有效。
9. Owing to the slump in commodity prices，我们可向你们开报下列物品。
10. You will note that these quotations are open for a week only，由于市场价格波动频繁。
11. 存货日见减少，so we suggest that you place your order without delay.
12. 此系特惠报盘 and cannot be repeated.
13. 由于供货充裕，we are able to offer you firm for immediate delivery.
14. 为复 5 月 20 日询价，we have the pleasure of quoting you 100 dozen nylon socks at ₤ 18 a dozen CIF Singapore.
15. 为盼扩大交易额，故报特低价。

Ⅲ. Translate the following sentences into English.

1. 本报盘 5 日内有效。
2. 以上报盘月底前有效。
3. 本报盘以收到你方订单时，货未售出为有效。
4. 此报价对我方无约束力。
5. 我方报价如有变更不另通知。

6．如果你方认为这一报盘可以接受，请即来电，以便我方确认。

7．按照你们的要求，我们报 50 吨大豆的实盘如下，以自本日起一周之内你方复到为准。

8．兹报实盘，以我方时间 10 月 5 日星期四上午 10 时以前答复为有效。

9．我们确认卖给你 50 吨苦杏仁。

10．你方所买的一批样货，按照商定办法，我们将开出即期汇票向你索款。

11．我们可以从现货中供应你 3000 打“天坛”牌男衬衫。

12．我们相信我们所报的价格会得到你方认可。

13．我们愿提请你们注意此事。

14．此系特惠报盘，我方通常折扣不使用此盘。

15．为了开展双方间具体的业务，我们很高兴向你方报特盘，以我方最后确认为有效。

Ⅳ. Write a letter to the buyers, stating that you have plenty of the goods they need and you can offer them.

Ⅴ. Translate the following letter into Chinese.

Ordering online

We have tried to make ordering our products online as easy as possible by providing an online shopping cart system to allow you to select the products you wish to order easily and quickly..

Once you have chosen the products you wish to order and they are in your shopping cart, proceed to checkout and complete your details.

Shipping: standard shipping is ￡25 + VAT per order

Availability: within 14 days of receipt of payment

Once we receive your order, one of our sales representative will call you to confirm price, total cost incl. Additional shipping costs, payment terms and delivery dates. If you have requested for us to provide you with a quotation to supply, you will be contacted regarding this too.

Ⅵ. Translate the following letter into English.

敬启者：

感谢贵公司 8 月 1 日寄来的询价单，该函及所附的样品均已收悉。

对该样品检验的结果，我们敢向贵公司保证，敝公司能够制造与该样品相同型号与品质的产品。

基于贵公司每年 100,000 双的需求量，我报盘如下：

价格：CIF 大连每双 25 美元

包装：塑料袋，外包装纸板箱

支付：凭即期的，不可撤销的，保兑的信用证

交货：收到订单后的 90 天内，即 11 月、12 月船期。

我们可向贵公司保证，此种价格是基于上述数量的最低价。其他技术性事项可参阅我公司的商品手册。

如有其他问题，请多多指点。

你真诚的……

（……敬上）

附件：商品手册一本

Chapter 5

Counter-Offers

Section 1 Business Knowledge 业务知识

对报盘信的答复有两种：一是有利答复（全部接受）；二是不利答复，虽然表示接受，但有添加、限制或其他更改的答复，这即构成还盘（counter-offer）。还盘也叫还价。受盘人在收到一项报盘后，往往对其中的某些内容不能完全同意，于是会提出不同的要求。这种口头或书面的要求一经提出，原来的报盘即刻失效，交易要在还盘的基础上重新开始。

还盘的内容不只是价格。对支付条件、装运期等主要条件提出不同的建议，也都属于还盘性质。一笔交易的成立，有时要经过多次还盘和反还盘的过程。

还盘究其本质是对发盘的拒绝。还盘一经做出，就构成了一项新的发盘。双方当事人的地位也即刻发生了变化，原来的发盘人（offerer）成了受盘人（offeree），而做还盘的一方又称为新的发盘人。

外商在回复发盘时很少用（counter-offer）的字样。这样正确识别出对方的还盘就非常重要。若将对方的还盘误认为接受（acceptance），并加以确认，这就意味着要以对方的条件成交，容易使自己陷于被动。在判断对方来函、来电时，只要其内容与自己的发盘有不一致的地方，即将其视为还盘。

怎样处理对方的还盘呢？这需要具体问题具体分析。如对方还盘的条件合理可行，且对自己又有利可图，应该尽早确认和接受。反之，若还盘条件过于苛刻，则可以拒绝，或不加以理会。这意味双方交易没有达成。

当我们对外商做还盘时，为了避免误解，可以只针对发盘提出不同意或需要修改的部分，已同意的内容在还盘中可省略。

下面是某年我国一公司与美国商人关于自行车买卖的往来电报，请据此案例来判断双方的交易是否达成。

8 月 15 日，我国某公司向美国一商人电报报盘，电文如下：出售 100 辆自行车，价格是每辆 45 美元，CIF 伦敦，装运期为 10 月。限 8 月 21 日复到。

8月17日对方回电，称：接受8月15日发盘，并提出每辆40美元，装运期可以推迟到12月。

我方未表态，于8月19日与另一商人达成交易。此时我方产品国际市场价格正不断上涨。

8月20日美商来电：表示接受我方8月15日的发盘。

我方即告之货已经售出，而美商认为已经接受了中方报盘，合同已经成立，要求我方履行合同，否则提出索赔要求。

请问，合同是否成立？为什么？

分析：

本案中美方8月17日的电报至关重要。电报对我方8月15日报盘提出了两项变更内容。一个是价格，一个是装运期。因此美方的8月17日电纯系还盘。如前面所讲，还盘是对发盘的拒绝。在前一章也曾提到，一项发盘在受盘人做出还盘的情况下会失去效力，发盘人将不再受其约束。由此可见，中方发盘在8月17日已经失效，中方公司当然可以与其他买家达成交易，美方商人无权干涉。至于美商8月20日的电报，尽管对中方8月15日盘又表示了接受，但是该接受不成立。因为一项发盘在已经失效的情况下，当事人不能再表示接受，必须经发盘人重新报盘，才可以继续磋商。况且，中方公司对美商的8月20日电并没有确认，而是详实告知，货物已经售出。至此，可以判定双方并没有达成交易，合同关系不成立。中方没有义务向美国商人供货，美商的索赔要求也纯属无理取闹，中方大可不予理会。

说到底，还盘就是讨价还价。买卖双方应在互让互谅的基础上讨价还价，互相协商，最后达成交易。在双方讨价还价的过程中，语气要和缓而坚定，绝不可使用绝对化的语气而导致断绝来往。双方应抱着“交易不成友谊在”的态度，为今后的贸易往来打下良好的基础。

那么，一封还盘信一般包括哪些内容呢？还盘是还实盘还是还虚盘呢？还是让我们到下面的样函中找答案吧。

Section 2 Specimen Letters 样函

（1）

Dear Sirs,

We wish to thank you for your letter of the July 4th, offering us 3,000 kilos[1] of walnutmeat at US$50 per kilogram.

We regret to say that we find your price rather high[2] and we believe we'll have a hard time[3] convincing our clients at your price.

Besides[4], there is keen competition from supplies in Korea and Thailand. You can't very well ignore[5] that. Should you be ready to[6] reduce your price by 5%, we might come to business[7].

Considering the long-standing business and relationship between us, we make you such a counter-offer. As the market is declining[8], we hope you will consider our counter-offer most favorable and fax us as soon as possible.

Yours faithfully,

Words, Expressions and Notes

1. kilo 千克

2. rather high 指价格过高

3. hard time 此处理解为很难让我方客户相信你们的价格

4. besides 此外、另外

注意，except, besides, except for 用法的关联和区别

作介词用法时，这三个词都有“除……之外”的含义，但 except 常与 do / does / did / have / has / had nothing 等词形成搭配用法，或者与全部肯定词 all，everything，everyone 等连用，或者与全部否定词 nothing、nobody 等连用，因此 except 加宾语作介词“除……之外”时常表示从整体中剔除一部分；而 besides 作“除……之外”时则表示“另外附加”的含义，相当于“in addition to”。试比较下列例句：

He did nothing except watch TV yesterday.

他除了看电视，其他什么也不做。

Besides（in addition to） us two, we need 3 more persons to finish the job.

除我俩人外（包括我俩在内），还需要 3 个人来完成这项工作。

作介词用法时的 except 后可接多种情况的介词短语。在这种情况下，except 后的介词是不可省去的，except 加介词的实际作用就相当于连词加相关的从句。例如：

The weather is fine today except in the northwest.

今天的天气除了西北部以外都很不错。

His mother never takes any exercise except that she has a dance on the floor.

除了跳跳舞，他的妈妈不做其他锻炼。

还需要强调的是 except 与 except for 的用法区别。

except 后排除的内容与主语往往是同一类的，而 except for 后所排除的内容与主语往往不是同一类的。例如，试比较：

All the buildings are excellent except this one.

所有建筑除了这栋楼都很好。

All the buildings are excellent except for their location。

所有建筑除了位置外都很好。

当 except 用在句首时往往改用 except for，例如：

Except for a policeman on his duty, there was no single person in the dark street that night.

那天夜里，除了值班警察，黑暗的街上没有一个人影。

5. ignore 忽视、不加以理会

6. be ready to 即将去做某事

7. come to business 达成交易

8. declining 这里指市场在衰退、萎缩

（2）

Dear Sirs,

Thank you for your letter of Oct 10th. As regards your counter-offer, we regret we are unable to accept it because our current price has already been proved workable[1] by many orders received from other buyers.

However, in order to meet you on this occasion[2], we are prepared to grant[3] you a special discount[4] of 2% on condition[5] that the quantity of the other order is not less than 1,000 pieces.

We hope this will enable you to enjoy[6] the benefit of special discount.

Yours sincerely,

Words, Expressions and Notes

1. workable 可行的
2. on this occasion 在这一场合
3. grant 准许，答应给予。名词有津贴、助学金的意思
4. special discount 特别折扣
5. on condition 以……为条件；若是，如果
6. enjoy 享受（后接名词或动名词），这里的意思是从特别折扣中获利

（3）

Dear Sirs,

200 Dozen "Youth" Ball Pens[1]

Your offer of April 10th for the captioned goods and the sample has been received, for which we thank you.

We would request you to give us a 10% commission instead of[2] 5% and to accept payment by D/P at sight[3], as we are working with[4] other suppliers on these terms.

We trust you will be glad to confirm the above terms by fax at an early date so that we may send in our formal order with detailed shipping instructions[5] accordingly.

Yours faithfully,

Words, Expressions and Notes

1. Ball Pens 圆珠笔
2. instead of 而不是；用……代替
3. D/P at sight 托收付款方式，可译为即期付款交单
4. working with 与某人合作
5. shipping instructions 装运指示，进口方对出口方如何装运货物所做的安排

（4）

Dear Sirs,

200 Dozen "Youth" Fountain Pens[1]

We thank you for your letter of April 21th and confirm our fax of April 28th, as per the copy attached[2].

As regards your request for a 10% commission and payment by D/P at sight, we regret being unable to meet your wishes[3] as we are doing business with other buyers on the basis of a 5% commission and payment by irrevocable letter of credit.

Consequently[4], we would suggest that you reconsider our terms and see your way[5] to fall in line[6] with other buyers.

Yours faithfully,

Words, Expressions and Notes

1. Fountain Pens 钢笔
2. as per the copy attached 如附件所示，内容详见附件
3. meet your wishes 满足你方的愿望
4. consequently 所以、因此
5. see your way to 有可能做，设法去做
6. fall in line with 与……保持一致

（5）

Dear Sirs,

Thank you for your letter of July 3th, and your order for 2,000 ream[1] MG Cap Paper[2].

Recently there has been a heavy demand for this kind of paper, and we are not accepting orders for August shipment[3]. We regret being unable to meet your wishes for September shipment.

However, in view of[4] our long connection and as the quantity involved is rather small, we are prepared to entertain your order at £… per ream CFR Amsterdam, provided[5] your friends accept November shipment. The date may appear somewhat[6] extended, but it is the best we can do under the circumstances[7].

If you find our offer acceptable, please fax us your acceptance before the end of the current month[8] for our final confirmation.

Yours sincerely,

Words, Expressions and Notes

1. ream 令，纸张的计量单位，1 令合 500 全张纸
2. MG Cap Paper 油光纸。cap paper 意为包装纸（粗纸）
3. August shipment 8 月份装运的货物
4. in view of 鉴于，考虑到，同 considering

例句：

In view of the unusual circumstances, they agree to waive their requirement.

鉴于特殊情况，他们同意放弃自己的要求。

We didn't ask you to cable remittance in view of the amount being very small.

鉴于金额很小，我们不要求你方电汇。

In view of the foregoing, we trust you will reconsider this question.

由于以上所述，我们相信你将重新考虑此问题。

5. provided 如果，假如，后面常接 that 引导的从句

注意：provided 不是过去分词，而是连词，作“假如，只要”解，在口语中常用 providing. provided that 与 if 的不同在于：provided that 所表示的“如果”，含有希望该条件实现的含义。例句：

We will be there before 10, provided we don't waste time.

如果我们不浪费时间，我们就能在 10 点之前到那儿。

We will go provided that the weather is fine.

假如天气好，我们就去。

Provided that no objection is raised, we will set back the program.

如果没人反对，我们就把这个项目推迟。

6. somewhat 稍微、有点儿，达到某种程度

7. under the circumstances 在这种情况下

8. current month 本月、当月，同 this month

（6）

Dear Sirs,

From your letter of March 22th, we are disappointed[1] at learning that you find our offer unacceptable because other suppliers are offering lower prices.

We are not in a position to accept your counter-offer because our price is reasonably fixed[2]. Regarding the qualities of the goods offered by others, we are rather doubtful[3] whether they are similar to or comparable with[4] those of ours. Please call the attention of your customers to[5] this point and convince them that not only price but also quality should be taken into consideration[6].

We hope to here from you before long[7].

Yours sincerely,

Words, Expressions and Notes

1. disappointed 失望
2. reasonably fixed 定价合理
3. doubtful 怀疑的，可疑的，未定的
4. comparable with 与……可比的，相当的
5. call the attention to 引起对某事的关注、注意
6. taken into consideration 把……考虑在内
7. before long 不久后，在短时间内；long before 表示很久之前

（7）

Dear Sir,

Subject: We regret that we cannot accept your counter-offer

In reference[1] to your e-mail of August 1st, we cannot make a better offer than the one we

suggested to you; we feel that offer itself is most generous[2] under the circumstances.

In checking our books[3], we find that you have purchased from us twice as much the first three months of this year as[4] you did in the first three months of last year. This indicates[5] to us that you have been successful in retailing our merchandise[6].

We hope that upon reconsideration you will be able to accept our offer. We have been very pleased to have you on our list of accounts[7].

Best regards,

×××

Words, Expressions and Notes

1. in reference to 关于，在某方面
2. generous 慷慨、大方，此处意思是我方报价最低
3. books 账目
4. as much…as… 与……一样多。因为前面有 twice，此处理解成：你们今年的头 3 个月在我处所购的货物是去年同期的两倍
5. indicates 说明、表明，指示
6. merchandise 商品、货物
7. list of accounts 这里是账目的意思，指愿将你们的名字留在我们的账目上，也即保留你方作为我们的客户

（8）

Dear Sirs,

We acknowledge receipt of both your offer of May 5th and the samples of Men's Shirts, and thank you for these.

While appreciating the good quality of your shirts, we find your price is rather too high for the market we wish to supply.

We have also to point out[1] that the Men's Shirts are available in our market from several European manufacturers[2]; all of them are at prices from 15% to 20% below yours.

Such being the case[3], we have to ask you to consider if you can make reduction in your price[4], say 10%. As our order would be worth[5] around Stg. 50000, you may think it worthwhile[6] to make a concession[7].

We await with keen interest your immediate reply.

Yours faithfully,

Words, Expressions and Notes

1. point out 指出，提出来
2. manufacturer 厂商，制造商，厂方
3. such being the case 事实既然如此

4. make reduction in price 降低价格

5. worth 名词表示价值或一定金额的数量，形容词意为：相当于……价值的、值得……的、有……的价值的

注意，worthiness 名词价值、值得

worthful 形容词可贵的，有价值的

worthy 形容词应得某事物的，值得做某事，可尊敬的

worth it 值得花时间、精力、值得干、有必要

worth one's salt 胜任、称职

worth the whistle 值得注意的

worthy of note 显著的，值得注意的

worth to fixed debt ratio 资本固定负债比率

worth to current debt ratio 资本流动负债比率

worthless 无价值的、无用的

valueless 无效果的、无价值的、没用的

priceless 极为贵重的、无价的

例句：

The actual worth of this parcel is well over us $ 100,000.

这批货的实际价值远远超过 10 万美元。

Last year we shipped to you ￡ 700, 000's worth of chemicals.

去年我们给你方装运了价值 70 万英镑的化工产品。

The sales contract was worth around us $ 300,000.

这份售货合同约值 30 万美元。

We don't agree with you that it is a mere trifle not worth bothering about.

我们不同意，这只是一件小事而不值得费心。

We should say that this new product of ours is well worth your effort to promote.

我方认为，我们的新产品很值得你方努力推销。

The order is too small to be worth the expense of opening an L/C.

这笔订单太小，不值得花钱开立信用证。

It is worth shipping. (It is shipworthy.)

它具备适航条件。

This contract is now worthless.

这份合同现在毫无价值了。

The necklace is valueless.

这条项链不值钱。

Good health is priceless to one's success.

健康对人的成功太重要了。

6. worthwhile 形容词的意思是值得花时间、精力的，值得去做

例句：

It is worthwhile to try again.

这值得再试一次。

7. make a concession to sb. 对某人做让步，此外 concession 还有特权（资源开采方面）的意思。

例句：

It is impossible for us to make any further concession in our price.

我们无法再在价格上让步。

China got oil concession in Saudi Arabia.

中国得到了在沙特阿拉伯的石油开采权。

The company owns valuable logging and mining concessions.

该公司拥有宝贵的伐木和采矿特许经营权。

（9）

Dear Sirs,

<u>Cotton Printed Shirting 2345</u>

We are in receipt of your cable dated 26th July from which we note your offer for the above item at Stg.××× per yard. Kindly note that all our competitors[1] are booking locally at Stg×××. In order to cope with[2] the prevailing heavy competition we had to book at Stg. ×××. We earnestly ask you to accept the above price.

With regard to the minimum quantity[3] of 10,000 yards per design which you asked for in your cable, we have to point out that in your previous[4] letter of 20th June the minimum was 7500 yards. We ask you to accept this lower minimum. We have booked a total of 45000 yards in six designs.

Please let us have your cable confirmation at your earliest convenience[5].

Yours faithfully,

Words, Expressions and Notes

1. competitor 竞争者，同 rival

compete 是动词，注意与 vie、rival 和 contest 的区别

compete 含义仅仅是为了争得名次、奖品，没有征服对手的意思

vie（with）与 compete 相比，词义弱得多，主要表示争夺中的兴奋、激动，常指嬉戏，争先恐后的意思

rival 主要意思是指对手，动词表示匹敌。

contest 主要含义是指竞赛，旨在比试技能、力气、耐久力等

例句：

We don't deem it advisable for you to compete with your Beijing Office in the same district on the same item.

我们认为你公司在同一地区对同种商品与你们北京公司竞争是不可取的。

After defeat of the new competitor, the prices can rise again.

新的竞争者被击败后，价格会重新上升。

The senior staff, instead of vying for the CEO's favor, sought to put the maximum distance between themselves and him.

公司的高管人员，不再竞相去讨得总裁欢心，而是极力与总裁保持最大距离。

They achieved more than they had ever dreamed, lending a magic to their family story no tale or ordinary life could possibly rival.

他们取得的成就比他们梦想的还多，这给他们的家族注入一股魔力，使得任何神话及日常生活都没法匹敌。

He contested with other bidders for the antique.

他与其他出价人竞争古董。

2. cope with 应付、适应，指有效地或成功的对付或应对；而 deal with 仅指采取行动去对付某人或事情，并不考虑成功与否。

例句：

We have too many orders to cope with.

我们要执行的订单太多了。

Please do your best to cope with the situation.

请妥善对待此情况。

We hope you will see your way to adjust the price so as to enable us to cope with competition.

我们希望你方设法调整价格以便使我们应付竞争。

To market such a product at this end, we have a number of difficulties to cope with.

在我地推销这种商品，有许多困难要克服。

Matters not provided for in this contract shall be dealt with in accordance with the Trade Agreement between the two countries.

凡本合同未尽事宜均按两国间的贸易协定办理。

3. minimum quantity 最低起订量

minimum 既是名词，也是形容词，表示最小量、最低、最少

例句：

Ten tons is the minimum quantity you have to take.

你方至少得买 10 吨。

This price is their minimum; they refuse to lower it any further.

这是他们的最低价，他们拒绝进一步降价。

4. previous 在前的、过早的，副词在……以前；precious 是珍贵的、贵重的

例句：

We touched on this subject in one of our previous letter.

在我们以前的信中曾提过此事。

I regret that a previous engagement prevent me from accepting your kind invitation.

我已有约在先，无法接受您的好意邀请，实在遗憾。

We need liberal samples previous to approaching the users.

在与用户联系之前，我们需要大量样品。

Our client is not prepared to place further orders previous to setting this claim.

在解决这项索赔以前，我方客户不打算进一步订货。

The gift given by you is very precious to my birthday.

你给我的生日礼物非常珍贵。

5. convenience 方便

at one's earliest convenience 尽早

例句：

Please send us some descriptive literature at your earliest convenience.

请尽早寄给我们一些说明书。

For convenience sake we will deduct these charges from the commission payable to you.

为方便起见，我们将从应付你方的佣金中扣除这些费用。

（10）

Dear Sirs,

Tin Foil Sheets[1]

We wish to thank you for your letter of 20th inst[2]. Offering us 50 long tons of the captioned goods at ￡135 per long ton CFR Shanghai, usual terms[3].

In reply, we very much regret to state that our end-users[4] here find your price too high and out of line with[5] the prevailing market level. Information indicates that some parcels[6] of Japanese make[7] have been sold at the level of ￡125 per long ton.

Such being the case, it is impossible for us to persuade[8] our end-users to accept your price, as material of similar quality is easily obtainable at a much lower figure[9]. Should you be prepared to reduce your limit by, say 8%, we might come to terms[10].

It is in view of our long-standing[11] business relationship that we make you such a counter-offer most favorably and cable us acceptance at your earliest convenience.

We are anticipating your early reply.

Yours faithfully,

Words, Expressions and Notes

1. Tin Foil Sheets 锡箔纸
2. inst.是 instant 的缩写，表示本月（this month），此外

   Prox.是 proximo 的缩写，表示下月 next month

   Ulti.是 ultimo 的缩写，表示上月 last month
3. usual terms 通常条件，这里指其他交易事项按照以往通常条件办理，意为双方是老客户了，曾有多次交易往来

例句：

On usual terms we could undoubtedly do further business.

在通常条件下，我们毫无疑问可以做更多交易。

4. end-users 最终用户
5. out of line with 与……不相符
6. parcel 包裹，一宗、一批，这里指一宗货物。动词表示打包

   parcel out 把……分成数份后分配

   parcel up sth. 捆扎，把某物打包

例句：

We are sending you a parcel of samples.

我们寄给你方一包样品。

We have sold many parcels on this basis.

我们曾按此条件出售过多批货。

This is the only parcel left.

这是仅剩下的 1 批货。

The goods may be sent by parcel post insured.

货物可以通过投保邮包险来发送。

Parcel out a shipment to several buyers.

把这一船货分发给几家买主。

7. Japanese make 日本制造，日本货。此处 make 意为制造的方法或式样，产品

例句：

They are interested in things of Chinese make.

他们对中国产品感兴趣。

If you can not offer, they will buy other makes.

如果你方不能报盘，他们将买别处的产品。

Some parcels of Japanese make have been sold at ￡150 per metric ton.

有几批日本货已按每吨 150 英镑出售。

8. persuade 说服，常指说服某人去做某事

例句：

We believe we can persuade users to divert their purchases to Chinese products.

我们相信能说服客户转而购买中国产品。

We regret we have not been able to persuade them to accept a substitution.

很遗憾，我方未能说服他们接受替代品。

9. figure 此处是指价格

10. come to terms 达成交易。表示成交的说服还有很多，如

come to business

close a bargain

close a deal

put the deal through

give one’s hands on bargain

11. long-standing 长期的、长久的

（11）

Dear Sirs,

Silicon Steel Sheets[1]

We learn from your letter of 10th October that our price for the subject article is found to be on

the high side[2].

Much as[3] we would like to cooperate[4] with you in expanding sales, we are regretful that we just can not see our way clear to[5] entertain your counteroffer, as the price we quoted is quite realistic. As a matter of fact, we have received a lot of orders from various sources[6] at our level.

If you see any chance to do better[7], please let us know. On account of[8] a limited supply available at present, we would ask you to act quickly.

In the meantime, please keep us posted of[9] developments at your end. We assure you that any further enquiries from you will receive our prompt attention.

Yours faithfully,

Words, Expressions and Notes

1. Silicon Steel Sheets 硅钢片
2. on the high side 这里指价格偏高，类似的表达方法还有：

Your price is a bit high. 你方价格有点高。

Your price is on the rise. 你方价格还在涨。

Your price is too high. 你方价格太高。

Your price is rather stiff. 你方价格相当高。

Your price is excessive. 你方价格过高。

Your price is prohibitive. 你方价格令人望而却步。

3. much as 复合从属连词，引导让步状语从句，意思是虽然很……

例句：

Much as I'm interested in your product, I can not place an order with you because of the high price.

虽然对贵方产品很感兴趣，因价格太高我们还不能订货。

Much as I should like to go, I can't go right now.

我虽然很想去，但现在还不能去。

此外，inasmuch as，insomuch as， in as much as， in so much as 均是复合从属连词，引导原因状语从句，表示：因为、既然……，例如：

Inasmuch as the debtor has no property, I abandoned the claim.

由于债务人没有财产，因此我放弃了债权。

He will resign insomuch as he is too old.

由于年事已高，他打算辞职。

4. cooperate 合作，同 work with

例句：

It is important that we cooperate closely.

我们双方紧密合作是很重要的。

We hope you will cooperate with us in promoting this new product.

我们希望你和我们合作推销这一新产品。

5. see our way clear to 有可能、有意愿办某事，努力设法办某事

例句：

We cannot see our way (clear) to increase the quantity.

我们无法再增加数量。

They do not see their way(clear) to extend the time of shipment.

他们不能再扩展装船期。

We hope you will see your way(clear) to granting our request.

我们希望你方能够答应我们的要求。

6. sources 来源，此处指货源

例句：

They used to purchase their requirements from other sources.

他们过去总是从别处购买需要的货物。

Where does this information take its source?

这一消息来自何处？

7. any chance to do better 字面意思是做得更好，此处意为能有机会出高一点的价格

例句：The price is the lowest possible, we can not do better.

这个价格已是最低限度，我们不能再让。

8. on account of　由于、因为

account 的习惯短语有：

for account of　为……，代……，受……委托

for sb's account（for the account of sb）由某人负担

take…into account　考虑、重视

on one's own account　为自己的利益，自行负责

not for any account　无论如何不

account for　说明原因；占一定比例

例句：

Oil exports account for 40% of the total export value.

石油出口占出口总额的 40%。

It is impossible for us to account for the delay.

我们无法解释耽误的原因。

Not on any account shall the safe be opened without my express orders.

没有我的明确指示，无论如何不能打开保险箱。

We buy this commodity for a friend of ours, not on our own account.

此项商品是我们代朋友买的，而不是为自己买。

One feature of modern enterprises is doing business on their own accounts.

现代企业的一个特点就是自负盈亏。

You should take into account not only the price but also the quality.

你们予以考虑的不只是价格，而且还有质量。

On account of difference in taste, your designs do not suit this market.

由于品位不同，你方设计款式不适合本地市场。

On account of lack of direct steamer, please allow transshipment in your L/C.

因为没有直达船，在你方信用证中请注明允许转船。

The arbitration fees shall be for the account of the losing party.

仲裁费用由败诉一方负担。

We hereby issue an irrevocable L/C in your favor for account of China Tading Co.,Shanghai.

兹受上海中国贸易行的委托，开给你方一份不可撤销信用证。

与 account 有关的专业短语：

auditing of account 查账

capital account 资本账户

common account 共同账户

keeping current account 流水账的登记

running account 流水账

sales for account 赊账

accountancy 会计学；会计工作

accountancy firm 会计机构

accountancy law 会计法

accountancy section 会计科，核算科

accountancy service 会计业务

accountant 会计师，会计员

certified public accountant 注册会计师

chartered accountant （英）注册会计师

general accountant 总会计师

accounting 会计学，会计、核算

accounting period 会计年度，会计结算期

economic accounting 经济核算

managerial/management accounting 管理会计学

9. keep us posted of 把情况随时通知我们，同 keep us informed of

（12）

Dear Sirs,

We confirm having received your telex No. LT/531 of May 17th, asking us to make a 10% reduction in our price for Men's Shirts. Much to our regret[1], we find it intolerable[2] to comply with your request because ours is the best possible price if you take quality into consideration. However, in order to develop our market in your place, we have decided to accept your counter-offer as an exceptional[3] case. We hope we can conclude contract[4] before long and await your prompt reply.

Yours truly,

Words, Expressions and Notes

1. much to our regret 让我们非常遗憾的是，much 在此处有争加语气的作用

2. intolerable 不能忍受的。Tolerance 也可表示公差

3. exceptional 例外的，异常的

exception 是名词，意为例外、除外，惯用搭配：

with the exception of 除……

without exception 一概，毫无例外

例句：

Please understand that this is an exceptional treatment.

此为破格的待遇，请理解这一点。

This is an exceptional offer.

这是一个特殊的报盘。

This is an exceptional case.

这是例外情况。

It is our practice to require sight L/C. we can not make an exception of this transaction.

用即期信用证结算是我们的惯例，这笔交易也不例外。

All the items listed are of interest to us with the exception of item 3.

除了第三项商品外，单上所列商品我们都感兴趣。

All the three orders without exception must be shipped in March.

这三笔订货一律都在 3 月装运。

4. conclude contract 达成合同、缔结合同，conclude 还有得出结论，做结论的意思。conclusion 是名词，表示结论、信念、观点。

例句：

We are glad to have concluded this transaction with you.

我们很高兴和你方达成这笔交易。

Since we have received no reply from you, we conclude that you have already covered your requirements.

由于没有接到你的答复，我们认为你已满足自己的需要。

I came to the conclusion that we must do business with foreign countries on the basis of equality and mutual benefit.

我认为我们应该在平等互利的基础上同海外各国做生意。

Section 3 Supplements 知识补充

Useful Sentences On Counter-Offers

1. We strongly advise you to accept catalogue XH100 as the type you selected is no longer obtainable.

我们郑重向你公司建议，接受商品目录中的 XH100 型，因为你公司所挑选的式样已无货可供。

2. If you can raise your order to 1000 we can offer you a price of CIF U.S.$ 30 per each.

倘若你公司能提高订购的数量到 1000，我公司便能提供每样 CIF 30 美元的价格。

3. Unfortunately we cannot accept your offer. Your prices are prohibitive.

很遗憾我们不能接受你方报盘，你方价格过高，不敢问津。

4. The prices you quoted are much higher than those of other manufactures.

你方报价比其他厂商所报的价格高很多。

5. Your top quality goods are priced too high for us . Please send us the prices of your average quality items.

对我公司来说，你们的高级品价格是太高了。故请寄来贵公司中级品的报价资料。

6. Your offer dated…is very attractive. However, the quantity offered is too small to satisfy our requirements. Would you be able to process a big order for a quantity of…item No…?

你公司……月……日所寄的报价但甚具吸引力，然而，供应量太少，无法满足我们的需要量。不知贵公司能否生产品目第……号，数量……的较大订单。

7. The packing of goods offered does not meet our standards. Could you use packing which is secure against breakage?

贵公司报价货物包装不符合我方标准。能否用防止破损的包装？

8. We can only accept your special offer if you assure improved packing of your goods.

如果你们能改善货物的包装，我公司将接受你公司的特价报价单。

9. Your quotation dated…sounds interesting but the listed payment conditions are not customary in our trade.

你公司……日的报价我们很有兴趣，但所列的付款条件不合我们的贸易习惯。

10. Please reconsider your payment conditions and let us have your revision of the offer dated… .

请重新考虑你公司的付款条件，并将你……日的报价单修改后寄给我们。

11. We are ready to accept your offer provided you extend the period of guarantee to 12 months.

如你公司延长保证时间至 12 个月，则我公司准备接受你们的报价。

12. Your offer lacks specifications on the type of shipping. We are looking forward to your clarification.

你公司的报价单中未指定运输方式，对此问题希望得到贵公司的澄清。

13. Owing to the present price of raw materials, we are unable to change the conditions of our offer.

由于目前的原料价格之关系，我们无法修正我公司报价单上的条件。

14. We are pleased to take care of your special request concerning the quality.

我公司很乐意考虑你对有关质量的特别要求。

15. Although we appreciate your having sent us samples of cotton piece goods, we are not interested at the present time.

感谢你方寄来了棉织品货样，但现在我们对此没有兴趣。

16. Let's have your counter-offer.

请你方还盘。

17. Your counter-offer is too low and we can't accept it.

你方还价太低了，我方无法接受。

18. Our offer is reasonable and realistic. It comes in line with the prevailing market.

我方报价是合理的、现实的，符合当前市场的价格水平。

19. If you insist on your price and refuse to make any concession, there will be not much point in further discussion.

如果你方坚持自己的价格，不作让步，我们就没必要再谈下去了。

20. We make a counter-offer to you of US$ 140 per metric ton FOB London.

我们还价为每吨伦敦离岸价 140 美元。

21. It's absolutely out of the question for us to reduce our price to your level.

我们不可能将价格降到你们要求的那么低。

22. Still, I think it unwise for either of us to insist on his own price.

不过，我认为彼此都坚持自己的价格是不明智的。

23. If the price is higher than that, we'd rather call the whole deal off.

如果价格比这还高，我们宁愿放弃这桩生意。

24. We ask for indulgence for 6 days to make a counter-offer.

我们要求宽限 6 天以便做出还价。

25. We regret to note that you have turned down our counter-offer.

我们很遗憾得知你方已经拒绝了我方还价。

26. How about meeting each other halfway?

能不能互相做出让步？

27. As a rule, the larger the order, the lower the price.

买得越多，价格越便宜，这是惯例。

28. The market is firm with an upward tendency.

目前市场坚挺，并呈上涨趋势。

29. Moreover, we've kept the price close to the costs of production.

再说，我们已经压到生产成本边缘了。

30. No other buyers have bid higher than this price.

没有别的买主出价高于这个价格。

31. The price you offered is above previous prices.

你方报价高于上次。

32. The package number and quantity are identical with each other.

包装号与商品数量相吻合。

33. Quantity matters as much as quality and price, doesn't it?

数量和价格、质量一样重要，不是吗？

34. The quantity you ordered is considerable.

你们订的数量还可以。

35. If the quantity of the goods does not confirm to that stipulated in the contract, the importer will refuse to accept the goods.

如果进口商发现货物数量与合同规定不符，他将拒收。

36. If there any quantity limitation for the import of cotton cloth from China?

从中国进口的棉布有数量限制吗?

37. You remarked yesterday you would sell on shipped quality, quantity and weight.
你们昨天强调你方售货以装船质量、数量和重量为准。

38. Useful quantities have changed hands.
较大数量商品已经转手。

39. A small order this year is also welcome.
小批订货今年也受欢迎。

40. We're prepared to purchase a shipment quantity of this material.
我们准备购买足够一次装运量的这种商品。

41. This year we can buy an extra 700 blue jeans.
今年我们可以多订 700 件牛仔裤。

42. The maximum quantity of cotton jerseys this year is about us $ 35,000.
我们今年最多能订购大约 35000 美元的棉毛衫。

Exercises

Ⅰ. Translate the following phrases and then make sentences.

worth while	at one's earliest convenience
make a concession to sb.	usual terms
cope with	parcel post
previous to	Japanese make
minimum quantity	at one's level
be prepared to	come to terms
in view of	on the high side
see one's way clear to	on account of
account for	for one's account
with the exception	

Ⅱ. Complete the following sentences in English.

1. We cannot see our way__________.

a．接受你方 9 月 10 日的还价

b．接受你方 3 月装船的建议

c．在尚未获得货源以前，接受大量订货

2. Please keep us posted of__________.

a．你处市场的货物供求情况

b．你们每月销售皮鞋的数量

c．你们市场行情的变化

d．你们每季度需要进口的数量

3. We assure you________________.

a．你们的订货将按照合同规定如期装运

b．我方所供货物价格公道，品质优良

c．我们要尽全力既促进贸易又增进友谊

4. Please rest assured________________________.

a．我们会把一切必要的事办好

b．我们就要准备这些货物

c．我们就要准备装运上述货物

5. Your price is found to be________________________.

a．偏高

b．脱离我处的市场行情

c．比日本货要高出30%

Ⅲ. Translate the following sentences into English.

1．只要你公司坚持所提出的价格，那我们将不能给你一个适当的报价。

2．我们以较低的价格提供较佳的产品。

3．我们不能配合你公司的要求使用特别的包装。无论如何你公司要我们特别注意的是：我公司应注意防止产品包装的损坏。

4．如果你公司能将9月3日的报价单的价格降低3%，我公司将乐意接受你们的报价。

5．你公司报价货物之包装不符标准，你公司能否使用可防止破损的包装?

6．由于我公司仓储能力的限制，货物需分三次分运。不知在这种条件下你公司份额报价是否有效。

7．你公司21日寄来的价目表很完整，但所列的付款条件不符合我们的贸易习惯。

8．我公司对于你公司30日寄来的报价单中的保险事项不甚满意，你公司能否对其重新考虑。

9．我们觉得，对于你公司的易腐货物，只适合于用冷藏卡车运输，请立刻让我公司知道此法是否可行。

10．由于考虑到我公司报你之价格为最低价格，故无法满足你公司的特殊要求。

11．很遗憾，我们无法履行你公司对我们30日所寄报价单中有关包装事项的特殊要求。

12．由于考虑到阁下将开出大量订货的订单，对于我们最近的报价单，将允许一定的折扣。

13．我公司的装运部门准备依从贵公司对运输路线的特殊要求，特此通知。

14．非常抱歉，我们无法依从你对有关包装的特殊要求，但愿意提供如下的特价报价。

15．尽管我公司无法满足你的特殊要求，但我们仍寄送另一份报价单给你。

Ⅳ. Translate the following essay into Chinese.

I'm afraid that I have to emphasize that we have already cut our prices to the minimum for the very fine products we are now putting on the market, and therefore it is quite impossible to reduce them any further without affecting their quality. As I feel sure you will appreciate, we do not wish to offer you a product that you will find difficult to sell or later have complaints about.

In order to ensure, therefore, that we are able to maintain the reputation we have had for a number of years till now for manufacturing footwear of superlative quality, we employ only the most skilled craftsmen and use only the finest materials. This has meant that our production costs have increased very considerably over the last few years, and yet we have been able to avoid raising prices. We have been happy to keep our prices as low as possible for the consumer, but as I have said, we would find it quite impossible actually to reduce them. We know that cheaper models are marketed by our competitors, but we have received no suggestion that they have been able to equal us in quality.

Our products have sold very well in the United States and Western Europe, and all the reports we have received suggest that the public appreciates being able to buy fine quality shoes at the very modest prices we quote. I very much hope that you will place at least a trial order with us, for I feel sure that you will find our shoes will sell as well as in the United Kingdom as they have elsewhere.

Ⅴ. Write a counter-offer according to the following particulars.

1. 回复对方 5 月 15 日关于 500 台海信电视机的来信。
2. 对价格和装运期满意，但要求变更付款方式。
3. 以前使用不可撤销的保兑信用证付款，花费很大。
4. 资金吃紧已达 3 个月，再加上银行利率很高，资金问题特别突出。
5. 建议对方接受“承兑交单”或“见票 60 天支付的远期付款交单”方式来支付货款。

Chapter 6

Conclusion of Business

Section 1 Business Knowledge 业务知识

在进出口业务中，洽谈交易程序一般按询盘→发盘→反还盘→接受→签订合同的环节来进行，习惯上把这 5 个环节称为交易洽商的一般程序。磋商的过程繁简不一，有的磋商没有询盘，有的磋商没有还盘。但是发盘与接受是交易达成不可或缺的环节。一般认为，在买卖双方谈判过程中，只要接受生效，合同关系就建立起来了。那么，什么是接受呢?

交易的一方接到另一方的发盘或还盘，并表示完全同意，这种口头或书面的表示，在进出口业务中称为接受（acceptance）。接受是达成交易和订立合同必不可少的环节。接受在法律上是一种承诺。它是指受盘人在发盘有效期内完全同意发盘的全部内容，愿意订立合同的一种表示。

怎样才能构成一项有效的接受呢? 一项有效的接受一般具备以下条件。

一、一项有效的接受必须是受盘人对一项实盘的完全认同。就是说，接受的内容必须同对方的实盘的各项条件严格一致，若接受中含有对原发盘内容的增加、限制或其他修改，接受均不能成立，应作为拒绝或还盘。

二、一项有效的接受必须是发盘所规定的受盘人表示才有效。任何第三者，针对该项发盘表示接受，均无法律效力，发盘人不受约束。但某些公开发盘除外，任何人都可以按规定办法表示接受。

三、一项有效的接受必须是受盘人在发盘的有效期内或合理的时间内表示接受才有效。假如一项实盘规定了明确的、具体的有效期限，发盘人只有在此期限内表示接受才有效。假如一项实盘未规定具体的有效期，应在合理时间内表示接受才有效。

四、接受应由受盘人采用声明或做出其他行为的方式表示，并且这种表示传达给发盘人才开始有效。缄默或不行动本身不是接受。所谓声明是指以书面文字表达上述意思；所谓行动是根据该发盘的意思或依照当事人之间已确立的习惯做法所做出的商业行为，例如，卖方用发运

货物或买方用支付货款等行为来表示同意。因此，采用某种行为的方式来表示接受并不是任意的行为，而是必须符合发盘书面文字内容的行为。

具体的业务中，交易双方经过磋商，一方的发盘或还盘被另一方接收后，交易立即达成，合同即告成立，双方就要承担法律责任。通常情况下，交易双方为明确规定各自的权利和义务，一般采用书面的形式把磋商过程中形成共识的所有交易条件确定下来，以备日后履约。由卖方按照双方认可的条款草拟的合同称为销售合同（sales contract）或销售确认书（sales confirmation），由买方拟定的合同称为购货合同（sales contract）或购货确认书（purchase confirmation）。不管是合同还是确认书，一般都是一式两份，经过双方签字，各执一份，据以执行，这种行为在进出口业务中，称为签订合同（to sign a contract）。

接受可以简单的表示，如“接受你方 × 月 × 日的实盘”。也可以较详细地表示，即在接受函中重述主要的交易条件。在表示接受时常用 accept 一词，在使用这个词时要注意其时态。如：

1. We accept you firm offer.

2. We have accepted your firm offer.

以上表明买方明确接受了卖方的报盘，即交易已宣告成立。

3. We are accepting your offer. 正在考虑接受，并没有肯定表示接受，因此交易尚未达成。

请注意下面的表述：

We accept your offer subject to December Shipment.这句话虽然 accept 一词是现在时，但是后面跟了一个条件：“以 12 月装运为条件，我们就接受你的报盘 。”这句话虽然用了 accept 一词，但又对一项重要条件即交货期做了修改，因此它不是一项接受，而是一项还盘。如未经发盘人确认，合同是不能成立的。

接受信函是订货与签订合同合二为一的，只要掌握好订货信和寄送合同，确认书信的写法即可。

订货信分为① 行文式：适合对单一商品的订购；② 列表式：适合对多种商品的订购；③ 填写订货单；④ 填写购货确认书。订货信是对报盘信的答复信，因而具备答复信的特点。

Section 2 Specimen Letters 样函

（1）

Dear Sirs,

We thank you for your letter of September 8th confirming your order for 40 long tons Talc in Lumps[1].

Price: US $…per long ton, CIF Liverpool.

Packing: in single gunny bag[2] of about 50 kgs. net each.

Although the current market price is a little bit higher, we accept the order on the same terms as before with a view to encouraging business[3].

As requested in your previous letter, we enclose our Sales Confirmation[4] No. 213 in quadruplicate[5]. Please send back one copy duly signed.

Please rest assured that your order will receive our careful attention.

Yours faithfully,

Encl.

Words, Expressions and Notes

1. Talc in Lumps 滑石块
2. single gunny bag 单层麻袋
3. encouraging business 促动业务、拉动业务
4. Sales Confirmation 售货确认书
5. in quadruplicate 一式四份

（2）

Dear Sirs,

We refer to our letter of 23 ult[1]. And your telex 6th inst[2]., we have pleasure in confirming the following order:

Commodity: Mou Tai Chiew[3]

Alcohol content: 45%~60%

Capacity[4]: 500 grams per bottle

Quantity: 100 dozen

Price: $… per doz. CIF Antwerp

Packing: in cases of 24 bottles[5]

Shipment: October, 2010

The relative letter of credit will be airmailed soon and you are required to ship the above lot[6] by the first available steamer upon receipt of our L/C.

Thank you in advance[7] for your prompt attention.

Yours faithfully,

Words, Expressions and Notes

1. ult. 上月
2. inst. 本月
3. Mou Tai Chiew 茅台酒
4. capacity 每瓶含量
5. in cases of 24 bottles 箱装，每箱 24 瓶
6. lot 这里指一批货物
7. Thank you in advance 预先致谢

(3)

Dear Sirs,

We are pleased in sending you the attached Order Confirmation No. 350 covering our recent purchase from you of 1,500 pieces of Mulehides[1].

We are going to buy this parcel for our own account[2], so as to distribute[3] the hides among several prospective[4] buyers. They are accustomed to[5] buying hides from Argentine, but we think we shall be able to persuade them to try your material. If the quality represented by your initial consignment[6] turns out satisfactory[7], we can assure you of repeated orders.

Yours faithfully,

Words, Expressions and Notes

1. Mulehides 骡皮
2. for our own account 为自己购买
3. distribute 分销
4. prospective 未来的、预期的，perspective 指观念、想法
5. be accustomed to 习惯于
6. initial consignment 首批来货
7. satisfactory 令人满意的

(4)

Dear Sirs,

We are pleased to have made with you an order for 200 metric tons of groundnut oil[1]. Enclosed please find our order sheet and the relative credit will be telexed to you within the next few days.

Our buyers have agreed to allow partial shipment[2] for this order, which will enable you to make shipment within the three months from April to June. If you could spread out[3] shipments by forwarding a proportionate quantity each month instead of making the whole lot of 200 metric tons be congested[4] into the same month, it would be of much assistance to our customers. It might interest you to know that the buyers concerned are among the leading importers of edible oils[5] in this city. It is very likely that they might want to duplicate their order[6] before the month is out[7].

Thank you for your cooperation. We hope we will have more businesses in the future.

Yours faithfully,

Words, Expressions and Notes

1. groundnut oil 花生油
2. partial shipment 分批装运
3. spread out 分散

4. congested 拥堵、拥挤

5. edible oils 食用油，常见各种食用油的说法：

peanut oil 花生油

sunflower seed oil 葵花籽油

rape seed oil 菜籽油

corn oil 玉米油

soy(a)bean/soybean oil 豆油

sesame oil (芝)麻油

almond oil 杏仁油

coconut oil 椰子油

flaxseed oil 亚麻籽油

6. duplicate their order 这里指再次订货

7. before the month is out 月底

（5）

Dear Sirs,

We refer to the recent exchanges of faxes between us and are pleased to confirm having concluded with you a transaction of 80 metric tons of groundnut kernels[1].

Enclosed is our Sales Contract No. 9031 in duplicate in which please countersign[2] and return one copy to us for our file[3]. We trust you will open the relative L/C at an early date[4]. As regards additional quantities we are working, we will let you have an offer sometime[5] next week.

Yours faithfully,

Words, Expressions and Notes

1. groundnut kernels 花生仁

2. countersign 会签，是指通过往来函电成交时，则先由一方缮制合同并签署，然后将合同正本一式两份寄交国外客户签署，而后退回一份以备存查，作为日后履行合同的依据。

3. for our file 供我方存档，同 for our record

4. at an early date 不久，在最近期间

5. sometime 将来或过去某一时候

sometimes 有时、间或

some time 在未来某时，经过若干时间

（6）

Dear Sirs,

We hereby confirm having sold to you the goods under mentioned[1], subject to terms stated below:

Quantity: 4,000 metric tons

Description: Canned Oat[2] of our usual standard, America

Price: US $ 50 per metric ton CIF New York

Weight: Net delivered[3]

Tare[4]: Actual

Shipment: Prompt shipment, sailing direct to port of destination, transshipment[5] not allowed

Payment: By an irrevocable letter of credit payable against presentation[6] of shipping documents[7]

Insurance: Marine insurance[8] to be covered by us

Conditions: We agree to settlement of disputes by…arbitration. No claim can be entertained unless made within 10 days of arrival of gods at the port of destination.

Remarks: Kindly sign and return one copy, each of the original and duplicate[9] here of evidence of your acceptance.

Yours faithfully,

Words, Expressions and Notes

1. under mentioned 下述的
2. Canned Oat 罐装燕麦
3. net delivered 净发货，此处理解为：产品重量以实际净发货数为准
4. tare 皮重，指货物包装物的重量

在外贸中，商品多数情况按照净重来计价，这就要根据实际情况来扣除皮重。计算和去除皮重的方法有以下几种。

第一，实际皮重法（actual tare）。即通过实际称量、逐一过磅得出总皮重，再从毛重里扣除。这种方法最精确，但也最麻烦，费用耗费也多。因此只有对单位价值较高的商品才适用。

第二，平均皮重法（average tare）。在包装材料、包装规格整齐划一的情况下，可以只称量其中一件商品包装物的重量，将其作为这批货物的平均皮重。然后再乘以商品的总件数，便能得出这批商品的总皮重。另外也可以抽取若干件商品包装进行称量，再取其平均值作为平均皮重。

第三，习惯皮重法（customary tare）。有些商品由于使用的包装比较规范，重量相对固定不变，并在长期的实践中为市场所公认。对于这类商品包装物，就不需要逐渐过称，而是直接把大家公认的重量作为皮重。例如，装运粮食的机制麻袋，国际公认每个重 2.5 磅。这个数字即为习惯皮重。

第四，约定皮重法（computed tare）。这是指买卖双方在合同中约定每件包装的重量，以此作为计算总皮重的基础。

5. transshipment 转运，即货物在中途某一港口换装另外一艘船，然后再驶往目的港
6. presentation 此处指票据的提示行为
7. shipping documents 装运单据
8. Marine insurance 海上保险
9. original and duplicate 正本和复件

（7）

Dear Sirs,

We thank you for your letter of 4th April, 2000 with which you enclosed your pricelist and catalogue, and for sample pairs of shoes[1] that we have also receive.

We agree that the quality is up to the standard[2] and the prices you quoted are satisfactory. We also note that you will allow us a discount of 5% on an order worth ￡5000 or more[3]. We therefore, have airmailed you our Order No.888 on Wednesday, it reads[4]

Commodity	Quantity	Article	Price	Total
Ladiesa and Children's Shoes	400 pairs	1021	￡12	￡4800
	400 pairs	1024	￡10.5	￡4200
	200 pairs	1025	￡9.5	￡1900
				￡10900
	Less 5% discount			￡545
				￡10355

Please note that as these goods are urgently required here, we should be most grateful if you could dispatch[5] the goods as soon as possible.

Yours truly,

Words, Expressions and Notes

1. sample pairs of shoes 样品鞋
2. up to the standard 符合标准，达到标准
3. ￡5000 or more 5000 英镑或高于 5000 英镑，类似的表达还有，

100 tons or there abouts　　100 吨上下

￡100 or less　100 英镑或少于 100 英镑

￡100 or above 100 英镑或多于 100 英镑

less than ￡100　少于 100 英镑

more than ￡100　多于 100 英镑

4. reads 此处理解为，订单内容如下所示
5. dispatch 这里指发货，此外还有速遣费、迅速办理的意思

例句：

Please do your best to hasten the dispatch of our Order No. 35 because the goods are urgently needed.

因为需要很紧迫，请尽力迅速发出第 35 号订单的货物。

Please act with dispatch.

请抓紧行动。

The furs ordered have been dispatched per air freight.

所订裘皮已由空运发出。

We will do our best to dispatch the shipment.

我们将尽量迅速装运。

Dispatch money has been paid according to the stipulated rate of ￡...per running day.

速遣费已按每一连续日…￡的规定费率付清。

（8）

Dear Sirs,

We want to say how pleased[1] we were to receive your order of April 15th for Ladies' and Children's Shoes.

We confirm supply of 1000 pairs of the shoes at the prices stated in your order No. 888 and will allow a 5% special discount on your order worth ￡5000 or above. Our Sales Confirmation No. BC-510 in two originals were airmailed to you. Please sign and return[2] one copy of them for our file.

It is understood[3] that a letter of credit in our favor covering[4] the said shoes should be opened immediately. We wish to point out that stipulations[5] in the relative L/C must strictly confirm[6] to the stated in our Sales Confirmation so as to avoid subsequent amendments[7]. You may rest assured that we will effect shipment without delay on receipt of your letter of credit.

We appreciate your cooperation and look forward to receiving from you further orders.

Yours truly,

Words, Expressions and Notes

1. how pleased 非常高兴，how 在此处表示程度

2. sign and return 签字并寄回

3. It is understood 不用说，大家都很清楚，据悉

4. covering 有关、关于

cover 作动词时有包括、适用、弥补、投保的意思。

例句：

our business activities cover a wide range of articles.

我公司经营的产品，品种繁多。

The rules cover all possible cases.

这些规则适用所有可能发生的情况。

They have to cover their short positions.

他们不得不补进卖空（期货）交易。

us $ 2000 is even not sufficient to cover the advertising fees, to say nothing of other expenses.

2000 美元连广告费都不够，更不用说支付其他费用了。

We agree to cover all the losses you sustained.

我们同意弥补你方遭受的一切损失。

The goods are to be covered against All Risks.

需要对货物投保一切险。

We have shipped on board s.s "Dayu"3,500 pairs of rubber shoes covered by your L/C No. 325.

你方第 325 号信用证项下的 3500 双胶鞋已装上“大禹”号货轮。

The inspection certificate covering this shipment states clearly that the goods were in sound condition when shipped.

关于这批货的商检证书清楚地说明货物在装出时情况良好。

We enclose our Sales Contract No. 99 covering this transaction.

兹附寄关于此项交易的我方第 99 号销售合同。

5. stipulations 规定

stipulate 是动词，后接从句要用虚拟语气。stimulate 是刺激、促进的意思。

例句：

The transaction is concluded on the stipulation that L/C should be opened 30 days before the commencement of shipment.

这笔交易达成的基础是在装船前 30 天开出信用证。

The contract stipulates for the use of the best materials.

合同规定要用最好的材料。

The contract stipulates that the goods be shipped entirely.

合同规定货物必须一次性全部装运。

6. confirm to 与……相符合、一致。conformity 是名词，习惯搭配

in conformity with/to，与……一致，依照……

例句：

In conformity with our desire to promote business, we have accepted your offer of 80 tons wool.

依照我们促进业务的愿望，我方接受你方 80 吨羊毛的报盘。

This is not in conformity with our arrangement.

这与我们商定的办法不相符。

This quality must confirm to the sample.

质量必须与货样一致。

It is necessary to confirm the specifications to the requirements.

规格必须与要求相符。

7. subsequent amendments 随后的修改。amendment 常指信用证、合同、宪法等重要文件的修改、修订。

例句：

We enclose amendment advice of L/C No. 39.

兹附寄第 39 号信用证的修改通知。

Please rush the amendment to the L/C.

请对信用证速作修改。

The wording of the agreement calls for amendment.

协议的措辞需要修改。

（9）

Dear Sirs,

We have duly received your Sales Contract[1] No.5630 covering 50 tons walnut meat we have booked with you. Enclosed please find the duplicate with our counter-signature[2]. Thanks[3] to mutual efforts, we were able to bridge[4] the price gap and put the deal through[5]

The relative L/C has been established[6] with the Bank of China, London, in your favor. It will reach you in due course.

Regarding further quantities required, we hope you will see your way clear to make us an offer. As an indication[7], we are prepared to order 80 tons.

Yours faithfully,

Words, Expressions and Notes

1. Sales Contract 销售合同，purchase contract 是购货合同
2. counter-signature 会签
3. thanks to 由于、多亏
4. bridge 这里指弥合价格上的差距

例句：

We have shown maximum flexibility in order to bridge the wide gap existing between the two sides.

为了弥合双方之间的巨大差异，我们已表现出最大的灵活性。

5. put the deal through 达成交易
6. established 这里指开立信用证。用于开证的表达方式还有：

open L/C　　issue L/C　　make out L/C

7. as an indication 顺便说一下，顺便提一下

（10）

Dear Sirs,

We acknowledge the receipt of your letter of the June 18th, for which we thank you. Since then a number of cables have been exchanged[1] resulting in our purchase from you of the following:

5000 pcs of Cowhide[2] RMB ¥….per pc. CFR London

These 5000 pieces of cowhides are to be packed in two lots[3], 2000 and 3000 and shipped on separate Bills of Lading[4] as they are intended for[5] two different customers.

Please mark[6] the bales with the lot number as given in the enclosed Order Sheet. It is necessary to take good note of[7] this lest[8] the parcel should be mixed up[9] on loading.

Yours faithfully,

Words, Expressions and Notes

1. a number of cables have been exchanged 双方之间大量的传真往来
2. cowhide 牛皮
3. in two lots 分成两批。lot 这里指一批货，同 parcel

lot No. 批号

odd lot 不成整数的某批货，散股（股票，1 个 lot 合 100 股）

carload lot 整车货物

例句：

We thank you for your kindness of receiving this last lot for us.

感谢你方为我们保留这最后一批货的好意。

This is the only lot available and others are after it.

这是可供应的仅有一批货，而且还有其他客户争相购买。

The goods are to be shipped in three lots of 300 tons each on separate B/L.

货物分三批装运，每批 300 吨，提单要分开。

4. Bills of Lading 提单

海运货物中，船方收到货后签发给托运人的收据，提单是货物所有权的凭证，通过转让提单可以完成在运货物的转销。

5. intended for 为……准备

6. mark 动词，在货物包裹外面加注标号、标记。作名词是标记、标准的意思。

post mark 邮戳　　price mark 价格标签

shipping mark 装运标记，唛头

trade mark 商标

例句：

The quality is up to the mark.

质量合乎标准。

Please fax marks (shipping mark) and destination.

请传真告知唛头及目的港。

Mark down the number of packages that are discharged into the lighter.

记下卸入驳船的货物件数。

This transaction, though small in amount, marks the beginning of our formal business relationship.

这笔交易金额虽小，却标志我们双方正式业务关系的开始。

Unless you advise to the contrary, we will mark the package the same as before.

除非你方另有通知，我们仍将在货包上刷以前的标志。

Goods are to be marked with our initials in a diamond.

货物应该标上我方缩写名称，外加菱形。

7. take good note of 认真留意、注意。note 作动词，表示记录、注意到、提到。关于 note 的一些常用短语：

account note 账单	bank note 钞票、纸币、银行券
booking note 订舱单	consignment note 铁路运单
counterfeit banknote 假钞	credit note 贷方通知单
delivery note 提货单	debit note 借方通知单
postal note 邮汇单	protest note 拒付通知
short-term note 短期票据	transfer note 汇票
treasury note 国库券	

例句：

Please take note of the above.

请对以上事项加以注意。

We have taken careful note of your shipping instructions.

我们对你方的装船要求已予以密切关注。

The matter is worthy of note.

此事值得注意。

Please note down all the details.

请记下全部细节。

You may have noted the market has dropped.

你方可能已注意到行市已经下跌。

We have received your letter of June 9th, contents of which have been duly noted.

你方 6 月 9 日来信已收到，内情尽悉。

Our products are noted for their attractive colors.

我们的产品以其鲜艳动人的颜色闻名。

In his speech he first noted the importance of the policy.

他在讲话中首先提到这项政策的重要性。

8. lest 以免，唯恐

lest 是从属连词，常用来引导目的状语从句，从句用虚拟语气，例如信文中的最后一句话：

It is necessary to take good note of this lest the parcel should be mixed up on loading.

有必要注意此事，以免货物在转运时放混。

9. mix up 混合，把（某人）搞糊涂、分不清

（11）

Dear Sirs,

"Parrot[1]" Brand White Cement

As a result of[2] our recent exchange of telegrams, we confirm having purchased from 1000 long tons (tons of 2240 Ibs) of the captioned goods on the following terms and conditions[3]:

Price: at ￡225 per long ton CFR Genoa, net shipping weight.

Packing: in 6-ply Kraft-paper bags[4] of about 110 Ibs net each.

Quality: against the seller's own guarantee[5] that the goods are fully up to the Chinese Export Standard.

Shipment: in one or two lots to be shipped from Qinghuangdao to Genoa during January, 2001, preferably[6] by direct steamer

Payment: by a confirmed and irrevocable letter of credit in your favor, payable by draft at sight.

We are pleased to have transacted this first business with your corporation and look forward to the further expansion of trade to our mutual benefit.

Yours faithfully,

Words, Expressions and Notes

1. parrot 鹦鹉

2. as a result of 由于……的结果

例句：

As a result of your delay in opening the L/C, we were unable to effect shipment in good time.

由于你们迟延开立信用证，我方未能如期装运。

The goods were eventually disposed of as a result of our repeated efforts.

由于我们一再努力，货物终于售出了。

3. terms and conditions 条款、条件

terms 和 conditions 时常连用。但是，terms 往往指大的方面，如支付方式采用信用证。conditions 经常指 terms 确定以后的具体条件，如什么时候通过哪家银行开证。

例句：

It was very unpleasant surprised to learn that the terms and conditions we finally agreed had been turned down by your company.

得悉我们双方最终商定的条款遭到你方拒绝，这让人感到惊讶、不快。

4. 6-ply Kraft-paper bags 6 层牛皮纸袋

ply 指（木的）层，（纸、布）的厚度，（绳或纱的）股，如 two plies of cloth 二层布；two-ply wood 二层胶合板；three-ply knitting wool 三股毛线

表示层、层面的单词还有很多，且用法有一定区别，例如：

coat/coating 指油漆或颜色形成的涂层，或表示与涂层厚薄相似的灰尘

deck 指类似甲板的地方（如公共汽车的层面）

layer 地质术语，通常指岩层、地层。

storey 计算建筑物高度的层，具体居住房屋的层

tier 指阶梯式的层，也表示社会阶层

veil 主要指妇女用的遮面纱，轻薄且随风拂动，又常常比喻云雾的薄层

a new coat of paint 一层新油漆

a coat of dust 一层灰

floating coat 中层漆

two coats of whitewash 两层白灰

the top deck of a double-decker bus 两层巴士的顶层

a layer of clay 一层泥土

layer of jam 一层果酱

a layer of snow 一层雪

a six-story building 六层楼

tiers of terraced fields 层层梯田

two tiers of arches 二层牌楼

the lowest tier of society 社会最底层

a veil of cloud 一层薄云

a veil of mist 一层薄雾

5. guarantee 担保、保证，guarantee 既可作名词，也可作动词

例句：

Increased demand is not always a guarantee of better prices.

需求增长并不一定保证能卖出好价钱。

If you guarantee payment, we will forward them the shipment on D/P basis.

如果你们担保付款，我方将按付款交单方式把这批货发运给他们。

It is not possible for us to guarantee the time of arrival.

我们不可能保证到达的时间。

We are ready to allow you a 5% commission provided you can guarantee yearly turnover of £85,000 for a start.

倘若作为开端，你方能保证一年营业额达到 85, 000 英镑，我方乐于给予 5%的佣金。

6. preferably 更可取的，更好的，宁可

例句：

The gloves are to be packed in dozen or in single pairs, preferably the latter.

这些手套按打或按副包装皆可，后者更好。

Please send us a full range of samples of your Men's Shirts, preferably by air.

请寄给我方你们男式衬衫的全套样品，最好空运。

（12）

Dear Sirs,

We thank you for your telegram duplicating[1] your order of October 12th for 500 doz. Rubber Shoes[2].

Although the prevailing quotations are somewhat higher, we will accept the order on the same terms as before with the view of[3] encouraging business.

As requested in your previous letter, we have made out[4] our Sales Confirmation No. 300 in duplicate[5] and shall thank you to send back one copy duly countersigned.

We are glad to know that a letter of credit will be established in our favor immediately. However we would like to draw your attention to the fact that the stipulations in the relative credit should strictly conform to the terms in our Sales Confirmation in order to avoid subsequent cable amendment.

We appreciate your cooperation and trust that the shipment which is to be dispatched after receipt of the relative letter of credit will turn out[6] to your entire satisfaction.

Yours faithfully,

Words, Expressions and Notes

1. duplicating 此处指重申、再次强调

duplicate 作动词，表示使重复、加倍；作形容词表示复制的、成双的、完全一样的，如 duplicate documents（单据副本），duplicate order（同样价格和条件的重复订货）；名词表示复制品、副本

例句：

We are sending you here with our Sales Confirmation No. 149 in duplicate.

随函寄去第 149 号销售确认书一式两份。

We hope you can duplicate our order No. 124.

我们希望你方能按我们第 124 号订单再供货一次。

We have some stock left, and shall be able to meet your requirements if you wish to duplicate your last order.

我们尚有一些存货，如你方愿意重复上次订单，我方能够满足你们的需要。

2. Rubber Shoes 胶鞋

3. with the view of 以…为目的，同 with a view to/of

例句：

We give this special accommodation with the view of cementing our relations.

我们给你方这个特殊照顾是为了加强我们的关系。

With a view to ironing out this misunderstanding, we explain as follows:

为了清除这一误会，我们作如下的解释。

4. made out 开列、填写、缮制

例句：

Please make out your sales Contract in three originals.

请将你们的销售合同按三份正本缮制。

5. in duplicate 此处指一式两份

6. turn out 结果是，成为……

例句：

We hope everything will turn out to be satisfactory in the end.

我们希望最终一切都令人满意。

（13）

A Specimen of Sales Contract
销售合同（样本）

SALES CONTRACT (ORIGINAL)

Contract No.: CE102 Date: Jun. 2, 20 × ×

Signed at: Qingdao

Seller: Sinochem Shandong Import & Export Group Corporation

20, Xianggangzhong Road, Qingdao, China

Buyer: Pacific Trading Co., Ltd。

1118 Green Road, New York, U.S.A.

This Sales Contract is made by and between the Seller and the Buyer whereby the Seller agrees to sell and the Buyer agrees to buy the under-mentioned goods according to the terms and conditions stipulated below:

1.

Name of Commodity Specifications & Packing	Quantity	Unit Price	Total Amount
Lithopone ZnS content 28% min. Paper-lined glass-fibre bags	100 M/Ts	USD360.00 per M/T CIFC3% New York	USD36,000.00

(The Seller is allowed to load 5% more or less and the price shall be calculated according to the unit price.)

2. Shipping Marks:

PTC
New York
No. 1-1000

3. Insurance: To be covered by the Seller for 110% of the invoice value against All Risks and War Risk as per the relevant Ocean Marine Cargo Clauses of the People's Insurance Company of China. If other coverage or an additional insurance amount is required, the Buyer must have the consent of the Seller before shipment, and the additional premium is to be borne by the buyer.

4. Port of Shipment: Qingdao, China.

5. Port of Destination: New York, U.S.A.

6. Time of Shipment: During August, 20 × ×, allowing partial shipments and transshipment.

7. Terms of Payment: The Buyer shall open with a bank acceptable to the Seller an Irrevocable Letter of Credit at sight to reach the Seller 30 days before the time of shipment specified, valid for negotiation in China until the 15th day after the aforesaid time of shipment.

8. Commodity Inspection: It is mutually agreed that the Certificate of Quality and Weight issued by the General Administration for Quality Supervision , Inspection and Quarantine of the People's Republic of China at the port of shipment shall be taken as the basis of delivery.

9. Discrepancy and Claim: Any claim by the Buyer on the goods shipped shall be filed within 30 days after the arrival of the goods at the port of destination and supported by a survey report issued by a surveyor approved by the Seller. Claims in respect to matters within the responsibility of the insurance company or of the shipping company will not be considered or entertained by the Seller.

10. Force Majeure: If shipment of the contracted goods is prevented or delayed in whole or in part due to Force Majeure, the Seller shall not be liable for non-shipment or late shipment of the goods under this Contract. However, the Seller shall notify the Buyer by fax or e-mail and furnish the latter within 15 days by registered airmail with a certificate issued by the China Council for the Promotion of International Trade attesting such event or events.

11. Arbitration: All disputes arising out of the performance of or relating to this Contract shall be settled amicably through negotiation. In case no settlement can be reached through negotiation,

the case shall then be submitted to the Foreign Economic and Trade Arbitration Commission of the China Council for the Promotion of International Trade, Beijing, China, for arbitration in accordance with its Provisional Rules of Procedure. The award of the arbitration is final and binding upon both parties.

12. Other Terms:

THE SELLER　　　　THE BUYER

(Signature)　　　　(Signature)

销售合同（正本）

合同号：CE102　　　　日期：20××年6月2日

签订于：青岛

卖方：中化山东进出口公司

中国青岛，香港中路20号

买方：太平洋贸易有限公司

美国纽约，格林路1118号

本合同由买卖双方签订。根据下列条件和条款，卖方同意出售、买方同意购买下述货物：

1.

品名、规格和包装	数量	单价	总值
锌贝白 氧化锌含量最低28% 用衬纸的玻璃纤维袋包装	100吨	每吨360美元 CIFC3%纽约	36 000.00美元整

（允许卖方溢短装5%，货值按单价计算。）

2．运输标志

PTC

New York

No. 1-1000

3．保险：由卖方根据中国人民保险公司的《海洋运输货物保险条款》的相关条款，按照发票金额的110%投保一切险和战争险。如果买方要求额外险别或增加保险金额，须在装运前取得卖方同意，并且支付额外保费。

4．装运港：中国青岛

5. 目的港：美国纽约

6. 装运时间：20××年 8 月，允许转船和分批装运

7. 付款条件：买方将通过卖方接受的银行开立一张不可撤销的即期信用证，装船前 30 天送达卖方，装船后 15 天之内在中国议付有效。

8. 商品检验：双方同意以中国国家质量监督检验检疫总局在装运港签发的品质和重量检验证书作为交货的依据。

9. 异议和索赔：买方对货物的任何索赔应于货物抵达目的港后 30 天之内提出，并提供由卖方认可的检验机构出具的检验报告。对于应由保险公司或轮船公司负责的索赔，卖方将不予考虑和受理。

10. 不可抗力：如因不可抗力使合同货物全部或部分未能交付或延迟交付，卖方将不对此负责。然而，卖方须用传真或电子邮件通知买方并于 15 日内用挂号航空邮件向买方提供由中国国际贸易促进委员会出具的不可抗力证明。

11. 仲裁：因履行该合同或与该合同有关的一切争议均通过友好协商解决。如友好协商不能解决，则提交中国北京中国国际贸易促进委员会的对外经济贸易仲裁委员会按其暂定程序规则进行仲裁，仲裁裁决对双方都是终局的和有约束力的。

12. 其他条款：

卖方　　　　　　　　　　　　　　　　　　买方

（签名）　　　　　　　　　　　　　　　　（签名）

(14)

Contract for Purchase

No. 3XQA7775OUS

This contract is made by and between China National Chemicals Import & Export Corporation, Erh Li Kou, His Chiao, Beijing, China, Cable Address: STNOCHEM BEIJING, (hereinafter called the buyer) and Unisobin Chemicals Export Corporation, 251 West Hasting Street, Vancouver, B.C., Canada, Cable Address: UNISOBIN VANCOUVER, (hereinafter called the seller) whereby the buyer agrees to buy and the seller agrees to sell the under-mentioned commodity on the following terms and conditions:

1. Name of Commodity and Quantity

Rock Phosphate, 100000 (One Hundred Thousand) Metric Tons—10% more or less at buyer's

option. The Buyer shall inform the Seller of this option within one month prior to the completion of this contract.

2. Specifications

Rock Phosphate must contain 72% Tribasic Phosphate of Lime ($Ca_3P_2O_8$), and the guaranteed content of Tribasic Phosphate of Lime in a dry state, i.e. dried at 105 °C : 72% min.

Phosphoric Anhydride (P_2O_5)	32.95%
Iron and Aluminum Oxides Combined:	2.8% max
Moisture	3% max
Fluorine (F)	3.65% max
Carbon Dioxide (CO_2)	3.8% max

Screen analysis: All Rock passing through one half inch mesh and retained on plus 150 meshes Tyler screen.

3. Price

US $12.00 (US Dollars Twelve) per M/T FOB stowed and trimmed

Vancouver B.C or Prince Rupert.

Total Value: US $ 1200000 (US Dollars One Million Two Hundred Thousand Only)

4. Destination: China Ports.

5. Period of Delivery

50000 M/T in October, 2005 at Vancouver Port

25000 M/T from October to December, 2005 at Prince Rupert Port

25000 M/T from January to March, 2006 at Prince Rupert Port

6. Weighing

The Rock Phosphate shall be weighed under the supervision of both seller's and buyer's representatives (the captain of the carrying vessel may be appointed as the buyer's representative), during loading operation at Vancouver or Prince Rupert by a self-acting balance, at the expense of the seller.

7. Inspection

The determination of quality of Rock Phosphate is subject to the results of analysis of representative samples drawn from the actually landed cargo, conducted by the China Commodity Inspection Bureau after arrival of the goods at the destination. The samples for testing moisture will be drawn during loading, two bottles of the same should be sent by the sellers, C/O the vessel, to the China National Foreign Trade Transportation Corporation at destination. The buyer shall have the right to claim against the seller for compensation of losses within 60 days after arrival of the goods at the port of destination, should the quality of the goods be found not in conformity with the specifications stipulated in the contract after reinspection by the China Commodity Inspection Bureau. The buyer shall have the right to claim against the sellers for compensation of short weight within 60 days after arrival of the goods at the port of destination, should the weight be found not in conformity with that stipulated in the Bill of Lading after reinspection by the China Commodity Inspection Bureau.

8. Invoicing

The provisional invoice will be made out for quality of 72% of $Ca_3P_2O_8$ and on shipped weight in B/L less 1%. Should the content of Tribasic Phosphate of Lime fall below the guaranteed 72%, and allowance on the basis of 2% of the sales price for each unit shall be calculated and deducted from the purchase price fractions prorate. Should the content of Tribasic Phosphate of Lime fall below the guaranteed 70%, the buyer has the right to refuse the cargo. In such case, all the losses and expenses arising therefrom shall be borne by the seller, or alternatively the price shall be renegotiated. If the Iron and Aluminum Oxides combined content exceeds 2.8%, an allowance on the basis of 2.8% of the sales price for each unit shall be calculated and deducted from the purchase price fraction prorate. At the time of loading, the moisture content of the whole cargo should be indicated in the quality certificate and should be also deducted from the invoiced weight.

9. Payment

The buyer shall open through the Bank of China, Beijing, an irrevocable letter of credit in favour of the sellers in US Dollars covering the FOB stowed and trimmed value of each shipment payable against receipt by the issuing Bank of the following shipping documents:

1) Full set (including three copies each of the negotiable and non-negotiable) of clean on board Bill of Lading or Charter Party Bill of Lading in accordance with the charter party, made out to order, blank endorsed, notifying the China National Foreign Trade Transportation Corporation at the port of destination.

2) Provisional invoice covering an amount corresponding to the full value of each shipment, weight 1% less than that in B/L, and quality based on 72% Tribasic Phosphate of Lime.

3) Certificate of quality and weight determination issued by the seller at the port of loading.

The buyer should open the relative letter of credit latest 20 days before the arrival of carrying vessel at the port of loading with validity for 90 days from the date of opening.

10. Terms of Shipment

1) Insurance to be covered by the buyer.

2) The buyer shall undertake to charter the carrying vessel. The buyer or its chartering agent shall advise the seller by fax or e-mail, 10 days prior to the arrival of the carrying vessel at the port of shipment, of the contract number, name of the carrying vessel, approximate loading capacity, laydays and port of loading, in order to enable the seller to make preparations for loading. The seller shall confirm by fax upon receipt of the above advice. The buyer's chartering agent shall make direct contact with the seller from time to time. Should for certain reasons the buyer not be able to inform the sellers of foregoing details 10 days prior to the arrival of the vessel at the port of loading or should the carrying vessel be advanced or delayed, the buyer or its chartering agent shall advise the seller immediately and make necessary arrangements.

3) Should the seller fail to effect loading in time when the vessel chartered by the buyer arrive at the port of shipment, the seller shall be held fully responsible for the dead freight, demurrage and

all other losses thus sustained.

4) Time to Commence: From 8 a.m. on the first working day following receipt of written notice from the Master during office hours that the vessel has entered port and is in free pratique and in every respect ready to load, whether in berth or not.

5) The ship-owner will pay light dues, extra quarantine dues, gratuities to pilots and boatmen, shore labour (if labour required by Master) as well as all ship's disbursement such as night watchmen, stores and provisions, laundry, medical assistance, telegraphic and postal expense. Pilotage fees at the rate of $ 50 per vessel.

6) It should be noted that the ship's draught will be as follows;

Vancouver port draft: 33 feet 6 inches max

Prince Rupert port draft: 33 feet 6 inches max

Vancouver port length: no restriction

Prince Rupert port length: 640 feet max

7) First opening and last closing of vessel's hatches to be performed by ship's crew at Owner's expense.

8) Loading rate: 10000 metric tons per weather working day of 24 consecutive hours (weather permitting), Sundays and holidays at the port of loading included.

9) Demurrage/Dispatch Money to be settled direct between the shippers and the owners according to charter party.

It is understood that all Charter Parties involved under this contract shall stipulate that dispatch money to be half the demurrage for all working time saved at loading port.

10) For any other clauses not stipulated in this contract, the parties concerned shall act in accordance with the Charter Party stipulations. The buyer shall furnish the sellers with one copy of each such Charter Party as soon as signed.

11. Advice of Shipment

1) Immediately after loading the goods on board the ship, the seller shall advise the buyer by fax of the contract number, name of commodity, net weight loaded, invoice value, name of vessel, port of departure and sailing date.

2) Should the buyer be unable to cover insurance in due time owing to the seller's failure to advise the buyer of foregoing details by fax, the losses thus sustained shall be borne by the seller.

12. Force Majeure

The seller shall not be held responsible for late delivery or non-delivery of the goods owing to generally recognized "Force Majeure" causes. However, in such case, the seller shall fax the buyer immediately and deliver in 14 days to the buyer a certificate of the occurrence issued by the Government Authorities or the Chamber of Commerce at the place where the accident occurs as evidence thereof.

13. Arbitration

All disputes in connection with this contract or the execution thereof shall be settled amicably by

negotiation. In case no settlement can be reached, the case under dispute may then be submitted for arbitration. The arbitration shall be conducted in the country of the defendant. In China, the China International Economic and Trade Arbitration Commission, Beijing, shall execute the arbitration in accordance with the Rules of Procedure of Arbitration of the said Commission. The decision of arbitration shall be accepted as final and binding upon both parties. The fees for arbitration shall be borne by losing party unless otherwise awarded.

In Beijing, China on 25th July, 2005

THE SELLER	THE BUYER
UNISOBIN CHEMICALS	CHINA NATIONAL CHEMICALS
EXPORT CORPORATION	IMPORT & EXPORT CORPORATION

Section 3 Supplements 知识补充

Useful Sentences On Conclusion of business

1. As a result of the exchange of letters between us, we have now come to terms.
通过双方信函往来，现已达成交易。

2. After long and friendly discussing we have now concluded business.
经过长期友好的讨论，现已达成交易。

3. Through lengthy and on-and-off negotiations we now finally have reached agreement.
经过长时间断断续续的谈判，我们现在终于达成了协议。

4. When looking back, we are happy to see we have come to a long way and finally succeeded in securing the transaction.
回顾过去，我们高兴地看到取得了巨大进展并最终达成交易。

5. In the course of our negotiations we have come to a much better understanding of each other, which bears a lot of our future business.
在谈判过程中，我们双方都给予了很好的谅解，这对我们今后的业务很有意义。

6. We are happy to have concluded business with you, our work was not wasted. The time-taking negotiations were worth our while.
与你方达成了交易，很高兴。我们的工作没有白做，这种费时的磋商还是值得的。

7. "No pains, no gains. " If not for the strenuous efforts from both sides, we wouldn't have come to this happy ending.
"一份辛劳，一分收获"。要不是双方竭尽努力，我们就不会达到这种美好的结局。

8. We are pleased to enclose herewith our contract No.4567 in two originals for your counter-signature. Please send one copy back to us at your earliest convenience.

现附上我方第 4567 号合同正本两份，请会签，并早日寄回一份。

9. Enclosed please find our Sales Contract No.HN768 in duplicate. If you find everything in order, please sign and return one copy for our life.

现随附我方销售合同第 HN768 号一式两份，请查收。如审查无误，请会签后退回一份存档。

10. We attach hereto our Purchase Contract No.3674 with our signature, please check and counter-sign. Then return one copy to us for our records as soon as possible.

今附上我方第 3674 号购货合同，我方已签字，请核实和会签，并尽快寄回一份存档。

11. We trust the current business is only a forerunner of a series of transactions in future.

相信这笔交易是未来一系列交易的先导。

12. The conclusion of the dealing is certainly not the ending. It is only the beginning, and a good one, of the long and friendly business relations between us.

这笔交易的达成当然不是结束。它仅仅是个开端，并且是我们之间长期友好业务关系的开端。

13. It is our belief that the current small business will lead to a series of larger dealings in the near future.

我们相信这笔小生意将带来今后一系列的大笔生意。

14. “A good beginning makes a good ending.” We hope that from now on we shall enjoy business relations profitable to both of us.

“好的开端带来好的结局。”我们希望从今以后我们之间的业务关系是互利的。

15. It is in view of out long-standing business relationship that we accept your counter offer.

只是鉴于双方长期的业务关系，我们才接受你方还盘。

16. We will certainly keep your requirement before us if we are able to get more goods next year.

如果明年能增加供应，我们一定考虑你方的要求。

17. I suggest that you buy this product instead of that.

我建议你方购买这种产品以替代那一种。

18. What is the minimum quantity of an order for your goods?

你们这种产品的最小起订量是多少？

19. In this case, we'll order 4,000 cases.

若是这样，我们就订购 4 000 箱。

20. I'm afraid we are not able to supply as much as you require.

你们要求的数量，我们恐怕无法满足。

21. May I suggest that you cut the quantity of your order by half ?

我建议您把订单的数量削减一半，怎么样？

22. We are in a position to accept a special order.

我们可以接受特殊订货。

23. We intend to book a trial order with you.

我们想从你方试订一批货。

24. We'd like to place a small order for the new varieties.
我们想少量订购些新产品。

25. We enclose a trial order. If the quality is up to our expectation, we shall send further orders in the near future.
兹附上我方试订单一份。如果质量符合我们的要求，近期内我方将寄出订单。

26. We are pleased to give you an order for the following items on the understanding that they will be supplied from current stock at the prices named.
兹订购下列各项产品，希望按既定价格供应现货。

27. We thank you for your quotation of 10th March andenclose herewith our order No.325 for TCL color TV set.
感谢你方 3 月 10 日的报盘，兹随函寄去我方订购 TCL 彩色电视机第 325 号订单。

28. Much to our regret, our customers can't accept your price and will turn elsewhere to cover their orders.
我方客户很难接受你方价格，他们已从别处订货，对此深表遗憾。

29. Owing to heavy commitments, we are not in apposition to accept new orders.
由于大量承约，我方不能再接受新订单。

30. We confirm having purchased from you Men's Shirts, for which a confirmation of order is enclosed for your reference.
我方确认已向你方订购男式衬衫，随函附上订购确认书，仅供参考。

31. We have received in due course your sales confirmation No.3557 in duplicate. As requested, we have countersigned and are enclosing one copy foe your file.
兹收到你方第 3557 号销售确认书一式两份。按你方要求，我们已会签，并随函退回一份供你方存档。

32. I shall be glad if you will forward fifty tons of coal, in accordance with your sample.
请按照你方公司提供的样品，供应我方 50 吨煤。

Exercises

Ⅰ. Make sentences with the following words and expressions.

by airmail	bridge the gap
countersign	mark down
thanks to	as a result of
terms and conditions	in duplicate
with the view of	with a view to
make out	conform to
conclusion of a deal	subsequent to
turn out	order sheet

Ⅱ. Complete the following sentences.

1. We are glad to say that 在近 10 年中我们已向你们购进了 5 万吨花生果。

2. Enclosed please find 我们通过在巴黎的中国银行开出信用证 13570 号。

3. Most of our customers 认为价格差距太大难以达成交易。

4. We hope 你方能想方设法在下半年再向我方供应 50 吨类似的产品。

5. The stipulations in the relative credit 应与我方销售合同的条款严格相符。

6. Please do your utmost to execute this order 因为它将带来其他交易。

7. We note that 你方打算照上次价格订购足球 2000 个。

8. If you guarantee payment. 我们将凭单付款把这批货发运给他们。

9. 为了清除这一误会，We explain as follows:

10. We give you this special accommodation 是为了加强我们的关系。

11. There is no question about 获得必要的进口许可证。

12. We would inform you that there is no possibility of 从我处官方获得电视机的进口许可证。

13. 请赶快办理必要事项 as to enable us to send you the covering contract at an early date.

14. As regards the captioned articles 随函寄给你第 146 号形式发票。

15. We are interested in 下列规格的永久牌自行车，请你方寄形式发票一式三份，以便我们申请进口许可证。

16. By confirmed, irrevocable, transferable and divisible L/C.信用证的卖方为受益人并允许分批装运和转船。

17. As we are badly in need of the goods，我们早就把有关信用证开出，谅必已经抵达你方，盼早日安排装运。

Ⅲ. Translate the following sentences into English.

1. 到明年第二季度，也许有可能大规模扩大生产。

2. 关于我方向你公司订购的 500 台缝纫机，我们已收到你方销售合同 484 号。

3. 我们正殷切地等候你方的信用证，收到后我们立即安排装运。

4. 我们今天已由伦敦的中国银行开出了一张以你方为抬头人的信用证，计 500 万美元。

5. 你们的不可撤销的信用证已及时收到，我们相信下周内可以安排装运。

6. 兹随函退回销售合同一份，该合同我们已会签。

7. 由于双方共同努力，我们达成了交易，希望这是我们双方之间贸易的良好开端。

8. 请电告你方最早装船日期，以便我方及时通过中国银行给你方开出信用证。

9. 经过很大的努力，最后我们才取得他们勉强的同意。

10. 我们感谢你方的这种友好态度。

11. 此试销订单，请先发来 35 台，以便开发市场，如成功，随后必有较大数量的订单。

12. 要完全按照我方指示的颜色办理，这是很重要的。

13. 请每批另寄发票一份。

14. 可以肯定，我们会非常认真地履行你方订单，以致完全满意。

15. 如蒙同情并谅解我们的困难，不胜感谢。

Ⅳ. Translate the following letter into English.

接到你公司 9 月 5 日印花细布订单，非常高兴，并欢迎你公司成为我公司的客户之一。

现确认按你方来信列明价格供应印花细布，并已安排下周由“公主号”轮装出。深信你公司收到货物后，定会感到完全满意。

你公司也许不甚知道我公司的经营范围，现附上目录一份。希望这首批订单将导致彼此更多的业务往来，展开愉快的工作关系。

Chapter 7

Terms of Payment

Section 1 Business Knowledge 业务知识

在对外贸易中，进出口交易的最终归结点是收取货款。如果这一点得不到保障，那么我们前面所讲的一切诸如建立业务关系→询盘→报盘→还盘→反还盘→订货等均毫无意义。同样，进出口货款如何支付也是买卖双方密切关注的主要问题之一。国际市场在长期实践的基础上，逐渐形成了一些人们习惯采用的，由不同的支付时间、地点和支付途径组成的支付方式。例如大家熟悉的汇付（remittance）、托收（collection）、信用证（L/C）等。这些支付方式的出现，都从不同的角度，在不同程度上，解决了买卖双方之间在支付问题上的矛盾，促进了国际贸易的进一步发展。

本章重点讲述 3 个问题：

- 我国在进出口贸易中常用的支付方式；
- 货款支付函电的写作与支付的联系；
- 相关函电的惯用表达法（详见样函）。

1. 我国在进出口贸易中常用的支付方式

我国在进出口贸易中常用的支付方式有汇付、托收和信用证。

（1）汇付（Remittance）

通过进出口商双方所在地银行的汇兑业务进行结算，即由进口人将货款交所在地银行，由该银行委托出口人所在地银行转交给出口人。汇款的当事人有四个，即汇款人、汇出行、汇入行和收款人。汇款人（remitter），是委托银行或其他机构将款项汇交给收款人的一方。通常是进口人。汇出行（remitting bank），是接受汇款人的委托，办理汇出款项业务的银行。汇出行有义务按照汇款人的指示，向自己的联行或代理行发出付款委托书，委托其向收款人解付汇款。汇出行对汇款中出现的延误、遗失、电讯传递失灵等情况不负责任，对自己的联行或代理行在

办理汇款业务中的失误也不负责。汇入行（paying bank），是指受汇出行委托，解付汇款的银行，也称付款行或解付行，汇入行一般都是汇出行的联行或代理行。

收款人（payee），是指接受汇款的人。进出口贸易中通常是出口人。

汇付方式有以下3种。

① 电汇（T/T，telegraphic transfer）汇出行应汇款人的申请，用电报通知汇入行，指示汇入行对收款人支付一定金额的一种汇款方式（由进口地银行发电通知出口地银行付款给出口人）。

② 信汇（M/T，mail transfer）由进口人将货款交给所在地银行，由该行用信件委托出口人所在地银行把货款付给出口人。

③ 票汇（D/D，demand draft）进口人向当地银行购买即期汇票，然后寄给出口人，出口人持票向汇票上指定的付款行提取货款。

汇付的方法虽分3种，但无论采取哪种方法，货运单据都是由出口人自行寄给进口人，银行并不经手，所以汇付又称为单纯支付（clean payment —simple payment）。

在国际贸易中，汇付的方式常用于以下几种业务中：

① 预付货款—payment in advance

② 随定单付现—cash with order （CWD）

③ 交货付现—cash on delivery （COD）

④ 记账交易—open account trade

采用预付贷款和随订单付现的方式，对出口人来说，是先收款后交货，资金不会积压，这是进口人对出口人信任的表示；反之，采用交货付现和记账交易时，对出口人来说，先交货后收款，资金就会积压，这是出口人对进口人信任的一种表示，但同时出口人自己也承担了一定的风险。

（2）托收（Collection）

托收是指，出口方根据外贸合同规定将货物装运出口后，开立以进口方为付款人的商业汇票并附上有关单据，委托当地银行通过进口方所在地银行向进口方代收贷款后汇回出口方的一种结算方式。

托收结算涉及的当事人主要有四方。一是委托人（principle），是指出具汇票和提供单据、并委托银行向付款人收取货款的人，也即货物交易的出口方。委托人在办理托收业务时，要与托收银行签订委托代理合同，并承担各项有关费用、承担付款人拒付的风险。二是托收行（remitting bank），是指接受委托人委托向付款人收取货款，同时又委托自己国外联行或代理行向付款人收款的出口地银行。托收行以委托人出具的托收申请书为依据，向国外的代收银行寄送托收委托书，委托人所有委托收款事宜均在托收委托书上面。托收行与代收行严格按托收委托书和托收国际惯例处理托收业务。三是代收行（collecting bank），是指接受托收行委托向付款人收款的进口地银行。代收行一般是托收行的国外分行或代理行。四是付款人（payer），即买卖合同下的进口人。

除了以上四方当事人外，有时根据需要还可能有提示行（presenting bank）。比如，当代收行与付款人不在同一地区或代收行不是付款人的开户行，代收行就需要委托另一家银行提示汇票和单据代为收取货款，受委托的银行称为提示行。

托收分为光票托收和跟单托收。光票托收是指收款时使用不附带任何货运单据的汇票或附有“非货运单据”，如垫款清单/商检证明。跟单托收使用较普遍，其含义是货款收取过程中要求随附

装运单据，依据交单条件不同可分为以下几种。

付款交单（D/P）代收行在收到进口方货款后，将汇票及所附的货运单据交付给进口方。按时间不同又分为即期付款交单和远期付款交单。

承兑交单（D/A）出口方在货物装运后，开具以进口方为付款人的远期汇票，连同各种货运单据一并交委托行寄往进口方代收行；代收行在进口方承兑汇票后，将跟单汇票交给付款人，进口方再于汇票到期日付清贷款。采用这种方式，进口方可先取单后付款，即进口方只要承兑汇票就可得到货运单据，而出口方此时即失去对货物的控制权，如果进口方在汇票到期日拒付，出口方有货、款全部落空的风险。

D/P 和 D/A 都是通过银行托收，按正常情况，出口人只要把汇票和装运单据交到托收行，就可以坐等收款了，可以不必再写信。但有时有些考虑周到办事认真的公司，往往还要再写信通知进口人一下，以便让对方做好准备，当然是付款或承兑的准备，同时也起到了提醒对方把合同履行到底的作用。

（3）信用证（Letter of Credit）

信用证是国际贸易中进口方银行用来保证本国进口商有支付能力的凭证。是进口方所在地银行，根据进口方的申请和担保，对出口方开出的一种信函式的凭证，通过出口方所在地银行，通知出口方，由开证行负责在出口方交付信用证规定的各种装运单据时，支付全部货款。信用证的结算方式属于银行信用，而前面讲的托收和汇付都属于商业信用。比较其他的货款支付方式，信用证结算有两个非常突出的作用。

第一，银行保证作用。信用证方式结算付款人是银行，银行信用高于以进口人为付款人的商业信用。通过信用证结算可以解决买卖双方互不信任的矛盾。可以使本来彼此不了解的进出口双方顺利达成交易。在一般情况下，买方多考虑先收到货物再付款；而卖方希望先付款再发货。信用证就是为了解决买卖双方的利益冲突和交易风险，由银行充当保证人的角色，银行作为付款人，凭借物权凭证的单据付款，对买卖双方都提供担保。只要卖方提供单据就可以收回货款；只要买方承诺支付货款就能获取单据提出货物。

第二，资金融通作用。在信用证业务中银行不仅提供信用担保，还可以提供资金融通服务。当受益人装运货物后取得运输单据，可以出具汇票连同运输单据到信用证规定的议付行办理出口押汇业务，这是议付行给予受益人的资金融通；在装运货物之前，受益人可凭银行打包贷款信用证（packing credit）办理打包融资业务，从而为出口人在装货前提供资金，便于其购买产品或支付加工费，这属于银行凭信用证给予的短期贷款。另外，在进口人收到单据后，在进口货物尚未到达以前，也可以凭物权单据在进口地银行办理进口押汇业务，等于为进口人在进口货物未出售之前融通资金。

应该指出，信用证在国际贸易结算中并不是完美无缺。有时买方不按时开证或不按合同约定条件开证或在信用证规定一些软条款和陷阱，可能使卖方无法履行合同或因单据不符点遭到银行拒付；在信用证业务下，出口方也有可能与承运人串通制造假单据对进口方施行诈骗。此外，使用信用证方式结算比汇款和托收手续复杂、费用高。无论是申请开证，还是审核信用证，审查单据，议付货款，都是技术性很强的工作，稍有不慎，就会出现疏漏，造成经济损失。

信用证是国际贸易活动中最主要的支付方式，其结算过程比较复杂，信用证本身又种类繁多，

关于信用证的具体内容将在本教材的第八章做重点讲述。

2. 相关信函的写作原则

关于货款支付方面的信函主要涉及两项主题。一个是付款条件，另一个则是催款。

（1）有关付款条件信函的写作原则

这类信函的写作，应把握下面 3 个要点。

第一，要明确说明目前的状况和面临的问题。（To state clearly the current situation and the problems you are facing.）

第二，应提出具体的要求。（To raise the specific requirement concerning payment.）

第三，做出明确答复。如果是拒绝付款的某些要求，最好用友善的口气讲明具体原因。To make a definite reply. If declining the request of payment, you'd better use the friendly wording that gives detailed reason.

（2）催款信的写作原则

催收对外贸易应收账款是很多公司面临的棘手问题，我们的海外欠账和海外坏账日益增多，在一定程度上与不善于拟写催款信函有关系。通常来讲写作催款信函，要遵循以下 4 个原则。

第一，有礼貌，不要恐吓你的客户。（Be polite and don't threaten your customer.）

第二，意思表达清晰明了。直接写出对方所欠的金额和你期望人家付款的日期。（Strive for clarity. To the point of asking for payment telling out the amount, the expected date of payment.）

第三，定期的发送催款信。（Send this kind of letter calling for payment at intervals.）

第四，有时候，在催款的同时对方已经向我们汇款了。为了避免伤害到你的客户，最好在催款信中加上一句："如果钱已汇出，请不要在意这份信。"（To avoid hurting your customer, you'd better add the sentence like this:" If money has been remitted, please don't mind this letter."）

Section 2 Specimen Letters 样函

（1）

Dear Sirs,

Referring to[1] our letter of enquiry dated September 24, we have received your proforma invoice[2] No.7695 and now wish to place an initial order for 5,000 Tapes[3] Type No, EM 137B. The order number is 4874.

We have instructed[4] our bank, the General Commercial Bank of Venezuela to open an irrevocable documentary letter of credit in your favor. The amount is US$8,900. This credit will be confirmed[5] soon by our bank's correspondent[6] in London. You are authorized to draw a 60 days' draft[7] on our bank against this credit for the amount of your invoice. Your draft must be accompanied[8] by a complete set of shipping documents[9], consisting of: a full set of clean shipped Bill of Lading[10], Commercial Invoice 5 copies and the Insurance Certificate 3 copies.

Our bank will accept your 60 days' draft on them for the amount of your invoice including the cost of freight and insurance, as agreed. Your bill[11] will therefore be at 60d/s for the full CIF invoice value. The credit is valid until the February 10 next year.

Yours faithfully,

Words, Expressions and Notes

1. referring to 针对、有关；提及、暗指；查阅差月，参考

2. proforma invoice 形式发票、估价发票

各类发票的说法：

commercial invoice 商业发票

custom invoice 海关发票

provisional invoice 临时发票

consular invoice 领事发票

official invoice 正式发票

3. Tapes 胶纸带

4. instruct 指示、通知

5. confirm 此处指信用证的保兑。是指开证银行开出的信用证请另一家银行对符合证上条款的单据履行付款义务。对信用证承担保证兑付义务的银行称为保兑行（confirming bank）。保兑信用证是开证行和保兑行共同对信用证承担付款责任。保兑银行通常是通知行，有时也可能是其他银行。保兑的手续一般是由保兑银行在信用证上加列保兑文句，如 the credit is confirmed by us.

6. correspondent 这里指我方银行设在伦敦的代理行。此外还有记者、通讯员的意思。correspondence 指信件、函件、通信

7. draw a 60 days' draft 开立见票 60 天付款的远期汇票

8. be accompanied by 与……随附，这说明汇票是跟单汇票

9. shipping documents 装运单据、货运单据，通常是代表货物所有权的海运提单或多式联运单据

10. clean shipped Bill of Lading 清洁已装船提单

11. bill 这里是指汇票，即 bill of exchange

（2）

Dear Sirs,

We thank you for your letter of 15th December, 2010.

We are pleased to receive your order, and wish to say that we have adequate[1] stocks of Type No, ED 167B Tapes in our warehouse[2]. As to the delivery, we think we can manage well.

Payment by irrevocable letter of credit at sight is not convenient[3] for us, and we shall draw a 40d/s bill on your bank[4].

We are now awaiting the arrival of your L/C, on receipt of which we shall make the necessary arrangements for the shipment of your order. Any request for further assistance or information will receive our immediate attention.

Yours sincerely,

Words, Expressions and Notes

1. adequate stock 充足的储备、足够的库存
2. warehouse 仓库、货栈
3. convenient 方便的、便利的
4. draw a 40d/s bill on your bank 向你方银行开立见票 40 天付款的远期汇票

（3）

Dear Sirs,

Further to our fax of January 12, attache please find[1] the final invoice for the shipment of 874-676 contract and the statement of your account[2] for your payment. We have instructed our accounting department[3] to send you by courier[4] the original final invoice (874-676) again for your payment.

Some of the items are overdue[5] for long time, but they are still being outstanding[6]. We are eager to have them settled without delay, so we invite your prompt attention to the matter and try your best to settle it.

Your kind and prompt attention of the issue will be highly appreciated.

Yours faithfully,

Words, Expressions and Notes

1. attached pleased find 随函附寄，请查收
2. statement of your account 关于你方账户的说明
3. accounting department 会计部门、核算部门
4. courier （传递信息或文件的）信使、通讯员
5. overdue 过期的
6. outstanding 未偿付的

（4）

Dear Sirs,

Account No.21637

We write to inform you that we do not appear to[1] have received your payment of ￡7000 for invoice 7781, dated 7 July. We would be grateful if you would give this matter your prompt attention.

If payment has been made in the past few days, please ignore[2] this letter and accept our thanks for your payment.

Should you have any queries[3] about your account, please do not hesitate to contact us.

Yours faithfully,

Words, Expressions and Notes

1. not appear to 似乎没有收到

2. ignore 这里是指别在意

3. queries 质疑、疑问

另外，关于货币金额的表示方法在这里详述一下

1）英镑

￡15， 15 英镑（货币符号￡放在数目前面）

36 p， 36 便士（p 放在数目之后，指 pence，单数形式是 penny）

￡88.66， 88 英镑、66 便士，不可写成￡88.66p

2）美元

$135，135 美元（货币符号$放在数目前面）

87 ¢，87 美分（¢代表 cent，放在数目之后）

$135.69, 135 美元、69 美分，不可写成$135.69 ¢

nickel 五分硬币

dime 一角硬币

coin 硬币

例句：

Last month I opened a checking account at a bank. My account number is 18639789. I made a deposit for $965; that is, $300 in bills (or currency), $660 in checks, $5 in coins. Ten days later I made a withdrawal for $556.78. I made out the required check, writing this amount both in figures and words.

上个月，我在银行开了一个支票账户，号码是 18639789。我存入了 965 美元，其中 300 美元是钞票，660 美元是支票，5 美元是硬币。十天后，我取出来 556.78 美元。我填写了一张取款单，写明所取款项的大、小写金额。

（5）

Gentlemen:

We refer to your Contract No. DSG 267 covering Enamelware[1] in the amount of ￡998.00 and Contract NO BSG 268 covering Basketware[2] ￡895.50 as both of these contracts are each of a value of less than ￡1000.00, we shall be glad if you agree to ship the goods to us as before on Cash against Documents[3] basis.

We hope that you will accommodate[4] us in this respect[5] and continue supplying us with Enamelware and Basket ware on the same basis.

We look forward to your early reply.

Yours truly,

Words, Expressions and Notes

1. Enamelware 搪瓷器皿

2. Basketware 篮筐制品

3. Cash against Documents 凭单证付款，与 cash 有关的短语有：

cash against delivery 货到付款

cash against order 交单付款

cash against shipping documents 凭装运单据付款

cash position 现金头寸

cash sales 现销

cash market 现货市场

cash in 兑现，收到……的货款

cash in on 利用，从中获利

例句：

U.S. executives cashed in some $5 billion worth of stock options last year in contrast to $3 billion in 2007.

美国主管去年将认股权换成 50 亿美元现款，而在 2007 年只有 30 亿美元。

Mr. John cashed in on people's great interest in camping and sold four hundred tents.

利用人们露营的兴趣，约翰先生卖出了 400 个帐篷。

He cashed in on his real-estate investment.

他在房地产投资上赚了钱。

4. accommodate 照顾、容纳、提供

例句：

Many foreign banks are now ready to accommodate China with long-term credit.

现在许多外国银行乐于给中国提供长期贷款。

The port is deep enough to accommodate ships drawing 25-30 feet.

这个港口的水深足以接纳吃水在 25 ~ 30 英尺的船舶。

We regret we can not accommodate you in this respect.

很抱歉我们不能在这方面给予你方照顾。

5. in this respect 在这一方面

（6）

Dear Sirs,

We are in receipt of your letter of March 8, contents of which have been duly noted.

With regard to Contract Nos. DSG 267and BSG268, we agree to D/P[1] payment terms for these contracts. However, we consider it advisable[2] to make it clear that for further transactions D/P will only be accepted if the amount involved for each transaction is below ￡1000.00 or its equivalent[3] in Renminbi at the conversion rate[4] then prevailing[5]. If the amount exceeds that figure[6], payment by Letter of Credit will be required.

We wish to reiterate[7] that it is only in view of our long friendly business relations that we extend you this accommodation. It is our sincere hope that we can enlarge[8] the business in these lines to our mutual benefit.

Yours faithfully,

Words, Expressions and Notes

1. D/P 付款交单，托收的一种方式

2. advisable 适宜的、可取的、明智的，后接从句时用虚拟语气

例句：

It is advisable that shipment be made in August.

以 8 月份装船为宜。

We think it advisable that you ship the goods at an early date.

我们认为，你方早日发货为好。

We find it advisable for you to pack the goods in wooden cases.

我方认为，你们用木箱包装货物为宜。

3. equivalent 既是名词也可作形容词，表示等值、等价、等价物

例句：

One US dollar is equivalent to RMB6.25 at the current exchange rate.

按当前汇率，1 美元相当于人民币 6.25 元。

4. conversion rate 指本币与外币的兑换比率，若专指两种外币之间的兑换率应该使用 cross rate

5. then prevailing 这里是指在当时通行的比率

6. figure 数字（有时也指价格），动词指计算、考虑。figure 的常用短语和习惯表达有：

figure out at 总计，合计

figure sth out 计算出，领会到

double figures 两位数

an income of six figures 六位数的收入

amount in figure 小写金额

in round figures 以整数或约数表示；大概、总之

例句：

We can't figure out the exact meaning of the last paragraph of your letter of May 5.

我们琢磨不出你方 5 月 5 日来函最后一段话的意思。

Could you figure out just how much the advertising expenses will be?

你能算出广告费要花多少吗？

Sales in the last three months figures out at about $30,000.

最后三个月的销售额合计约 30 000 美元。

The figure quoted by you is too high.

你方开出的价格太高。

7. reiterate 重申、再次强调

8. enlarge 扩大

（7）

Dear Sirs,

The goods which you ordered on 2nd October have been shipped to you today by s.s[1] "Seafarer[2]", due[3] at Lagos on 5th November.

We have taken special care to include in the consignment[4] only items suited to conditions in Nigeria. We hope you will be pleased with our selection and that this, your first orders will lead to further[5] business between us.

From the enclosed copy of invoice you will see that the price of £1880 is well within the maximum figure you stated. We have drawn on you for this amount at sight[6] through the bank of Nigeria, which has been ordered to hand in[7] documents when you make presentation of the draft[8]. We hope you will understand when we explain that the urgency of your order left with insufficient time to make the usual enquiries and that we therefore had no choice but to[9] follow our standard practice[10] with new customers of placing the transaction on a cash basis[11].

We look forward to your further orders. And, subject to satisfactory references[12] and regular dealings,we would be prepared to consider open account terms with quarterly settlements[13].

Yours faithfully,

Words, Expressions and Notes

1. s.s 指船舶，是 steamship 的缩写

2. seafarer 航海者、航海家、船员，这里指船名

3. due 适当的，（票据）到期的，所欠的，预期的；overdue 表示逾期，同 pastdue

例句：

We trust the shipment will reach you in due course.

我们相信这批货将按期到达你处。

After due consideration, we have decided to grant your request.

经过适当考虑，我们决定答应你方的要求。

The draft will fall due on May 30.

汇票于 5 月 30 日到期。

The remittance is in payment of all commissions due to you up to date.

这笔汇款是迄今为止付讫前你方的各项佣金。

The steamer is due at 21:00.

轮船应该在 21 点到达。

Fresh supplies are due to arrive early next month.

新货应于下月初到。

4. consignment 这里指所发出的这批货

5. further 促进，其形容词和副词表示更多的、进一步的，继……再

例句：

Further to our letter dated June 20, we have pleasure in informing you that we have got the export license.

继我方 6 月 20 日函，兹再奉告，我方已经得到了出口许可。

Further heavy buying of cash and forward lifted the latter to the day's high.

现货与期货的进一步大量购进把后者提高到当天的最高价。

We trust to be favored with your further orders.

今后尚希望不断地惠予订购。

Further particulars are necessary.

需要更多的细节。

The talks were characterized by a warm and friendly exchange of views to further mutual trade interest.

这次谈判在热烈友好气氛下交换了意见，以促进双方业务。

6. drawn on you for this amount at sight 向你方开立此金额的即期汇票
7. hand in 递交、呈上
8. make presentation of the draft 提示汇票
9. had no choice but to 别无选择、只好
10. standard practice 惯例
11. cash basis 按现金交易去成交
12. references 此处意指资信证明
13. quarterly settlements 按季度结算

（8）

Dear Sirs,

We wish to place with you an order for 1000casks Iron Nails at your price of US $150.00per cask CFR C5%[1] Lagos for shipment during July/August.

For this particular order we would like to pay[2] by 30 days L/C[3]. Involving about US $150000, this order is comparatively a big one. As we have only moderate means[4] at hand, the tie-up of funds[5] for as long as three to four months indeed presents a problem to us.

It goes without saying[6] that we very much appreciate the support you have extended us in the past. If you can do us a special favor[7] this time, please send us your contract, upon receipt of which we will establish the relative L/C immediately.

Yours faithfully,

Words, Expressions and Notes

1. US $150.00per cask CFR C5% 每桶 150 美元，拉各斯成本加运费、含 5%佣金
2. pay 付款，支付，合算，给予，payment 是名词形式

习惯短语：

pay in advance 预付

pay in cash 付现金

pay by check 凭支票付款

pay in installment 分期付款

pay on delivery 货到付款

例句：

It doesn't pay to buy in small quantities.

小量购买不合算。

If this change is effected, we will have to pay rather heavy expenses.

如果做这项改变，我们将不得不付出相当高的费用。

We enclose a cheque for US$4,000 in payment of all commissions due to you up to date.

兹随函寄去 4000 美元支票一张，支付截至目前欠你方的全部佣金。

3. 30 days L/C 见票后 30 天议付的信用证。同样的意思还可以表述成：

L/C available by draft at 30 days after sight

L/C at 30 days after sight

L/Cat 30 days

远期信用证可用 usance L/C, time L/C 或 term L/C 表示

即期信用证可用 letter of credit payable against sight draft; letter of credit available by sight draft; letter of credit payable against draft at sight 表示，在外贸信函中常简称为 sight L/C

4. moderate means 这里是婉转表达手头资金有限（现钱不多）

此外，means 还有资力，财产，手段，方式，工具等含义，如：

means of production 生产资料

means of transport 运输工具

by all means 务必，尽一切办法

by means of 用，借助，依靠

by no means 决不，一点也不

例句：

This firm is quite reliable. It never does business beyond its means.

这家公司比较可靠，在经营方面一向量入为出。

You are required to ship the goods in October by all means.

请你们务必在 10 月份发运这批货。

He will pay the transaction by means of sight L/C.

他将用即期信用证来支付这笔交易。

Your last shipment was by no means satisfactory.

你方上次发货并不令人满意。

5. tie-up of funds 占压资金。tie-up 是束缚、停顿的意思，用法很多，如：

tie-up in negotiation 谈判僵局

tie-up of traffic 交通停顿

tie up property 冻结财产

例句：

The request for easier payment terms is compelled by their funds being tied up in numerous commitments.

由于资金被许多业务占用，他们迫不得已要求较宽松的付款条件。

6. It goes without saying 不用说（表示非常确定）

7. special favor 特别关照

（9）

Dear Sirs,

We are the largest department store[1] in Kuwait and have recently received a number of enquiries for your stainless-steel cutlery[2]. We think there are good prospects[3] for the sale of this cutlery, but at present it is little known here and as we can not count on[4] regular sales we do not feel able to make purchase on our own account[5].

We are therefore writing to suggest that you send us a trial delivery for sale on D/A[6] terms. We make the proposal hoping to place firm orders[7] when the market is established[8].

We believe our proposal offers good prospects and hope you will be willing to give it a trial. As to our standing[9], you may check[10] it with our bankers, the National Bank of Kuwait.

Yours faithfully,

Words, Expressions and Notes

1. department store 百货商店；chain store 连锁店；franchised shop 特约加盟店

2. stainless-steel cutlery 不锈钢刀具、餐刀

3. prospects 前景、景象

4. count on 指望、依靠

5. on our own account 自负盈亏、为自己的利益，同 at one's own risk

6. D/A（Documents against Acceptance）承兑交单

7. firm orders 此处指实际或实质意义上的订货

8. established 这里的意思是说市场成熟、建立起来

9. standing 此处意为资信状况。此外还有状况、身份、名望、期间、持续的意思，形容词指长期有效的、固定的。standing 的习惯搭配有：

standing charges 固定的费用

standing orders 常年订单

standing permit 长期准许证

credit standing 资信状况

例句：

What is their financial standing?

他们的财务状况如何?

You may refer to our bank, the Bank of China in London for our financial and credit standing.

你方可向我方银行—伦敦中国银行查询我们的资信情况。

10. check 检查、盘查。check 的常用短语有：

check up （check up on）查对、核对

check with (tally with) 经查，与……相符

check in 登记、报到；托运、寄存

check out 付账后离开，检验后无误、合格

例句：

The engine has checked out.

发动机已经检验合格。

I'm ready to check out from the hotel.

我已准备好结账离开宾馆。

What do you check in? Just these two suitcases.

您托运什么？就这两个手提箱。

Passengers are requested to check in at the airport at least one hour before the plane takes off.

请旅客们至少在飞机起飞前一小时到机场办理登机手续。

Your account of sales does not check with our account.

你方销货账与我方账目不符。

We will check up on our stocks and see whether we can offer you anything.

我们要查对存货，再看能否向你方报盘。

Please check up the figures.

请核对这些数字。

（10）

Dear Sirs,

Since our Mr. Brown's return, we have thoroughly considered the terms of payment discussed with your Mr. Wu. We are in agreement with[1] your proposals and hereby give you in writing the terms and conditions which have been agreed upon as follows:

1. Your terms of payment are confirmed, irrevocable letter of credit with draft at sight instead of D/P at sight.

2. The price quoted to us is net[2] with no discount whatsoever[3].

The above terms of payment were approved by our manager and will be acted upon[4] accordingly. The relative order is now being prepared[5] and will be sent to you in the course of next week.Taking this opportunity[6], we would like to inform you that our representative at the forthcoming[7] Guangzhou Fair will still be Mr. Brown, who will doubtlessly[8] write to you about it. We sincerely hope that future discussions between our two houses[9] will result in further business to our mutual advantage.

Yours faithfully,

Words, Expressions and Notes

1. in agreement with 与……一致

agreement 是协议、协议书；agreeable 是形容词表示同意的，合意的；agree 是动词表示同意

常用短语

come to (reach) an agreement 达成协议

agree with sb. 同意某人意见

agree to 同意或接受（建议、办法、条件）

agree on（upon）双方同意或商定

agree in 对某事有相同看法或取得一致意见

例句：

We are glad that, through exchange of letters, we have come to an agreement.

我们很高兴通过互换信函和你方达成协议。

The duration of this agreement is five years.

本协议有效期为五年。

As agreed, we are drawing on you at 30 days D/P.

按双方商定，我们将开出30天汇票以付款交单方式向你方索款。

We agree with you on this point.

在这一点上我们同意你们的意见。

We regret we can not agree to your terms.

抱歉，我们不能接受你方的条款。

L/C terms were agreed on.

双方商定用信用证付款。

There is one point in the contract in which we do not agree.

在合同中有一点我们没有取得一致意见。

We are agreeable to your suggestion.

我们同意你们的建议。

The design is agreeable to taste of the market.

这种设计适合此地市场的品位。

The goods are not up to the agreed specifications and quality.

这批货未能达到商定的规格和质量。

2. net 指净价（不含佣金、折扣）

3. whatsoever 无论什么，这里理解成不含任何佣金。

4. be acted upon（on）按照……行事、执行，例如：

The buyers were acting on our advice.

买方是听了我们的劝告行事的。

Acting upon your recommendation, we have decided to place a trial order.

按照你们的建议，我方决定试订一批货。

5. being prepared 正在备制、正在准备

6. taking this opportunity 借此机会，以此为契机

7. forthcoming 即将到来的，现成的、唾手可得

8. doubtlessly 无疑地、肯定的

9. houses 此处指公司、商号。house 的常见用法：

banking house 银行大楼

branch house 分号、分店

brokerage house 经纪行

clearing house 票据交换所

commercial paper house 证券交易所，商业票据商号

commission house 代办行，证券经纪公司

confirm house 保兑公司

finance house 金融公司

investment house. 投资公司、投资商号

(11)

Dear Sirs,

Our past purchase of Mild Steel Sheets[1] from you has been paid as a rule[2] by confirmed, irrevocable letter of credit.

On this basis, it has indeed cost us a great deal. From the moment to open credit till the time our buyers pay us, the tie-up of our funds lasts about four months. Under the present circumstances, this question is particularly taxing[3] owning to the tight money condition[4] and unprecedented[5] high bank interest.

If you would kindly make easier payment terms[6], we are sure that such an accommodation would be conducive to[7] encouraging business. We propose either "Cash against Documents on arrival of goods" or "Drawing on us at three months sight".

Your kindness[8] in giving priority[9] to the consideration of the above request and giving us an early favorable reply will be highly appreciated.

Yours faithfully,

Words, Expressions and Notes

1. Mild Steel Sheet 低碳钢板、软钢
2. as a rule 作为惯例
3. taxing 棘手的，难于负担的，感到有压力的，例如：

Such an amount is taxing for a firm of moderate means.

这样一笔数额对一个只有一般财力的商号是有压力的。

tax 指税收、税；taxable 形容词，表示应纳税的、可征税的

常用短语和表达方法：

tax avoidance 避税

tax abatement 减税

tax dodger 偷税人

tax evasion 逃税

tax heaven 避税天堂

tax holidays 免税期

to levy a tax on sth. 对某物征税

surtax 附加税

taxable earnings 应纳税的收入

taxation 课税、税制、税金

taxation bureau 税务局

double taxation 双重课税

4. tight money condition 紧张、吃紧的资金状况
5. unprecedented 前所未有的
6. easier payment terms 较为宽松的付款条件

7. be conducive to 对……有帮助的；conduce 是其动词形式

例句；

We believe personal contact will be conducive to the promotion of better understanding.

我们认为亲自接触将有助于促进更好的理解。

Investigation will conduce to a better analysis of the business situation.

调查会促使更好地分析商业形势。

Accumulation of information is conducive to success in business.

积累信息对业务的成功有帮助。

8. kindness 好意、善意，友好的行为

9. priority 重点，优先考虑的事。习惯用法有：

top priority 重中之重，最优先考虑的事

give priority to 优先考虑……，给……以优先权

enjoy priority in 在……享有优先权

例句：

We are unable to appoint you as our agent in your district, but you may enjoy priority in our offers.

我们不能指定你方作为在你处的代理人，但是你方可在我公司报盘方面享有优先权。

The question of payment will take top priority in our discussion.

支付问题将在我们的讨论中占最重要地位。

（12）

Dear Sirs,

We note from your letter of August 2nd that you wish to have a change in payment terms.

Actually, there is nothing unusual in our original arrangement[1]. Counting from time you open credit till the time shipment reaches your port, the interval[2], which is quite normal, is only about three months. Besides, your L/C is opened when the goods are ready for shipment[3]. In this case, we are sorry that we can not meet your wishes.

As we must adhere to[4] our customary practice, we sincerely hope that you will not think us unaccommodating[5].

As soon as a fresh supply[6] of Mild Steel Sheets comes in, we will contact you.

Yours faithfully,

Words, Expressions and Notes

1. original arrangement 原先商定的办法，原先的安排

2. interval 间隔的时间。interval 的常用短语有：

at intervals 每隔一会儿

at interval of 每隔……时间

at regular intervals 每隔一定（固定）时间

例句：

Shipments are arranged at intervals of one month.

装运货物按每隔一个月来安排。

We hope you will succeed in working up some business in the interval.

我们希望在此期间你们能成功地逐步发展一些业务。

3. ready for shipment 货物收妥待运

4. adhere to 恪守、遵循

5. unaccommodating 不肯通融的，不肯照顾的

6. fresh supply 新货

Section 3 Supplements 知识补充

Useful Sentences On Terms of payment

1. Please note that our terms of payment are by irrevocable L/C, payable by sight draft (by draft at…days' sight) accompanied by shipping documents at the bank of China at the port of shipment.

请注意，我方支付条款是用不可撤销的信用证，即期跟单汇票（或：××天期票）在装运港中国银行付款。

2. We advise caution in granting credit terms.

关于赊购条件以我方忠告（小心）为要。

3. As agreed, the terms of payment for the above orders are letter(s) of credit of 60 days' sight or D/P sight draft.

双方同意，上述订货货款以 60 天信用证或即期付款交单方式支付。

4. We can not proceed without settling first the terms of payment.

不首先解决付款条件，我方无法进行。

5. The documentary bill of exchange has been drawn upon you a 60 days under L/C No. DO24R and has been delivered to the Royal Bank of this city. Documents:

(1)Full set of Clean "On Board" Bill of Lading with insurance cover.

(2)Commercial Invoice in triplicate.

(3)Inspection certificate issued by Logic Inspection House.

我们已按第 DO24R 信用证规定向你开出 60 天见票付款的跟单汇票，并已提交本市皇家银行。

单据为：

（1）连同保险单在内的全套清洁，"已装船" 提单。

（2）商业发票一式三份。

（3）检验证书（由洛吉检验所签发）。

6. In compliance with your request, we exceptionally accept delivery against D/P at sight, but this should not be regarded as a precedent.

按你方要求，我们破例接受即期付款交单，但只此一次，下不为例。

7. In as much as the amount involved is rather small, we agree to draw on you by documentary sight draft.

由于金额很小，我们同意向你方开出即期跟单汇票。

8. The shipping documents will be handed to you by Midland Bank of your city against your accepting our 3 months' draft for £2300.

你方承兑了我方金额为 2300 英镑见票 3 个月付款的汇票后，你处米德兰银行就会把装船单据交付你们。

9. Our Bankers in Tokyo, Ohiro Bank, will accept your draft on then on our behalf.

我方东京大平银行将代表我方承兑你们开给他们的汇票。

10. We enclose a bank draft for RMB ¥34980, being the amount less 2% discount.

我们附寄银行汇票一纸，金额计人民币 34980 元，已扣除 2%折扣。

11. We thank you for your draft on Nova Scotia Bank for us $80000 in settlement of your account up to and inclusive of November 30th.

你方用以清偿截至 11 月 30 日为止的账目，金额计 8 万美元的诺沃・思科西亚银行汇票一纸收到，谢谢。

12. The beneficiaries have written us to the effect that they are without the L/C to this date. Please do your utmost to ensure the payment without delay.

受益人来信称他们至今未收到信用证，请尽力保证及时付款。

13. Our delay in payment was due to temporary accounting difficulties. The amount of…will be paid at the beginning of next week.

我们的延迟付款是由于在清理账务上的暂时困难所致。金额……元将在下周全部支付给你公司。

14. Your invoice dated…was filed incorrectly and, therefore, was not paid. Would you kindly excuse this error?

你公司…月…日开的发票有误，因此，我公司并未付款，请原谅。

15. Will you please let us have your cheque for the amount of the enclosed statement?

请以支票支付账单所载款项。

16. Since the total amount is so big and the world monetary market is rather unstable at the moment, we can not accept any terms of payment other than a letter of credit.

因为这次交易金额巨大，而且目前国际金融市场很不稳定，所以我们除了接受信用证付款外，不能接受别的付款方式。

17. We would suggest that for this particular order you let us have a D/D, on receipt of which we shall ship the goods on the first available steamer.

此次订货，我们建议你方使用即期汇票。收到汇票后，我们将把货物装上第一艘可订到的船。

18. In order to conclude the business, I hope you will meet me half way. What about 50% by L/C and the balance by D/P?

为了做成这笔交易，希望双方各让一步。50%货款用信用证支付，其余 50%按付款交单支付

怎么样？

19. For such a large amount, L/C is costly. Besides, it ties up my money. All this adds to my cost.
开这样大数额的信用证，费用很大。再说资金也会积压，这些都会增大成本。

20. Your proposal for payment by time draft for Order No.23 is acceptable to us.
对于第 23 号订单，我们可以接受你方远期汇票付款的提议。

21. We shall draw on you at 60 days sight after the goods have been shipped. Please honor our draft when it falls due.
货物装运后，我们将向你方开出见票 60 天内付款的汇票，请到期即付。

22. The bank has just advised us that our draft No.4 was declined (rejected, refused).
我们刚收到银行通知，我方第 4 号汇票被拒付了。

23. Under the installment plan, 20% of the contract value is to be paid with orders.
根据这个分期付款计划，合同总值的 20%应在订货时付讫。

24. Please indicate that the L/C is negotiable in our country.
请注明信用证在我国可以议付。

25. Your request for D/P payment has been considered and we agree to grant you this facility.
我们已经考虑过你方付款交单的要求，并同意给予你方这个方便。

26. We can't accept payment on deferred terms.
我们不能接受延期付款。

27. You ought to pay us the bank interest once payment is wrongly refused.
如果拒付错了，你们应该偿付我方的银行利息。

28. Of course payment might be refused if anything goes wrong with the documents.
如果单据有问题，当然可以提出拒付。

29. The equipment will be paid in installment with the commodities produced by our factory.
设备以我们厂生产的产品分期偿还。

30. We can't agree to draw at 30 days D/A.
我们不同意开具 30 天期限的承兑交单汇票。

31. The draft was discounted in New York.
汇票在纽约贴现。

32. The draft has not been collected.
这张汇票的款项尚未收进。

33. We'll be unable to meet these drafts.
我们无力兑付这些汇票。

34. We have drawn a clean draft on you for the value of this shipment.
我们已经开出光票向你方索取这批货的货款。

35. The draft has been handed to the bank on clean collection.
汇票已经交给银行按光票托收。

36. We've already remitted the amount by cheque.

我们已用支票将货款汇出。

37. For payment we require 100% value, irrevocable L/C in our favor with partial shipment allowed clause available by draft at sight.

我们要求用不可撤销的、允许分批装运的、金额为全部货款并以我方为抬头（受益人）的信用证，凭即期汇票支付。

Terms Used in Making Payment

deferred payment	延期付款
cash payment	现金付款
delay in payment	延期付款
down payment	付款定金
extension of payment	延长付款
full payment	全额付款
interim payment	中期付款
non-payment	不付款
partial payment	部分付款
payment in kind	分类付款
payment in account	账面付款
payment in advance	预付货款
pay by installments	分期付款
account payable	应付账款
account receivable	应收账款
cash account	现金账
credit account	贷方账
debit account	借方账
running account	流水账
mail transfer	信汇
telegraphic transfer	电汇
demand draft	票汇
collection	托收
drawer	出票人
drawee	受票人
holder	持票人
payer	付款人
payee	受票人
clean bill	光票
fictitious bill	空头支票

documentary bill	跟单汇票
sight draft	即期汇票
time draft	期汇票
bank's bill	银行汇票
commercial bill	商业汇票
D/P at sight	即期付款交单
D/P after sight	远期付款交单
trust receipt(T/R)	信托收据

Exercises

Ⅰ. Give Chinese equivalents for the following words and expressions and then make sentences.

for the amount of	due at
at one's figure	open account terms
figure out at	in payment for
in payment of	by all means
by means of	by no means
tie up	count on
on one's own account	credit standing
check with	in agreement with
agree in	act on
agreeable to	at intervals of

Ⅱ. Translate the following sentences into English.

1. 由于资金被许多业务占用，他们不得不要求放宽付款条件。
2. 我方抱歉不能接受货到目的港后凭单付款的支付方式。
3. 如果你方能同意按即期信用证方式付款，我们即能达成交易。
4. 鉴于双方长期友好关系，此次我们例外接受 60 天付款交单付款。
5. 中国商人决不会自负盈亏采购货物。
6. 瑞典一进口商要求我们按承兑交单方式运去一批试销商品。
7. 为确保早日交货，我们附寄银行汇票一纸，计 3000 美元。
8. 我们今日已通知我方银行电汇给你方全部金额，收到后请回信。
9. 请在扣除你方应收手续费后，将货款贷记我方 1008 号账户。
10. 你 3 月 12 日汇票已承兑，到期应照付。

Ⅲ. Translate the following into Chinese.

We are very interested in your automatic blankets, for which we believe there is a good market. As we can't count on regular sale, we don't feel able to make purchase on our account.

We therefore suggest you send us the goods on consignment basis. That means we would settle accounts of sales every month and send you payment due after deducting expenses and commission at a rate to be agreed.

Ⅳ. A foreign buyer whom you do not want to lose has regularly paid his accounts promptly by banker's draft, but payment of his last account is now eight weeks overdue. You wrote to him one month ago, but received no reply. Send him a second letter.

Chapter 8

Establishment of L/C and Amendment

Section 1 Business Knowledge 业务知识

1. 开证方式与信用证的内容

信用证是开证银行根据开证申请人的请求或开证行以自身名义向受益人开立的在一定金额和一定期限内凭规定的单据承诺付款的书面文件。信用证没有固定格式，内容也不完全一致，各开证行参照国际惯例拟定的"开立标准 L/C 格式"进行开证。根据开证人的要求和指示，开证银行通常采用两种开证方式。

第一，信函开证。这是一种传统开证方式，即以银行信件形式把信用证内容打印在固定格式上，经业务负责人签署后，以航空挂号形式邮寄给通知行，由通知行转交给受益人。（详见 Section 2（12））

第二，电开信用证。开证行以电报、电传、或 SWIFT 系统等方式开出信用证。银行把信用证内容通过电报和电传通知给通知行，这种方式比信函开证速度快。近些年使用 SWIFT 开证情况逐渐增多，过去采用电报、电传开证，各国银行标准、条款和格式不尽相同，文字烦琐。采用 SWIFT 系统后，使信用证格式标准化、固定化和统一化，而且传递速度快、成本低。（详见 Section 2（13））

尽管信用证没有固定格式，但内容大体一致，其主要内容有以下几方面。

（1）开证行名称、开征地点和日期。

（2）出口方名称、地址或通知行名称。

（3）信用证的性质/号码。

（4）开证文句：开证说明受何进口商的委托开立信用证。

（5）汇票文句：受益人应凭借汇票取款，汇票的支付人是谁，金额多少，汇票是即期还是远期。

（6）跟单文句：汇票应附有哪些单据、各需几份、货物的名称、品质、数量、重量、包装和价格。

（7）分批装运及转船：说明是否允许分批装运和转船。

（8）装船期限及信用证有效期文句。

（9）开证行负责文句：确定开证行的付款责任。

（10）开证行对议付行或代付行的提示文句，要求议付行在议付或代付时应该注意办理的事项。

（11）附加条款：如保兑条款、限制船只国籍条款，限制航程条款、履行保证条款等。

2. 信用证的当事人

信用证结算方式的基本当事人有：开证申请人、开证行、通知行、受益人。此外，还有其他关系人：保兑行、议付行、付款行和偿付行。

保兑行：根据开证行的要求，在信用证上加具保兑（confirm）的银行。保兑行在信用证加具保兑后，必须承担付款或议付的责任。

议付行：应信用证受益人的请求，依据信用证规定条款，审核单据无误后予以议付（negotiate），然后将单据寄给开证行或指定银行，收回垫款的银行。

转递行：将开证行开立的信用证原件传给受益人的银行。

通知行：在收到开证行的信用证后，以自己的通知书格式照录后通知受益人。

付款行：信用证规定的付款银行，也可能是其他银行。

偿付行：指接受开证行的委托，偿还议付垫款的银行。

3. 信用证的种类

信用证分类依据很多，所以它的种类也的确不少。国际贸易中经常用到的信用证有以下几种。

（1）光票信用证与跟单信用证

光票信用证：这种信用证是指受益人根据信用证的规定，在收取货款时只需开具汇票或者附发票等非装运单据，即可索回货款。因为不用随附装运单据，出口人可以在货物装运前开具汇票收款。光票信用证上通常规定：payment in advance against clean draft is allowed 等文句。

跟单信用证：这种信用证是指受益人根据信用证规定，在议付货款时，除开出汇票外，还要随附装运单据。国际贸易结算使用的信用证绝大多数都是跟单信用证。

（2）不可撤销信用证与可撤销信用证

不可撤销信用证：是指开证行一经开出信用证，在有效期内，未经受益人或有关当事人的同意，证上内容不得随意修改或撤销。只要受益人按照证上要求，提供单据和汇票，开证银行或其指定银行要保证付清货款。未注明"可撤销"与否的信用证应视为不可撤销。国际贸易里普遍使用不可撤销信用证。

可撤销信用证：指开证行开出的信用证，在有效期内，可不经过受益人或其他当事人的同意，修改或撤销证上内容。如证上有如下条文：the credit is subject to cancellation or amendment at any time without prior notice to the beneficiary. 但是，开证行对被指定的银行或授权银行在接到修改通知或撤销通知以前，已经根据表面符合要求的单据付款、承兑或议付，则撤销无效。

（3）即期信用证与远期信用证

即期信用证：泛指信用证规定受益人可凭即期汇票收取货款。有些即期信用证含有电报索偿条款（L/C with T/T reimbursement clause），这种情况下，开证行把最后审单付款的权力交给议付行。只要议付行审单无误，即可以用电报向开证行或其指定付款行索偿收款。所以电索信用证比一般即期信用证收汇快，有时当天就可收回货款。

远期信用证：指凭远期汇票收取货款的信用证。使用远期信用证，如果受益人想于汇票到期前收取货款，可以贴现汇票，但贴现费用和迟期付款利息由受益人承担。远期信用证又细分为 3 种情况。

第一，银行承兑远期信用证。是以开证银行作为远期信用证付款人。证下的汇票在承兑前，银行对出口人的权利和义务以信用证为准；在承兑后，银行作为汇票的承兑人，按票据法规定，将对持票人、背书人、出票人承担付款责任。

第二，迟期付款信用证。是指规定货物装运后若干天付款或开证行收取单据后若干天付款。这种信用证一般不要求出口方出具汇票，即便开出远期汇票也不能贴现，所以出口人不能利用贴现市场资金，只能自行垫款或向银行借款。

第三，假远期信用证。指信用证规定受益人开具远期汇票，由付款行负责贴现，并规定贴现利息和费用及承兑费用由开证人负责，又称为买方远期信用证。这种信用证的特征是有如下类似条款："drawee banker's discount charges and acceptance commission are for the account of the applicant and therefore the beneficiary is to receive value for usance draft as if drawn at sight."。注意受益人接受这种信用证，要承担汇票到期前被追索的风险。

（4）保兑信用证与非保兑信用证

保兑信用证：是指开证银行开出的信用证请另一家银行对符合证上条款的单据履行付款义务。对信用证承担保证兑付义务的银行称为保兑行。关于付款责任，一般的不可撤销信用证是由开证行承担付款责任；保兑信用证是开证行和保兑行共同对信用证承担付款责任。保兑银行通常是通知行，有时也可能是其他银行。保兑的手续一般是由保兑银行在信用证上加列保兑文句，如"the credit is confirmed by us"。证上若没有加注类似文句，将视作非保兑信用证。

（5）可转让信用证和不可转让信用证

可转让信用证：指信用证的受益人（第一受益人）可以要求授权付款、延期付款责任、承兑或议付的转让银行，或当信用证自由议付时，可以要求信用证中特别授权的转让银行，将信用证全部或部分转让给一个或数个受益人（第二受益人）使用的信用证。可转让信用证的第一受益人往往是中间商，他把信用证转让给实际出口人（第二受益人）。由出口人办理装运交货和收款事宜。我国有些出口商品由各大总公司统一对外成交、签订合同，然后再由口岸或地方分公司履行交货，这样国外进口方应该开立可转让信用证，由总公司作为第一受益人转让给口岸或地方贸易公司，由口岸或分公司作为第二受益人就地交货、议付货款。根据 UCP600 的规定：由开证行在信用证上明确注明"可转让（transferable）"，信用证方可转让。在申请转让时并且在信用证转让之前，第一受益人须不可撤销的指示转让行，说明它是否保留拒绝允许转让银行将修改通知给第二受益人的权利。如果转让银行同意按此条件办理转让，它必须在办理转让时，将第一受益人关于修改事项的指示通知第二受益人。对拒绝接受修改的第二受益人而言，该信用证视作未被修改。该惯例还规定，转让银行所涉及转让费用，除另有规定外，应由第一受益人支付，除非信用证另有说

明，可转让信用证只能转让一次。

可转让信用证除信用证金额、单价、到期日、最后交单日期及装运期限等任何一项或全部均可减少或缩短外，信用证只能按原证中规定的条款转让。但第一受益人有权用自己的发票和汇票替换第二受益人提交的发票和汇票，其金额不得超过原证金额，如信用证对单价有规定，应按原单价出具发票。

不可转让信用证：是指受益人不能将信用证的权利转让给他人使用的信用证。凡信用证未注明“可转让”字样，则不能转让。

（6）议付信用证、付款信用证、与承兑信用证

议付信用证：指信用证规定由某一银行议付或任何银行都可议付的信用证。指定某一银行议付的称为限制议付信用证（restricted negotiation credit）；任何银行都有权议付的称为公开议付信用证（open negotiation credit）或自由议付信用证（freely negotiation credit）。议付信用证有效期的失效地点通常在出口国，汇票的付款人可以是开证行或其指定的其他银行。UCP600 规定：开立信用证时不应以申请人作为汇票付款人，如信用证仍规定汇票付款人是申请人，银行将此汇票视为附加单据。

付款信用证：是指信用证规定开证银行保证当受益人向开证行或其指定付款行提交符合规定的单据时进行付款，或受益人开具汇票而不准议付的信用证。在付款信用证中有一种延期付款信用证（deferred payment credit），它是指受益人提示符合信用证规定单据后，由付款行在规定的将来时间进行付款的信用证。这种付款信用证不要求受益人出具远期汇票或即使出具汇票也不能贴现，只能待汇票到期受益人才能收到货款，这是出口方对进口方的信贷支持，以便于资本性货物的出口。

承兑信用证：是指使用远期汇票的跟单信用证。开证行或其指定付款行在收到符合规定的单据和汇票时，先履行承兑手续，待汇票到期日再行付款。它与延期付款信用证一样，都是远期信用证。但不同的是，承兑信用证必须有远期汇票，而延期付款信用证不一定要求出具汇票。

（7）背对背信用证

简称对背信用证。它是指出口人（中间商）凭进口人开来的信用证作抵押，要求出口地银行再向实际出口商开出另一信用证。两个信用证在出口地银行是“背对背”形式。进口人开来的信用证称为母证，出口中间商向实际出口人开出的信用证称为子证。母证金额一般大于子证金额，其交货期母证要长于子证。对背信用证主要适用于中间商经营进出口业务的需要。对背信用证的受益人可以是国外的，也可以是国内的，其装运期、信用证到期日、金额和单价等较母证有变化。但两证中货物的质量、数量必须一致。子证的开证申请人通常是以母证项下收到的货款来偿付子证开证行已垫付的资金。所以，子证的开证行除了要以母证作为开证抵押外，为防止母证发生意外收不到货款，要求子证开证人缴纳一定数额的押金或提供担保。由于子证受母证的约束，子证受益人如果要求修改证上内容，须征得母证开证人和母证开证行的同意。如发现单证不符，子证的开证行也须征求母证开证行的意见，若母证开证行不同意付款，子证开证行可能遭到拒付风险。因此，子证受益人在缮制单据时必须特别谨慎，不能疏忽。

（8）循环信用证

指当受益人全部或部分使用完信用证金额以后，其信用金额又恢复到原金额可再被受益人使

用，直至达到规定次数或累计总金额为止。循环信用证主要用于长期供货，实行分批装运和分批收款的情况，开证申请人为了免交多次开证费用、节省开证押金，才使用此种信用证。循环信用证的循环方式有 3 种。

第一，自动循环（automatic revolving）是指受益人在规定期限内每次使用信用证议付货款，无须等待开证行通知，即可自动恢复到原金额供受益人使用。例如，证上有如下规定，"the total amount of this credit shall be restored automatically after date of negotiation."。

第二，半自动循环（semi-automatic revolving）指受益人每次议付货款若干天内，开证行未发出停止恢复原金额的通知，即自动恢复原金额，这种半自动循环信用证，开证行具有保留停止使用信用证的权利。例如，信用证规定："Should the negotiating bank not be advised of stopping renewal within seven days after each negotiation, the unused balance of this credit shall be increased to the original amount."。

第三，非自动循环（non-automatic revolving）是指受益人每次议付货款后，要等开证行发出恢复原金额通知后，才能使用的信用证。例如，证上规定："the amount shall be renewal after each negotiation only upon receipt of issuing bank's notice stating that the credit might be renewal."。

除以上 3 种，还有根据时间循环和按照累计总金额限制使用的循环信用证。

（9）对开信用证

对开信用证是指在对等贸易中，交易当事人互为买卖双方，双方对其进口部分，向对方开出信用证，这两个信用证称为对开信用证。对开信用证有两种情况：一种是同时生效的，即一方开出信用证后，虽然已被受益人接受，但暂时不能生效，必须等对方开出回头信用证且被其受益人接受时，两证才能同时生效；另一种情况是对开信用证可以分别生效，即一方开出证后被受益人接受即可使用，无需等待对方开出回头信用证。分别生效的信用证，虽然是两个受益人，但互有联系、互有约束、互为条件。双方必须承担购买对方货物的义务，双方成交金额相等或大体一致，可有一定差额。这种信用证多用于易货贸易、补偿贸易和加工装配贸易。

4. 信用证支付程序

信用证结算货款，从开证申请人向银行申请开立信用证到开证银行付清货款，需要经过很多业务环节，并需办理各种手续。由于信用证种类不同，信用证条款有着不同规定，其业务环节和手续也不尽相同。但从信用证支付方式的一般程序看，主要有 8 大环节。

（1）进口商要求其银行开立以出口商为受益人的信用证。

（2）进口商银行开立信用证，并将其寄给出口商国家的往来银行。因进口商银行开立信用证，故被称为开证行。

（3）出口商银行收到开证行的信用证并辨别真伪后将其递交出口商。由于该银行把信用证通知递交给了出口商，因而该银行被称为通知行。

（4）出口商审核信用证无误后，按证上要求完成装运并准备汇票及所有的装运单据，然后把汇票和装运单据递交通知银行要求议付。通知行帮助出口商获得货款。

（5）通知行把汇票及装运单据寄给开证行要求支付。

（6）开证行收到汇票及装运单据后把他们递交给进口商。

（7）开证行，此时被称为付款行，把货款汇给通知行。

（8）通知行收到货款后交给出口商。

5. 信用证的修改

受益人收到信用证后，应该以买卖合同为依据详细审查信用证与买卖合同条款是否相符。如发现有不符点，应及时要求进口人通过开证行进行修改。改证的途径是将信用证的问题通知开证人与开证银行，由开证人指示银行进行修改，开证行再将修改通知书寄交出口方通知行，并由通知行交给受益人。这时信用证修改生效，原证有关规定作废。有时在信用证开立后，买方会主动修改信用证，此时卖方不想接受这种单方面修改，应在银行3个工作日内将信用证修改通知按原来路线返回，否则即被认为接受修改，原证有关规定失效。若信用证内容经审查无误，即可按规定条件装运货物。受益人装运后要按照信用证要求缮制各种单据并开出汇票，在信用证有效期内向议付行交单议付货款。

6. 信用证的结算特征特点

信用证作为银行信用的支付方式，具体来说在结算环节有3大特点。

（1）开证银行负有第一性付款责任

信用证是由开证银行以自己的信用做出付款保证的。所以在此条件下，银行就负有第一性付款责任。UCP600规定，信用证是一项约定，不论其如何命名或描述，是开证行应开证申请人的要求和指示或以其自身名义，在与信用证条款相符情况下，凭规定单据向受益人或其指定人付款，或承兑并支付受益人出具的汇票，或授权付款行付款、或承兑汇票，或授权另一家银行议付。可见，开证银行是首先的付款人。

（2）信用证是一种独立自足文件

信用证的开立以买卖合同为依据。但一经开出，即成为独立于买卖合同和其他合同之外的另一种契约，不受买卖合同和其他合同的约束。根据UCP600的规定：就性质而言，信用证与可能作为其依据的销售合同或其他合同，是相互独立的交易。即使信用证提及某合同，银行与之完全无关，不受其约束。因此，一家银行做出付款、承兑并支付汇票或议付或履行信用证项下其他义务的承诺，不受申请人与开证行或与受益人之间在已有管辖下产生索偿或抗辩的制约。所以，信用证是一项独立自足文件，开证银行和参与业务的其他银行只按信用证规定履行自己的义务。

（3）信用证是一种单据交易

在信用证结算中，实行凭单付款原则。在信用证业务里，有关各个方面处理的是单据，而不是与单据有关的货物、服务或其他行为。所以，信用证是纯粹的单据业务。银行虽有义务“合理小心的审核一切单据”，但这种审核只是用以确定单据表面是否符合信用证条款，开证银行只“根据表面符合信用证条款的单据付款”。因此，银行对任何单据的形式、完整性、准确性、真实性以及伪造或法律效力概不负责，对单据上规定或附加的一般/特殊条件，也不承担责任。信用证结算下所谓的单据“严格相符”原则，就是“单证一致、单单一致”。

Section 2 Specimen Letters 样函

（1）

Dear Sirs,

Re: Our sales Contract No. C145

Referring to the 5,000 tons of Red Beans[1] under our S/C No.C145, we wish to draw your attention to the fact that the date of delivery is approaching, but we still have not received your covering Letter of Credit up to date[2]. Please to try your best to expedite[3] the L/C, so that we may execute[4] the order smoothly.

We hope to receive your favorable news soon.

Yours faithfully,

Words, Expressions and Notes

1. Red Beans 红豆，也即小豆
2. up to date 到目前为止
3. expedite 加速、加快
4. execute 履行、执行

（2）

Dear Sirs,

We refer to the faxes dated 12th of April and 22nd of May, asking you to open the relevant L/C regarding the captioned order, we regret to say up till now[1] we have not received any news from you.

We have to remind[2] you that it was agreed that you would establish the required L/C upon receipt of our Sales Confirmation. It is a pity that you failed to do as what you have agreed. As the goods have been ready for shipment for quite some time, it behooves[3] you to take immediate action to issue the L/C in order that we can conclude the business to mutual benefits.

We are expecting good news from you at an early date.

Yours faithfully,

Words, Expressions and Notes

1. up till now 直到目前
2. remind 提醒，使想起
3. behooves 适宜

（3）

Dear Sirs,

We thank you very much for your order No. 289 of May 13th with which you have set us your shipping instructions.

The goods of your order are being manufactured for shipment[1]. You informed us that you will arrange to open an irrevocable L/C in our favor, valid until August 13th[2] and ask you to send it promptly.

Upon arrival of the L/C we will pack and ship the goods urgently as requested in accordance with your shipping instructions. We assure you that we will make complete shipment[3] so that we can give you perfect satisfaction[4].

Yours faithfully,

Words, Expressions and Notes

1. being manufactured for shipment 要发运的这批货正在制造、生产过程中
2. valid until August 13th 信用证的有效期至 8 月 13 日
3. complete shipment 完成装运
4. perfect satisfaction 令人完全满意

（4）

Dear Sirs,

L/C No.BSW6170

We have received your letter of July 8th and regret to learn that you are unable to extend[1] the subject L/C.

As is known to you, there is only one vessel sailing from your port each month and it usually leaves here in the first half of a month[2]. So far as we know[3], the only vessel available this month will leave here in a day or two and the deadline[4] for booking sipping space[5] is long past. Therefore it is impossible for us to ship the goods this month, and we would like you to do your best to extend the L/C as requested in our letter of June 28th.

Please act promptly and let us have your reply by return fax.

Yours faithfully,

Words, Expressions and Notes

1. extend 指延展信用证的期限
2. first half of a month 某月的上旬
3. so far as we know 据我们所知
4. deadline 最后期限

5. booking shipping space 订舱

在货物成交量不是很大时一般租用班轮运输，此时船方出租的不是整条船，而是船上某个舱位，称为 shipping space。当货物成交量很大时，采用包租船运输（charter transport），按照船舶经营特点，包租船又分定程租船（voyage charter）和定期租船（time charter）

（5）

Dear Sirs,

We would like to explain the matter of L/C amendment.

According to the L/C we received, the payment was to be made at 120 d/s[1]. but we want it to be made at sight[2]. This was agreed on by you and expressly[3] mentioned in your order sheet. Therefore, please amend it as stated[4]. The goods will be shipped by 20th of this month. We should be obliged[5] for your immediate amendment of the L/C as requested by us.

Please reply by fax.

Yours faithfully,

Words, Expressions and Notes

1. at 120 d/s 见票后 120 天付款
2. at sight 即期付款
3. expressly 明确的，清楚的
4. as stated 按照规定，请按要求
5. obliged 这里表示感激、感谢的意思

（6）

Dear Sirs,

Our Sales Confirmation No. TE151

With reference to[1] the 4000 dozen shirts under our Sales Confirmation No. TE151, we wish to draw your attention to the fact that the date of delivery is approaching but up to the present[2] we have not received the covering L/C. please do your utmost to expedite its establishment[3] so that we may execute the order within the prescribed time[4].

In order to avoid subsequent amendments, please see to it[5] that the L/C stipulations are in exact accordance with[6] the terms of the contract.

We look forward to receiving your favorable response[7] at an early date.

Yours faithfully,

Words, Expressions and Notes

1. with reference to 关于、涉及
2. up to the present 到目前为止
3. establishment 建立、开立，此处意为信用证的开立。开立信用证最常见的说法是 open an L/C，从银

行角度可以用 issue an L/C。establishment 表示开证是较为正式的说法，其动词形式是 establish

例句：

We shall be glad to establish business relation with you.

我们乐于同你方建立业务关系。

We are pleased to have done some business with you since the establishment of our business relationship.

自从建立业务关系以来，我们与你公司做了一些交易，对此感到高兴。

This year is the 30th anniversary of the establishment of our firm.

今年是我公司创建 30 周年。

Application has been made by us to the bank for the establishment of L/C.

我们已向银行申请开证。

We admit that you deserve some credit for establishing this brand in your market.

这一新品牌能在你方市场打开销路，我们承认是你们的功劳。

4. prescribed time 规定的时间里

prescribe 指合同、文件及章程方面的规定；也可表示医生开药、开立处方；其名词是 prescription

例句：

The contract prescribed that the goods be shipped in September.

合同规定这批货在 9 月份发运。

This prescription doesn't work for your disease.

该处方对你的病不管用。

5. see to it 确保、保证

6. exact accordance with 与……完全相符

7. favorable response 积极的回应

response 表示反应、回应，固定搭配短语为 in response to，动词形式为 respond

例句：

In response to your request, we make a firm offer as follows:

应你方要求，我们报实盘如下：

Please keep us advised of the response to our new products in your market.

请随时告知你方市场对我们新产品的反应。

（7）

Dear Sirs,

We have receive your L/C No. 145/88 issued by the Yemen Bank for Reconstruction & Development for the amount of ￡13720 covering 16000 dozen Stretch Nylon Socks[1]. On perusal[2], we find that transshipment and partial shipment[3] are not allowed.

As direct steamers[4] to your port are few and far between[5], we have to ship via[6] Hong Kong more often than not[7]. As to partial shipment, it would be our mutual benefit because we could ship immediately whatever we have on hand instead of waiting for the whole lot[8] to be completed.

We, therefore, are cabling this afternoon, asking you to amend the L/C to read[9]:

"TRANSHIPMENT AND PARTIALSHIPMENT ALLOWED"

We shall be glad if you see to it that amendment is cabled[10] without any delay, as our goods have been packed ready for shipment[11] for quite some time.

Yours faithfully,

Words, Expressions and Notes

1. Stretch Nylon Socks 弹力呢绒袜
2. on perusal 经审核、查对
3. transshipment and partial shipment 转运与分批装运
4. direct steamers 直达货轮
5. few and far between 这里是指轮船航次稀少，而且船舶之间的时间间隔长
6. via 由，取道，通过（某种手段或某人）

例句：

As requested, we have forward the samples via your Shanghai Office.

按照要求，我们已将样品通过上海公司转寄你方。

The goods are to be shipped to Vancouver, thence via Overland to Montreal.

货物由船运至温哥华，之后再由该处经陆运至蒙特利尔。

7. more often than not 时常，往往，多半
8. whole lot 整批货
9. amend the L/C to read 把信用证内容修改为；amend 后也可接 as

例句：

The amount of the L/C has been amended as US$ 4836.

信用证金额已修改为 4836 美元。

Please amend the quantity of the L/C to read" 2% more or less".

请将信用证上的数量改为"允许 2%溢短装"。

10. amendment is cabled 电改信用证，即用电报方式来修改信用证
11. packed ready for shipment 货物打好包装已备转运

pack 作名词指小包、小箱、小盒、包装量；package 指包装用料，中小型的包裹、包、捆；packaging 是包装方面的装潢，美观、高效的包装法。

包装的惯用表达方式有：

a pack of canned goods 一小箱罐头食品

a six-pack of beer 半打装啤酒

packaging industry 装潢业

packaging designing 装潢设计

seaworthy packing 适合海运的包装

packing list 装箱单，花色码单

outer packing 外包装

inner packing 内包装

export packing 出口包装

insufficient（improper，faulty，poor）packing 包装不良

例句：

You are outdistanced in the packing and packaging of the material.

在货物包装及装潢方面你们很落后。

When the shipment arrived, the packages were all intact, but many of them were found short of weight.

货到时，包装完好无损，但发现很多包短重（重量不足）。

The shirts will be packed each in a polyethylene bag, five dozen to a cardboard case.

每件衬衫装一塑料袋，五打装一硬纸板箱。

（8）

Dear Sirs,

Re: Our Order for ….

Immediately on receipt of your telegram dated June5 advising that the covering export license[1] had been issued, we opened telegraphically L/C No.889 for ￡1500 in the customary manner.

Please see to it that shipment of this order is effected during this month, since punctual[2] shipment is one of important considerations[3] in dealing wit our market.

As called for[4] in our L/C, please mark all drums[5] conspicuously[6] with the shipping mark××× and the word "POISONOUS[7]". Your compliance[8] in this respect will do much to facilitate our taking delivery[9] of the goods on arrival.

We should be glad if you could manage to arrange shipment by s.s. "Morning Star" sailing[10] on or about the 24th inst, and cable us your shipping advice immediately after the departure[11] of the vessel.

Yours faithfully,

Words, Expressions and Notes

1. export license 出口许可证
2. punctual 准时的、正点的，严守时刻的
3. considerations 考虑的因素
4. called for 要求、需要；call on 是拜访的意思；call 还可以指船舶的停靠

例句：

This steamer will call at your port.

此船将在你方港口停靠。

There is no call for us to adjust the price.

我们无需调整价格。

For this steamer, Dalian is not a port of call.

大连不是这条船中途停靠的港口。

The wording of the agreement calls for some revision.

协议的措词需稍做修改。

Our representative will call on you while in Shenyang.

我们的代表在沈阳停留期间将去拜访你。

5. drums 桶，指产品的包装桶

6. conspicuously 显著的、明显的

7. POISONOUS 有毒的，产品外包装上的警告性标志

8. compliance 服从、顺从、听从、合规

9. taking delivery 提货

10. sailing 起航，（轮船的）航班

11. departure 离开、背离

例句：

Which is the departure platform for the 8:00 train?

八点钟的列车从哪个站台出发？

The expected time of departure of 1224 flight is 9:30 a.m.

1224 次班机预计开航时间是上午 9 点 30 分。

It is a gross departure from your promise.

这严重背离了你方的承诺。

（9）

Dear Sirs,

As per[1] the instructions from Brown & Sons, received through our Hong Kong office, we have opened an irrevocable letter of credit for ￡20000 in your favor, valid until 30 November next. You have authority[2] to draw on us at 60 days against this credit for the amount of your invoice upon shipment of 2000 tons of Steels to Browning & Sons.

Your draft must be accompanied[3] by the following documents, which are to be delivered[4] to us against our acceptance[5] of the draft. Bill of Lading in triplicate[6], Commercial Invoice, Insurance Certificate and Certificate of Origin are required.

Provided you fulfill[7] the terms of the credit we will accept and pay on maturity[8] the draft presented to us under this credit and if required, provide discounting facilities[9] at current rates.

Yours faithfully,

Words, Expressions and Notes

1. as per 根据、依照

2. authority 权力、职权、当局（复数）

对外贸易有关主管机构的说法有：

port authorities 港务当局

money authorities 金融当局

licensing authorities 签发许可证当局

exchange control authorities 外汇管理当局

customs authorities 海关当局

competent authorities 主管当局

例句：

The buyer has already applied to the authorities concerned for import license.

买方已向有关当局申请进口许可证。

He has the authority of his home office for immediate decision.

他的国内公司授权他可以当即做出决定。

Please give us authority to settle the matter as we see fit.

请给我们以相机处理此事的权力。

3. accompanied 兼带、陪衬、伴随

例句：

The credit is available by beneficiary's drafts, drawn on us, in duplicate, without recourse, at sight, for 100% of the invoice value, and accompanied by the following shipping document:

本信用证需由受益人开具以我行为付款人且无追索权的即期汇票，汇票一式两份按发票金额全额开立，并须附有下列装运单据：

Each bid shall be accompanied by a Bid Guaranty.

每份投标需附有投标保证书。

The accompanying letter has got our immediate attention.

此附函已得到我方即刻处理。

4. deliver 递送，交付

例句：

The documents have already been delivered to the bank.

单据已交付银行。

All notices of the Marine Arbitration Commission to the parties shall be delivered by courtier, registered mail.

海事仲裁委员会对当事人的一切通知以特快信使、挂号信送达。

The quantity to be delivered next month must not be less than 3,000 tons.

下月应交付的货物数量不得少于 3000 吨。

5. acceptance 此处指承兑汇票

此外还有许可，承认，接受，验收的意思。

例句：

Kindly send us 2 bills of lading by separate posts, together with your draft at 30 days for acceptance.

请将两份提单分别寄来，同时开立 30 天（见票后 30 天付款）汇票以便承兑。

The items of the verification and acceptance test are as follows:

考核与验收试验项目如下：

The design has met with favorable acceptance in many countries.

这种设计已在许多国家受到欢迎。

We strongly recommend acceptance for our stock is running low.

由于存货日渐减少，我们极力劝你方接受。

6. in triplicate 一式三份

类似的表达还有：

in three copies 一式三份

in duplicate 一式两份

in quadruplicate 一式四份

in quintuplicate 一式五份

in sextuplicate 一式六份

in septuplicate 一式七份

in octuplicate 一式八份

in nonuplicate 一式九份

in decuplicate 一式十份

一式几份还可以用 fold 表示，如 in three fold 一式三份

7. fulfill 履行、遵守

8. maturity（票据等）到期，成熟

例句：

We do not think the time for negotiating sole agency has come to maturity.

我们认为商谈独家代理的时机尚未成熟。

We are pleased to inform you that your draft has been duly honored on maturity.

兹乐于奉告，你方汇票已于到期日全数兑付。

9. discounting facilities at current rates 以当前利率提供汇票贴现的便利

（10）

Dear Sirs,

Your L/C No. 1417-10 M/T Frozen Rabbit Meat

…thank you for your L/C for the captioned goods. We are sorry that owing to[1] some delay[2] on the part of[3] our suppliers at the point of origin[4], we are not able to get the goods ready before the end of this month. As a result, we sent you a cable yesterday reading:

LC1417 PLSCABLE EXTENSION SHIPMENT VALIDITY 15/31 MAY RESPECTIVELY LETFOLLOWS[5]

It is expected that the consignment will be ready for shipment in the early part of May[6] and we are arranging to ship it on s/s "Dongfeng" sailing from Dalian on[7] or about 10th May.

We are looking forward to receiving your cable extension[8] of the above L/C thus enabling us to effect shipment of the goods in question[9].

We thank you for your cooperation.

Yours faithfully,

Words, Expressions and Notes

1. owing to 由于，owing 表示未付的、欠着的

2. delay 耽误、延迟、拖延，既是名词也可作动词。

3. on the part of 在……方面，就……而言

例句：

On our part, we always keep to our promise.

就我们这方面说，我们总是遵守诺言的。

The fault is on the part of the shipping company.

这是轮船公司的错。

4. point of origin 指货物的产地

5. LC1417 PLSCABLE EXTENSION SHIPMENT VALIDITY 15/31 MAY RESPECTIVELY LETFOLLOWS

这句电报文稿的意思是：此电针对你方第 1417 号信用证，请把信用证的装运期和有效期分别延展至 5 月 15 日和 5 月 31 日。相关信函随后寄发。

6. in the early part of May 在五月上旬，同 early in May；表示下旬可以说 in the late part of May 或者 late in May

7. on or about 10th May 5 月 10 日左右；UCP600 规定“在或大概在（on or about）”或类似用语将被视为规定事件发生在指定日期的前后五个日历日之间，起讫日期计算在内，所以装运期在 5 月 5 日至 15 日之间都是允许的。

8. cable extension 电展信用证，指用电报方式延展信用证的期限

9. in question 所提到的、提及的

（11）

Dear Sirs,

With reference to our Sales Confirmation No.7904 dated August 8, 2004, we regret to say that your letter of credit has not yet reached us up to the time of writing[1]. This has caused us much inconvenience[2] as we have already made preparations for shipment according to the stipulations of the said Sales Confirmation.

You must be aware that the terms and conditions of a contract once signed should be strictly observed[3], failure to abide by[4] them will mean violation of contract[5]. If you refer to[6] our Sales Confirmation, you will see the clause reading;

“The buyer shall establish the covering Letter of Credit before 30th August, 2004, failing which the Seller reserves the right[7] to rescind the contract without further notice[8].”

The goods you ordered have been ready for quite some time and demand of late[9] has been so great that we find it hard to keep them for you any longer. However, in consideration of our friendly business relations, we are prepared to wait for your L/C, which must reach us not later than October 5, 2004. if we again fail to receive your L/C in time, we shall cancel our Sales Confirmation and ask you to refund[10] to us the storage charges we have paid on your behalf[11].

Your co-operation in this respect will be appreciated.

Yours sincerely,

Manager

China National Import & Export Corp.

Words, Expressions and Notes

1. up to the time of writing 直到写这封信为止

2. inconvenience 不便、麻烦的事；动词表示使感到不方便，使感到麻烦

例句：

If it does not inconvenience you, please send your samples at an early date.

如果不麻烦的话，请你方早日寄送样品。

Needless to say, we have been put to no little inconvenience by the delay in delivery.

毋庸讳言，耽误交货让我方遭受很大不便。

3. observe 这里指遵守、遵循

4. abide by 遵守，例如：

One of our guiding principles in doing business is to abide by contracts and keep a good faith.

我们做生意的一项指导原则就是重合同，守信用。

5. violation of contract 违约，违反合同，用法同 breach of contract

6. refer to 这里指参考、查阅

7. reserves the right 保留权利

8. rescind the contract without further notice 取消合同而不做另行通知

表示"撤销、取消"意思的词汇有很多，但用法上存在区别。rescind 表示运用正当权力进行废除或废止活动。在法律上意为合同的废止，并且表示该合同似乎从未生效；annul 是指在法律上不再有效，可用于某种权力、婚姻、契据、凭证、法规或条例等；cancel 表示彻底否定某事物的行为，强调通过法律宣布无效或者撤销、解除效力；withdraw 指把发出去的东西又追回，使其失效；revoke 表示召回、废除。

例句：

The king revoked his decree.

国王取消了他的法令。

My driving licence was revoked due to drunk driving.

因酒醉驾车，我的驾驶执照被吊销了。

We should withdraw dirty banknotes from circulation.

应该收回破旧钞票使其不再流通。

As the time of shipment you proposed is too late for our customer to accept, we wish to cancel our order No.341.

由于你方所提装运期太晚，我方客户不接受，因此撤销我方第 341 号订单。

If you fail to effect shipment at latest by the end of this month, the contract is to be considered annulled.

若你方最迟至本月底不能发货，该项合同被视为无效。

Either party may rescind this contract by notice in writing.

任何一方都可以用书面方式通知解除本合同。

9. demand of late 最近以来的需求

10. refund 退款，归还给

例句：

The money shall be refunded if seller fails to provide good title.

如果卖方不能提供可靠的所有权凭证，这笔款项应被归还。

The buyer demanded a refund on the inferior goods.

买方对劣等货物要求退款。

I want to refund this ticket because I will stay in school instead of go home during holidays.

假期我因为不能回家要待在学校里，所以想退掉这张车票。

11. paid on your behalf 替你方支付

（12）

信开信用证

THE BANK OF TOKYO, LTD.

New York Agency

100 Broadway New York, N.Y. 10005

Date: June 21, 20 × ×

<table>
<tr><td>IRREVOCABLE
DOCUMENTARY CREDIT</td><td>Credit number of issuing bank
110 LCI 985467</td><td>Of advising bank</td></tr>
<tr><td rowspan="3">Advising bank
Pre-advised by: Telex Through
Bank of China
Qingdao, China

Beneficiary

China National Textiles Imp. &
Exp. Corp.
No.78 Jiangxi Road, Qingdao, China</td><td colspan="2">Applicant
Kanematsu- Gosho (Canada) Inc.
400 de Maisonneuve Blvd. W.
Montreal, Quebec,Canada</td></tr>
<tr><td colspan="2">Amount
Abt.CAD174,000.00 (ABOUT CANADIAN DOLLARS ONE HUNDRED SEVENTY FOUR THOUSAND AND 00/100)</td></tr>
<tr><td colspan="2">Expiry
For negotiation before August 15, 20 × ×</td></tr>
</table>

Dear Sirs,

We hereby issue the Irrevocable Documentary Letter of Credit which is available by beneficiary's drafts on us for full invoice value at sight bearing the credit number and date of issue, and accompanied by the following documents:

Signed Commercial Invoice in quintuplicate;

Canadian Customs Invoice in quintuplicate;

Packing list in quintuplicate;

Weight and Measurement Certificate in quintuplicate;

Full set of clean on board Bills of Lading issued to order of shipper marked "Freight prepaid" and notify consignee.

Evidencing shipment of:

About 300,000 yards of 65% Polyester, 35% Cotton Grey Lawn as per buyer's order No.S-0578,

CFR Montreal.

We are informed insurance is to be covered by buyer.

Shipment from China to Montreal latest July 31, 20××	Partial shipment permitted
	Transshipment permitted

All other bank charges are for the account of beneficiary.

Documents must be presented to negotiating bank or paying bank within 15 days after the on board date of Bills of Lading, but within validity of letter of credit.

Special Conditions:

Two sets of non-negotiable shipping documents must be airmailed direct to Kanematsu-Gosho (Canada) Inc., Montreal and beneficiary's certificate to this effect is required.

Special instructions for reimbursement:

We will pay the negotiating bank as per their instructions upon receipt of documents.

The amount of any draft drawn under this credit must, concurrently with negotiation, be endorsed on the reverse hereof, and the presentment of any such draft shall be a warranty by the negotiating bank that such endorsement has been made and that documents have been forwarded as herein required.

We hereby engage with the drawers, endorsers and bona fide holders of drafts drawn and negotiated under and in compliance with the terms of this credit that the same shall be duly honoured on due presentation to the drawee.

The advising bank is requested to notify the beneficiary without adding their confirmation.

Yours faithfully,

THE BANK OF TOKYO, LTD.

此信开证的译文

东京银行纽约分行

纽约百老汇大街 100 号, N.Y. 10005

日期：20××年 6 月 21 日

不可撤销跟单信用证	开证行信用证号码 110 LCI 985467	通知行信用证号码

通知行	申请人 Kanematsu-Gosho (Canada) Inc. 400 de Maisonneuve Blvd. W. Montreal, Quebec, Canada
由中国银行青岛分行电传通知	
受益人	金额 大约 174,000.00 加拿大元（大约壹拾柒万肆仟加拿大圆）
中国纺织品进出口公司 中国青岛江西路 78 号	有效期 20××年 8 月 15 日以前议付有效

执事先生：

现开立不可撤销的跟单信用证，凭受益人向我行开立的发票全额的即期汇票付款，汇票上具明本信用证号码和开证日期，并由下列单据伴随：

签署的商业发票一式五份；
加拿大海关发票一式五份；
装箱单一式五份；
重量和尺码单一式五份；
全套清洁已装船提单，凭托运人指示，著名“运费预付”，并通知收货人
证实下列货物的装运：

买方订单 S-0578 项下的大约 30 万码原色细麻布，65%化纤，35%棉，成本加运费到蒙特利尔。

保险由卖方负责。

最迟于 20××年 7 月 31 日由中国运往蒙特利尔	允许分批装运
	允许转船

其他银行费用均由受益人承担。

单据必须在提单日期后 15 日之内、并要在本信用证有效期内提交议付行或付款行。

特殊条款：

受益人必须将两套副本装运单据直接航寄给 Kanematsu-Gosho (Canada) Inc., Montreal，并出具已航寄证明。

关于偿付特殊规定：

收到单据后我们会向议付行进行偿付。本信用证下开立的所有汇票的金额，必须在议付的同时在本信用证背面背书，该汇票的提示即作为议付行的担保，证明该背书已作出，单据已经按此处要求寄出。

我们向汇票的出票人、背书人以及善意持有人保证，在本信用证项下并按本信用证要求开立、议付的所有汇票，都将在向受票人提示时得到支付。

我们要求通知行在不加保兑的情况下向受益人发出通知。

东京银行

谨上

（13）

SWIFT 格式信用证

ZCZC BSDDF1 0002090643【1】

P3 SDAAOC
SWIFT BSDDF1 0002090643
99 E N 701 99 S

BASIC HEADER F 01 BKCHCNBJA500 9690 630741
APPL. HEADER O 700 1747000208 TDOMCATTBMTL 4242 982370 0002090647 N
+ TORONTO DOMINION BANK MONTREAL【2】
+QUEBEC CANADA
(BANK NO: 8020006) +MONTREAL, CANADA

:MT: 701 ----------ISSUE OF A DOCUMENTARY CREDIT ----------

SEQUENCE OF TOTAL :27 【3】: 1/2【4】
FORM OF DOCUMENTARY CREDIT :40A: IRREVOCABLE【5】
DOCUMENTARY CREDIT NUMBER :20 : I1757119【6】

DATE OF ISSUE	:31C:	000208【7】
DATE AND PLACE OF EXPIRY	:31D:	000415NEG BANK【8】
APPLICANT	:50C:	C AND G LINGERIE (1998) INC.,【9】
MONTREAL, QUEBEC H2S 3L5		
BENEFICIARY	:59 :	SHANDONG GARMENTS IMP. AND EXP. CORP.【10】 70 SICHUAN ROAD, QINGDAO THE PEOPLES REP OF CHINA 266002
CURRENCY CODE, AMOUNT	:32B:	CAD32453.60【11】
AVAILABLE WITH…BY…	:41D:	AVAILABLE WITH【12】 ANY BANK BY NEGOTIATION
DRAFTS AT…	:42C:	DRAFTS AT SIGHT【13】
DRAWEE	:42D:	OURSELVES【14】
PARTIAL SHIPMENT	:43P:	PARTIAL SHIPMENTS ALLOWED【15】
TRANSSHIPMENT	:43T:	TRANSHIPMENTS ALLOWED
LOADING/DISPATCH/TAKING/FROM	:44A:	
THE PEOPLE'S REP. OF CHINA		
FOR TRANSPORTATION TO…	:44B:	
MONTREAL, QUE., CANADA		
LATEST DATE OF SHIPMENT	:44C:	000331【16】
DOCUMETNS REQUIRED	:46A:【17】	

DOCUMENTS

COMMERCIAL INVOICE IN TRIPLICATE

CANADA CUSTOMS INVOICE OF DEPARTMENT OF NATIONAL REVENUE/CUSTOMS AND EXCISE IN TRIPLICATE

PACKING LIST IN TRIPLICATE

FULL SET OF CLEAN ON BOARD MARINE/OCEAN BILLS OF LADING TO ORDER BLANK ENDORSED MARDED FREIGHT PREPAID NOTIFY

C AND G LINGERIE (1998) INC. AND DATED LATEST MARCH 31/2000.

EXPORT LICENSE

INSURANCE POLICY OR CERTIFICATE COVERING MARINE RISKS, ALL RISKS, FOR 110 PERCENT OF THE INVOICE VALUE

CHARGES	:71B:	ALL BANKING CHARGES OUTSIDE CANADA ARE FOR APPLICANT'S ACCOUNT
PERIOD FOR PRESENTATIONS	:48 :	DOCUMENTS TO BE PRESENTED【18】

WITHIN 15 DAYS AFTER DATE OF
SHIPMENT BUT WITHIN
CREDIT VALIDITY

CONFIRMATION INSTRUCTION :49 : WITHOUT【19】

INSTRUCTION TO BANK :78 :

NEGOTIATING BANK TO AIRMAIL (1) DRAFT(S) AND COMPLETE SET OF DOCUMENTS (2) REMAINING DOCUMENTS BY NEXT MAIL TO US

ON RECEIPT OF DOCUMENTS IN ORDER AT OUR COUNTER WE SHALL PAY A DEPOSITORY OF NEGOTIATING BANK'S CHOOSING

TRAILER【20】

MAC: 4678C676 CHK:982922E807BA

NNNN

ZCZC BSDDF1 0002090643

P3 SDAAOC

SWIFT BSDDF1 0002090643

99 E N 701 99 S

BASIC HEADER F 01 BKCHCNBJA500 9690 630741

APPL. HEADER O 700 1747000208 TDOMCATTBMTL 4242 982370 0002090647 N

+ TORONTO DOMINION BANK MONTREAL
+QUEBEC CANADA
(BANK NO: 8020006) +MONTREAL, CANADA

:MT: 701 ----------ISSUE OF A DOCUMENTARY CREDIT ----------

SEQUENCE OF TOTAL :27 : 2/2【21】

Documentary Credit Number :20 : I175119

DESCRPT OF GOODS/SERVICES :45B:【22】

16/84 PCT COTTON/POLYESTER WOVEN SATIN FLEECE, LADIES SLEEPWEAR, S/C 20SGC5102

1020 PCS PYJAMA STYLE 1539 AT CAD8.90 PER PC.

240 PCS NIGHT SHIRT STYLE 1540 AT CAD5.40 PER PC.

600 PCS HOUSECOAT STYLE 1541 AT CAD8.90 PER PC.

964 PCS PYJAMA STYLE 1542 AT CAD8.90 PER PC.

420 PCS NIGHT SHIRT STYLE 1543 AT CAD6.40 PER PC.

240 PCS NIGHT SHIRT STYLE 1544 AT CAD5.00 PER PC.

480 PCS HOUSECOAT STYLE 1545 AT CAD8.90 PER PC.

C.I.F. MONTREAL

ADDITIONAL CONDITIONS :47B:【23】

SPECIAL CONDITIONS

CONTAINER SHIPMENT ALLOWED

INSURANCE TO BE COVERED BY SHIPPER

SHIPMENT ONLY ON ANY ONE OF THE FOLLOWING FOUR SHIPPING LINES IS ACCEPTABLE 1. MITSUI O.S.K., 2. SEALAND, 3. AMERICAN PRESIDENT 4. KASE SHIPPING ENTERPRISE LTD.

BENEFICIARY'S CERTIFICATE ADDRESED TO ISSUING BK CONFIRMING THEIR ACCEPTANCE AND/OR NON-ACCEPTANCE OF ALL AMENDMENTS MADE UNDER THIS LC QUOTING THE RELEVANT AMENDMENT NO.,

IF THIS LC IS NOT AMENDED SUCH STATEMENT IS NOT REQUIRED.

ALL DOCUMENTS CALLED FOR UNDER THIS CERDIT, EXCEPT THOSE WHICH THE CREDIT SPECIFICALLY STATES CAN BE "COPIES", MUST BE CLEARLY MARKED ON THEIR FACE AS "ORIGINAL".

A DISCREPANCY HANDLING FEE OF

CAD45.00

IS PAYABLE BY THE BENEFICIARY ON EACH DRAWING PRESENTED WHICH DOES NOT STRICTLY COMPLY WITH THE TERMS AND CONDITIONS OF THIS VREDIT AND HAS TO BE REFERRED TO THE APPLICANT.

TRAILER

MAC:233E646C CHK: 50198DC6F8D2

NNNN【24】

Notes:

【1】银行代码

【2】开证行

【3】条款代码

【4】表示共有两页，此为第一页

【5】信用证是否可以撤销，此证是不可撤销信用证

【6】信用证号码

【7】开证日期

【8】到期日与到期地点

【9】开证申请人

【10】受益人

【11】信用证金额

【12】是否自由议付，此证可自由议付

【13】汇票是远期还是即期，这里是即期

【14】受票人是谁

【15】是否允许分批装运和转船

【16】装运期

【17】所需单据包括哪些

【18】交单日期

【19】信用证是否要保兑，改证不需保兑

【20】表示信用证第一页结束

【21】表示共有几页，此为第二页

【22】货物描述

【23】特殊条款

【24】表示信用证结束

Section 3 Supplements 知识补充

Useful Sentences On Establishment of L/C and Amendment

1. We will open the L/C upon receipt of your reply.
待收到你方答复后立即开立信用证。

2. The goods under S/C No.3697 has been ready for quite some time. Please have the Letter of Credit opened with the least possible delay.
第 3697 号合同项下货物早已备妥，请赶快开立信用证。

3. In spite of our repeated requests, still we have not received your letter of credit up to now. Please open the credit by cable immediately, otherwise, we cannot effect shipment in January.
尽管再三催请开证，信用证仍未收到，请立即电开，否则不能 1 月交货。

4. If your L/C fails to reach us by the end of July, we will be forced to cancel your order.
如果信用证不能在 7 月底前开到我处，将被迫撤销订货。

5. The time limit for opening the Letter of Credit against Contract No.44078B is drawing near.
44078B 合同项下货物开证期正在到来。

6. Please open the Letter of Credit promptly at the contract price, or we cannot apply for export license.
请按合同价格迅速开证，否则不能申请出口许可证。

7. Today we have opened an irrevocable Letter of Credit in the amount of US$35000 covering our order No.9876 with the Bank of China, Changchun.
9876 号订单项下货物，今天已通过长春的中国银行开立了不可撤销的信用证，金额为 35000 美元。

8. We request you to have L/C No.H2284 amended as follow:

(1) Extend the time of shipment till 31 May.

(2) Extend the validity of the L/C till 15 June.

Await your amendment advice.

请对 H2284 号信用证做下列修改：

（1）将交货期展至 5 月 31 日。

（2）将有效期展至 6 月 15 日。

等候修改通知书。

9. Your L/C No.5466 calls for shipment in two equal monthly lots while S/C No.1101 stipulates shipment in a single lot to be made not later than 1September. Please amend accordingly.

第 5466 号信用证规定两批装运，每月一次，每次数量相等，而 1101 号合同规定 9 月 1 日前一次装运，请对信用证作相应修改。

10. Please amend L/C No.4776 as follows:

(1) Amount is to be increased by RMB ¥506.

(2) The words "12 dozen per carton" are to be replaced by "20 dozen per carton."

请对 4776 号信用证作如下修改：

（1）金额增加人民币 506 元。

（2）每箱装 12 打改为每箱装 20 打。

11. Your Letter of Credit stipulates 60 days sight, whereas our contract shows 30 days sight, So you are requested to make necessary amendment to the L/C and advise us by telex before 3 December.

你方信用证规定 60 天期汇票，而合同规定 30 天期汇票。请对信用证作必要修改，并于 12 月 3 日前电告我公司。

12. Please amend by telex L/C No.137/24/85 as allowing transshipment and partial shipments.

请电传修改 137/24/85 号信用证，允许转船和分批装运。

13. We request you to see to it that L/C is opened by cable whenever order is placed with us.

请注意做到你方无论什么时候向我们订货，就得开信用证。

14. Because of the recent fire in the factory, all the stocks were destroyed. In this case, we cannot make shipment as arranged before. Please extend the date of shipment and the expiry date of L/C No.44779 to 30 April and 15 May respectively.

由于最近工厂发生火灾烧毁了全部库存，已不能按照原安排交货。请将装运日期和 44779 号信用证有效期分别展至 4 月 30 日及 5 月 15 日。

15. Please delete from the L/C the clause, "All bank commissions and charges are for beneficiary's account". Such should be paid by the importing party only.

请从信用证中删去此条款，“所有银行佣金和费用由受益人支付”，因这些费用理应由进口方承担。

16. One non-negotiable set of documents should be forwarded through carrier and relative carrier receipt should be enclosed with the non-negotiable set of documents.

应向承运人提交一整套不可转让单据，相关承运人的收据应当同整套不可转让单据一起提交。

17. Beneficiary should inform the applicant the following details by fax directly after shipment within 10 days.

受益人应该在货物装船后 10 天内以传真告知开证申请人下述细节。

18. All documents must be English unless specified otherwise and must mention our L/C number and date.

除另有说明，所有单据要使用英语，而且必须提到我方信用证编号和日期。

19. Free spare parts should be shipped and a copy of the invoice should be faxed after shipment.

免费备用配件应一同装船，装船后用传真发出发票副本。

20. Shipping mark, net weight, gross weight, and country of origin should be mentioned in each box.

每箱都要注明唛头、净重、毛重和原产地国家。

21. It is stipulated clearly in the Sales Confirmation that the relevant L/C must reach us not later than the end of August. Although the reaching time of the L/C is overdue, we would like still to ship your goods in view of long-standing friend relationship between us.

在销售确认书上清楚的规定信用证应不迟于 8 月底开抵我处。虽然你方信用证到达期限已过，但鉴于我们之间的长期友好关系，我方愿意装运你方的订货。

22. Extra copy of invoice for issuing banks file is required.

另外提交一份发票作为开证行留档。

23. Should the applicant waive the discrepancy, we will release documents to the opener.

如果开证申请人接受不符点，我们就放单给开证人。

24. Beneficiary must courier one set of non-negotiable documents to the applicant.

受益人必须快递一套不可转让单据给开证人。

25. We hereby engage with drawers and/or bona fide holders that drafts be negotiated in conformity with the terms of this credit.

开证行承诺汇票出票人或善意的持票人将在单证相符情况下得到议付。

26. Provided such drafts are drawn and presented in accordance with the terms of this credit, we hereby engage with the drawee, endorsed and bonafide holders that the said drafts shall be honored on presentation.

凡根据本信用证条件开出并提示的汇票，本银行保证对受票人、背书人及善意持有人付款。

27. After we have checked the L/C carefully, we request you to make the following amendments.

1) The quantity should read: 1000M/T, 5%more or less at Seller's option

2) Partial shipment is allowed.

我们在认真审核信用证后，请你方做如下修改：

1）数量为：1000 吨，允许 5%溢短装，由卖方决定

2）允许分批装运

28. After checking this figure up with the total value in S/C No.248, we find that there is deficiency

of USD 300 in your credit. Please instruct the opening bank to make up the deficiency by cable.

在核对信用证与第 248 号销售合同的总金额后，我方发现证上金额短少 300 美元。请通知开证行用电报方式补充所缺金额。

29. Please amend the foregoing L/C to read piece length in 30 yards instead of 40 yards.

请把上述信用证条款里匹长 40 码改为 30 码。

30. Documents have to be presented within 14 days after the date of issue of the bill of lading or other shipping documents.

单据必须在提单或其他装运单据签发日后 14 天内提示。

Exercises

Ⅰ. Make Sentences.

in response to	more often than not
few and far between	call at
at maturity	owing to
on the part of	abide by
facilitate	refund

Ⅱ. Translate the following sentences into English.

1. 信用证必须由我方公司可以接受的银行加以保兑。
2. 为了避免随后修改信用证，务请注意下列事项。
3. 兹通知你方，以你方为受益人的信用证已由伦敦巴克莱银行开出。
4. 在收到信用证后的一个月内，你们至少应装运这笔订货的一半。
5. 开证行以一旦收到此信用证要求的单据并经审查认为无误时，即予以电汇偿付。
6. 信用证 2356 号请修改：（一）按合同，长吨改为吨；（二）展装运期到九月底并准许分运转船。
7. 信用证 3855 号，请来电取消“银行费用由受益人负担”的条款。
8. “和平”轮定于本月 25 日起航开往欧洲。因为你们的信用证修改书迄今未到，我们恐怕赶不及将货物装该船。
9. 由于我们的疏忽，开立信用证有错误，很抱歉。
10. 信用证 560 号修改书未到，请即电改，以便早日装运，电复。

Ⅲ. Translate the following letter into Chinese.

Re L/C 1234 issued by District Bank

We acknowledge receipt of the captioned Letter of Credit for the amount of £2500 covering your order No.215 for 8 metric tons Walnutmeat.

It appears that the amount in your L/C is insufficient as the correct total CIF value of your order comes to £2960 instead of £2500 the difference being £460.

In view of the above, please increase the amount of your L/C by £460. On receipt of your

amendment we shall arrange shipment without fail.

Ⅳ. Write a reply to the above letter with the following particulars.

1. 由于我们的粗枝大叶（oversight），开立的信用证有错误，很抱歉。
2. 今天早晨已通过我方银行用电报修改第1125号信用证。
3. 我方需货甚急，望即准备装运。
4. 倘若这批船货到达后，买主觉得满意，很可能将续订。

Ⅴ. Examine the following L/C with the following contract to see whether the stipulations in the L/C are exactly the same as those in the contract. If not, please write a letter to ask for proper amendment.

The First National City Bank

New York, USA

No. 6524/89

Date: 15 June 2009

Documentary Letter of Credit

Confirmed, Irrevocable

To: Shandong Ceroilfood

Imp. & Exp. Corp.

Qingdao, P.R. China

Advising Bank: Bank of China, Qingdao Branch

Dear Sirs,

You are authorized to draw on Messrs. Macdonald & Evans Co., for a sum not exceeding US$80,700(SAY US DOLLARS EIGHTY THOUSAND SEVEN HUNDRED ONLY) available by draft drawn in duplicate on them at 30 days after sight, accompanied by the following documents:

1. Full set of clean on board Bill of Lading made out to order and blank endorsed, marked "freight prepaid".
2. Signed commercial invoice in triplicate, including S/C No.95/3456 dated May 13, 2009.
3. Weight Memo/Packing List in duplicate, including gross and net weight of each package.
4. one original insurance policy/certificate

Packing: Packed in seaworthy wooden cases.

Shipment from Qingdao to Boston. Partial shipment and transshipment are allowed, through B/L required. Shipment to be made on or before July 10, 2009.

This credit is valid in China on or before July 10, 2009, for negotiation and all drafts drawn hereunder must be marked DRAWN UNDER THE FIRST NATIONAL CITY BANK, Credit No, 6524/89

Yours faithfully,

Sales Contract

No. 95/3456

Date: May 3, 2009

Seller: Qingdao Ceroilfood Imp. & Exp. Co

Buyer: Messrs. Macdonald & Evans Co.

Specification: A Grade, Art. No.123

Quantity: 3,000 cartons 24 can each

Unite Price； US$ 27 per carton CIF New York

Total Value: US$ 81,000(Say US Dollars Eighty-one Thousand Only)

Packing: in seaworthy reinforced cardboard box

Insurance: to be effected by the sellers for 110% of the invoice value against All Risks as per China Insurance Clauses of January 1, 2008

Shipment: to be effected in July, 2009 from Qingdao to New York, part shipment is allowed and transshipment is prohibited.

Shipping Marks: at the buyer's option.

Terms of Payment: by confirmed and irrevocable sight L/C

This contract is signed in Qingdao on this third day of May, 2009.

The seller　　　　　　　　　　The buyer

Chapter 9

Packing, Shipping Marks and Shipment

Section 1 Business Knowledge 业务知识

1. 货物的装运（Shipment）

（1）装运时间（time of shipment）

在对外贸易中，按时装运进出口货物，及时将货物从装运地运到目的地，对完成进出口任务，满足市场需要，减少货物积压和提高商品的竞争力，都具有重要意义。在当前市场竞争十分激烈的情况下，我们必须加快货运，抢运应市，以快制胜。特别是对某些鲜活商品或季节性商品的运输，更要抢时间、争速度，及时完成运输任务，以免造成经济上的损失和信誉上的不良影响。如果不能及时装卸，运输迟缓，到货慢，就会影响贸易的开展，甚至会减少销路或丢失市场。

卖方应该按照同买方约定的时间，地点和运输方式将合同规定的货物交付给买方或其代理人。装运一般是指将货物装上运输工具，它与交货是两个不同的概念。但是，在国际贸易中，由于采用 FOB/CIF/CFR 三种价格术语时，卖方只要根据合同的有关规定将货物装上船，取得提单，就算交货。提单签发日期亦即为交货日。因此装运一词常被用来代替交货概念。这种凭单交货被称为象征性交货。凭单交货时，装运期和交货期是一致的（实际交货是指货物运抵目的地，因而，装运时间与交货时间并不是一致的）。在买卖合同中，合理地规定装运期（交货期）是很重要的。装运期（交货期）可分为：定期装运、近期装运和不定期装运。

第一，定期装运即明确规定具体期限

① 限于某月或某几个月内装运

例：For shipment during October 2010

② 限于某月某日前装运

例：Shipment on or before 15 November 2009

第二，近期装运：采用某些术语表示装运期

Immediate shipment 立即装运

Prompt shipment 即期装运（各国对它的解释不尽相同。美国指合同签订后三周内装船，而英国是签约后两周内装运）

Shipment as soon as possible 尽快装运

对上述表达法，建议我们在实际业务活动中尽可能避免，因为这种表述意思含糊而又容易引起不必要的贸易纠纷。

第三，不定期装运，即规定在收到信用证后若干天装运

例：Shipment within 30 days after receipt of the L/C

（2）装卸港口（ports of loading and unloading）

除了装运期，装卸港口也是货物装运的重要条件。装卸港包括装运港和目的港。装运港（port of shipment）又称装货港，是指货物起始装运的港口；目的港（port of destination）又叫卸货港，是指合同规定的最后卸货港口。装卸港口的规定与贸易术语相关，是贸易术语不可缺少的组成部分，同时也与贸易双方承担的运输责任有关。为便利卖方安排货物运输，方便买方接货和转售货物，一般情况下装运港的规定先由卖方提出，经买方同意后再确定；目的港则由买方先提出，经卖方同意后再确定。通常装卸港口各规定一个。例如，

port of shipment: Shanghai port of destination: London

如果成交量特别大，根据业务需要可以规定两个或两个以上的港口，例如

Port of shipment: Dalian/Qingdao/Shanghai

Port of destination: London/Liverpool

有时候交易磋商过程中难以明确装卸港口，此时可采用选择港（optional port），即从某几个港口中任选一个或规定某一航区中的任一港口作为装卸港。如，CIF London/Hamburg/Rotterdam，这时买方最后的目的港要在开立信用证时明确或在载货船舶到达第一个卸货港前若干小时（通常是 48 小时）通告最终目的港。备选港口一般不超过 3 个，而且应是同一航区、同一航线上比较靠近的港口。

针对大宗货物交易中所采用的程租船运输以及某些特殊情况，还需要约定装卸时间、滞期费、速遣费、装卸费用；分批装运和转船；运输单据和装运通知等内容（详见 Section 2 中的有关样函）。

2. 货物的包装及唛头（packing and shipping mark）

包装是对外贸易中一个重要的环节，它包括运输包装（习惯称外包装或大包装）和销售包装（习惯称小包装或内包装）。它们都是为了保护商品的品质完好和数量完整而采取的措施。具体来说。运输包装不仅要起到防止货物运输途中受损的作用，同时，也应具备方便装卸、储存和防盗的功能。销售包装形式多样，用料各异，既要便于携带和使用，又要美观新颖达到促销的目的。在商品的外包装上要刷上包装标识，主要有运输标志（唛头），指示性标志和警告性标志，其中运输标志是必不可缺的。按照国际标准化组织（ISO）建议，为了简化单证，便于用打字机一次做成，运输标志不宜用几何图形。一般包括 4 行，每行不超过 7 个字母，包括数字和符号。标准唛头应包

含 4 项信息：收货人或发货人的代号名称；合同号码或信用证号码；目的港名称：货物件号、序号。

对于易损、易变质的商品，常用醒目的图形和简单的文字提醒有关人员在装卸、搬运和储存时应注意的事项。这种标志属于指示性标志。警告性标志是对一些易燃、易爆、有毒等危险品在其包装上清楚而明显地刷制的标示，以示警告。

在国际贸易中，还有一种中性包装，它是在商品包装上既不注明生产国别、地名和厂名，也不注明原有商标和牌号的包装。中性包装分无牌中性包装和定牌中性包装。其目的是为了打破进口地区所实施的关税与非关税壁垒或为了满足买方的特殊需求而采取的措施。

有关包装事项，在合同的包装条款中应作详细的规定，主要涉及包装方式、材料、费用的负担及运输标志等内容。

自从集装箱日益发展以来，上述对外包装的要求有了较大的变化，有时甚至可以完全省去外包装，但对内包装的要求则不断从结构造型、色彩向更新潮化的方向发展。目前，已有堆叠式、挂式、展开式、开窗式、易开式、喷雾式、套式、礼品式或复用式等新颖包装。

Section 2 Specimen Letters 样函

（1）

Dear Sirs,

Sales Contract No. 88A/341

We thank you for your letter dated November 10, enclosing the above sales contract in duplicate we wish to state that the packing clause[1] in the contract is not clear enough. The relative clause should read:

Packing: Seaworthy export packing, suitable for long ocean transportation[2]

In order to avoid possible future trouble, we would like you to make clear beforehand[3] our packing requirements as follows:

The shirts under the captioned contract should be packed in plastic bags[4], five dozen to one carton[5], 20 cartons on a pallet[6], 10 pallets in ECL container[7]. On the outer packing please mark our initials[8] LHCK in a triangle[9], under which the port of destination and our order number should be stenciled[10]. In addition, directive marks[11] like KEEP DRY AWAY FROM PRESSURE[12], etc. should also be indicated.

We have made a footnote[13] on the contract to that effect[14] and are returning herein one copy of the contract, duly countersigned by us. We hope you will find it in order and pay special attention to the packing.

We look forward to receiving your shipping advice and thank you in advance.

Yours sincerely,

Words, Expressions and Notes

1. packing clause 包装条款
2. long ocean transportation 长途远洋运输
3. beforehand 预先、事先

4. plastic bags 塑料袋

5. carton 纸板箱

6. pallet 托盘，是指用木材、金属或塑料制成的托板

使用时将货物堆放于托板上，用箱板纸、塑料薄膜或金属绳索加以固定，从而形成一件托盘包装。托盘装载容量为 1 ~ 1.5 吨。托盘下面有插口，供铲车装卸使用。托盘也有一次性使用和可回收周转使用两种。托盘规格分为 3 种 80′ × 100′，80′ × 120′，100′ × 120′

7. ECL container ECL 公司的集装箱

8. our initials 我方公司名称缩写

9. triangle 三角形

10. stenciled 刷上、钢印、印制上

11. directive marks 指示标志，也可以写作 indicative mark

由于某些产品自身比较精贵，稍不注意就可能破损。所以为了提示人们在装卸、运输、保管过程中引起注意，就需要用醒目、明了的简单图形和文字在外包装上进行标注。这类标志就成为指示标志。（例如小心轻放、此端向上、防止潮湿）

12. KEEP DRY AWAY FROM PRESSURE 防潮怕压

13. footnote 注释、脚注、批注

14. to that effect 按照…的意思，这里指在上一段关于包装的指示标志的规定

（2）

Dear Sirs,

We are glad to inform you that 300 cases of handsaws[1] you shipped to Sydney on 1st June have arrived in perfect condition[2]. It shows that you have made improvement in packing.

As for the hand drills[3] to be shipped to us, we would like you to have them packed in boxes of 2 dozen each, 50 boxes to a wooden case[4]. We are certain that you will give special care to the packing in order to avoid any damage in the process of transportation.

Please let us know by fax if you can meet our requirements.

With best regards.

Yours faithfully,

Words, Expressions and Notes

1. handsaws 手工锯子

2. in perfect condition 指货到时状况良好

3. hand drills 手工钻头

4. wooden case 木头箱，对外贸易中货物的常用包装造型有：

fiber board case 纤维板箱	veneer case 胶合板箱
kraft paper bag 牛皮纸袋	plywood case 胶合板箱
polyethylene bag 聚乙烯袋	jute bag 麻袋
wooden box 木箱	crate 板条箱
bales 捆包	paper bag 纸袋

barrel 鼓形桶	cask 桶（常用装酒精、饮料）
tub 木樽、桶	cylinder 圆通、钢桶
bottle 瓶	can 罐
basket 篓	carboy 大玻璃瓶、酸瓶
jar 瓮，广口瓶	demijohn 坛子
tin 听	drum 桶
keg 小桶	hogshead 大桶、大啤酒桶
straw bag 草包、草袋	gunny bag 麻袋
sack 布袋、麻袋	chest 箱子、茶箱

（3）

Dear Sirs,

We regret to inform you that of the 200 cartons of Iron Nails[1] you shipped in Dubai on February 22, thirteen cases were badly damaged, which of course is not your fault.

But we have to write to you in regard to the packing of these nails, which we feel necessary to clarify[2] so as to avoid the same damages in the future transactions.

The packing for Dubai is to be in wooden cases of 112 Ibs net, each containing 7 Ibs×16 packets[3]. For Malta, we would like you to have the goods packed in double gunny bags[4] of 50/60 kilos each. As for the British market, our buyers prefer 25 kilo cartons.

We should be grateful if you let us have your opinions about these requirements.

Yours sincerely,

Words, Expressions and Notes

1. Iron Nails 铁钉
2. clarify 澄清、说明
3. packets 小盒、小包
4. double gunny bags 双层麻袋

（4）

Dear Sirs,

We thank you very much for your letter dated July 3rd. We have immediately passed the information onto[1] our clients who are now actively working on your counter price.

Meanwhile, our clients wish to know the details of the packing of your Lotus-nuts[2], i.e.

a. How are the goods packed and packaged?

b. What measures will you take to protect the goods from dampness or rain?

c. What measures will you take to prevent the inner packing[3] from being torn apart[4]

Please provide us with any information regarding the above by return mail. We look forward to hearing from you soon.

Sincerely yours,

Words, Expressions and Notes

1. passed the information onto sb. 把信息转给某人
2. Lotus-nuts 莲子
3. inner packing 内包装
4. torn apart 被撕裂

（5）

Dear Sirs,

We noted your letter of October 27 carefully and approached our clients about the packing. After our repeated explanation[1], they say they will have no objection[2] to your packing of the garments in cartons if you guarantee that you will pay compensation in all cases they can not get indemnification[3] from the insurance company for the reason that the cartons used are not seaworthy[4].

We deem it our duty to inform you of this and consider it a tacit understanding[5] that should the insurance company refuse compensation; you would hold yourselves responsible for the losses our clients might sustain[6] on account of your using such cartons.

We think you will understand that our candid[7] statement is made for our mutual benefit as packing is a sensitive subject[8], which often leads to trade disputes[9].

We appreciate your cooperation.

Yours sincerely,

Words, Expressions and Notes

1. repeated explanation 反复解释
2. objection 反对
3. indemnification 赔偿、保障、赔偿物
4. not seaworthy 不适合海运
5. tacit understanding 默契
6. sustain 遭受
7. candid 坦诚的、坦率的
8. sensitive subject 敏感话题
9. trade disputes 贸易争端

（6）

Dear Sirs,

We are pleased to have received your L/C No.6771, covering 1,000 dozen "Tiger Head" brand Flashlights[1] under our sales confirmation No. FV0934 and inform you that shipment was made on S/S "Dongfeng" on August 4 for transshipment at Hong Kong.

Enclosed is a set of the duplicate shipping documents consisting of:

A non- negotiable copy of bill of lading[2]

A signed invoice No.998

Packing list[3]

Certificate of origin[4] No. 10001

Insurance policy[5]

Availing ourselves of this opportunity, we wish to assure you of our close cooperation.

Yours faithfully,

Words, Expressions and Notes

1. Flashlights 手电筒
2. A non-negotiable copy of bill of lading 一份提单副本
3. Packing list 装箱单
4. Certificate of origin 货物原产地证明
5. Insurance policy 保险单

（7）

Dear Sirs,

We learn from your shipping advice that the antique potteries[1] and porcelain-ware[2] we ordered on March 10 have been shipped by s.s. "Fenghua". According to the shipping schedule, it is expected to arrive in a day or two. However, after several contact with the local forwarding agent, we are surprisingly told that the sail vessel has not yet at all[3] arrived in Shanghai, let alone[4] finished loading and set sail for[5] Osaka. As the matter of fact that the goods are still lying at the dock[6] in Shanghai waiting for shipment, these copies will not do you any good. On the contrary, they will prove deceptive manner in handling this transaction.

You may recall that we have time and again[7] emphasized the vital importance of punctual shipment because these antique potteries and porcelain-ware are for display at an international exhibition[8] to be held in Tokyo on July 11. we think it absurd to dispute with you over the delay in shipment on the present occasion when time is so pressing[9]. The only remedy[10] for avoiding non-performance of the contract we signed with the exhibition administration is to send the goods by air at once and at any cost, please permit us to say that your cooperation in this regard is mandatory[11], for failure to have the antique potteries and porcelain put on display at the exhibition will not only cause us a heavy loss economically but also spoil your reputation and image as a famous porcelain manufacturer.

To be fair, we are prepared to pay for the airfreight, while you should be responsible for the other expenses such as shifting goods from the dock to the airport.

We have instructed our bank to insert in the L/C the wording: "Shipment either by sea or by air" and are looking forward to receiving your confirmation that punctual arrival of the goods at Tokyo is guaranteed, i.e. on or about July 7.

Yours faithfully,

Words, Expressions and Notes

1. antique potteries 陶瓷古玩
2. porcelain-ware 瓷器
3. at all 根本
4. let alone 更不用说
5. set sail for 向……起航、航行
6. dock 码头
7. time and again 屡次、反复
8. international exhibition 国际展览会
9. pressing 紧迫的，迫切的
10. remedy 补救、挽回
11. mandatory 强制性

（8）

Dear Sirs,

Your letter of June 20 has received our best attention. We apologize for the delay and also for the false information that the antique potteries and porcelain you ordered have been shipped by s.s. "Fenghua".

The sail vessel is tramp run[1] by a foreign forwarding agency to sail the Pacific. In the past it did serve us to our satisfaction; for instance, a few shipments of glass-ware[2] that required special care were handled in a way much better than what was expected. In light of experience, we therefore, entrusted "Fenghua" to effect the shipment. Unfortunately, it should have failed our expectation.

According to the forwarding agency, the duplicate copies of the B/L were sent by mistake as a result of confusion[3] in work. They in no way[4] implied any attention of deceiving the client. Nevertheless, we have cancelled the shipping space and firmly requested compensation for the losses we both have sustained.

Now the goods have been shifted to the airport waiting for dispatch to Tokyo tomorrow by Shanghai Airlines[5], Flight SJA-354. We believe this is the best solution of the case. All documents will be mailed by special express[6] as soon as they are ready.

Yours faithfully,

Words, Expressions and Notes

1. tramp run 不定期货轮
2. glass-ware 玻璃器具
3. confusion 混淆
4. in no way 决不
5. Shanghai Airlines 上海航空公司
6. special express 特快邮件

(9)

Dear Sirs,

Referring to our letters and telexes covering Order No.1986 for 3,000 tons of Tin Foil Sheets[1], so far we have not had definite information from you about the exact delivery time, although these goods are contracted for shipment before the end of last month. Our L/C was opened with the Bank of China[2] as early as in May, 2009.

We have been inconvenienced by the delay. Please tell us immediately of the earliest possible date of shipment. Otherwise we reserve our right to cancel the order and lodge claims[3] for our losses.

Please look up the matter[4] and give us your definite reply without further delay.

Yours sincerely,

Words, Expressions and Notes

1. Tin Foil Sheets 锡箔纸
2. open L/C with the Bank of China 由中国银行开出信用证
3. lodge claims 提出索赔
4. look up the matter 查清这件事

(10)

Dear Sirs,

It gives us much pleasure to advise you that the 500 dozen Shirts under Order. HAC-86 packed in cartons[1] were shipped on board s.s "Fengqing" on the 25th July to be transshipped at Antwerp. We shall appreciate it if you will inform us of the condition of packing as soon as the consignment arrives at your end.

In regard to packing the goods in question in cartons, we wish to give you our comments as follows:

1. Packing in cartons prevents skillful pilferage[2]. As the trace of pilferage will be more in evidence[3], the insurance company may be made to pay the necessary compensation[4] for such losses.

2. Cartons are quite fit for ocean transportation, and they are extensively used in our shipment to other ports to the entire satisfaction of our clients. Such packing has also been accepted by our insurance company for WPA and TPND[5].

3. These cartons are well protected against moisture[6] by plastic lining[7].

The very fact that they are made of paperboard induces[8] special attention in handling and storage. Thus shirts packed in such cartons are not so susceptible to[9] damage by moisture as those packed in wooden cases.

4. Since cartons are comparatively light and compact[10], they are more convenient to handle[11] in loading and unloading. Besides, they are not likely to be mixed with wooden cases while in transport or storage, so that the rate of breakage[12] is lower than that of wooden cases. In view of the above

reasons, it is believed that your clients will find packing in cartons satisfactory and their fears unwarranted[13].

We are awaiting your further comments.

Yours faithfully,

Words, Expressions and Notes

1. carton 包装用的纸板箱

2. skillful pilferage 惯盗

3. be more in evidence 更显著，更加显眼

4. compensation 补偿、赔偿，如 compensation trade 补偿性贸易

5. WPA and TPND 水渍险与偷窃及提货不着险；WPA= With Particular Average，TPND = Theft，Pilferage and Non-Delivery

6. moisture 潮湿、湿气，也可以指含水量，例如：

The wheat you shipped per s.s. "Star" contains too much moisture.

你方由“明星”号货轮运来的小麦含水量太高。

7. plastic lining 指包装箱内的塑料衬里

8. induces 促使，诱导，导致，诱发

例句：

Please try to induce buyers to accept the price.

请努力促使买方接受这一价格。

Your price has failed to induce our interest.

你方价格未能引起我们的兴趣。

9. be susceptible to 易受影响的，敏感的

susceptible 与 liable，subject，prone 几个词的含义相近，但在用法方面有一定区别。

susceptible 强调由于人或事物的本质、特性、素质或性格而失去抵抗力或遭受某种痛苦。

liable 指人们遇到或可能遇到的事情是由于服从权势或因其生活状况，屈从于某种无法控制的力量而引起的后果。

subject 指由于某种原因诸如社会、政治或经济地位、性情特点而趋向于必然遭受、忍受或经历某些事情。

prone 很少指物，通常指人在不同程度上受到某事物倾向性制约。

例句：

One is more prone to make mistakes when he/she is tired.

当人们疲劳的时候做事就比较容易出毛病。

Perished goods are subject to damage in transit.

易腐烂的货物在运输途中容易损坏。

The goods you packed in wooden cases are susceptible to damage by moisture.

装在木箱中的这批货容易被潮气损坏。

Prospective buyers are liable to judge the quality of goods by appearance.

潜在买主容易从外观判断货物质量。

10. compact 结实的，紧凑的

11. handle 这里是指理货

12. rate of breakage 破损率

13. unwarranted 没根据的，未经授权的，无保证的

（11）

Dear Sirs,

We returned for your file the counter-signed copy of contract No. DG-5081 on September 15th.

Please mark[1] the bales with our initials SCC in a diamond[2], under which comes the destination Bremen with order number 4424 below again.

This is to apply all orders unless otherwise specified[3].

Yours faithfully,

Words, Expressions and Notes

1. mark 此处是指在包裹外刷制唛头

2. diamond 此处指菱形，经常用作唛头上的几何图形。有关唛头的常用语有：

triangle 三角形；circle 圆形；rectangle 长方形；hexagon 正六角形

cross 十字形；downward triangle 倒三角形；star 星形；square 正方形

heart 心形；oval 椭圆形；three diamond 三菱形

This side（end）up 此面向上

Handle with care 小心轻放

With care 小心搬运

No hook（use no hook）请勿用钩

Keep cool（keep in cool place）放置冷处；保持冷藏

Keep dry 保持干燥

Keep/store away from boiler 远离锅炉

Inflammable 易燃货物

Fragile 当心破碎

Fusible 易熔物

Explosive 易爆炸货物

Glass with care 小心玻璃

Poison 小心有毒

Open here 从此处开启

Sling here 此处吊索

To be kept upright 竖立安放

Keep away from heat 隔离热气

Perishable 易坏货物

Guard against damp（wet）勿使受潮

No smoking 严禁烟火

Keep flat（stow level）注意平放

Not to be thrown down 不可抛弃

3. unless otherwise specified 如果没有其他规定

（12）

Dear Sirs,

Your shipment of 1000 c/s Tinned Goods[1] ex[2] s.s "Changchun" under Contract No. JB-558 has arrived at our end safely and in good condition[3].

The goods are found to be of excellent quality, while the packing is only middling[4], having a certain leeway[5] to make up[6]. You will understand that with many brands of the same commodity competing for sale here, merchandise is forced not only to give value but to be seen to give value[7].

Yours faithfully,

Words, Expressions and Notes

1. 1000 c/s Tinned Goods 1000 箱罐头食品

2. ex 从…，在…

货物由某货轮运来多用 ex；货物由某货轮运走多用 per。

例句：

The price is £200 per ton ex warehouse London.

在伦敦仓库外交货每吨价格是 200 英镑。

The goods ex s.s. "Changchun" have been reinspected.

由"长春"号货轮运来的货物已经过复验。

3. in good condition 指货物到达时状态良好。类似的说法还有：

in sound/perfect condition 状况良好

in a damaged condition 损坏状态

in a mouldy condition 受潮、发霉状态

4. middling 一般般，这里是指包装很平常

5. leeway 差距、余地，例如：

When opening letter of credit, please allow 3% leeway in quantity and amount.

开信用证时，请允许在数量和金额上有 3%上下的增减余地。

6. make up 这里是指弥补、补足，此外还有化妆、整理、配制、构成的意思

7. not only to give value but to be seen to give value 不仅要有价值，而且看上去也应物有所值。此处的含义是说商品不但要质量好，而且外表（指包装）要美观考究

（13）

Shipping Instructions

Dear Sirs,

Re: your Sales Confirmation No. C215 Covering 4000 Dozen Shirts

We have for acknowledgement your letter dated 19th August in connection with[1] the above subject.

In reply, we have the pleasure of informing you that the confirmed, irrevocable Letter of Credit No. 7634, amounting to[2] £3500 has been opened this morning with the District Bank, Ltd. Manchester. Upon receipt of the same[3], please arrange shipment of the goods booked by us without the least delay[4]. We are informed by the local shipping company that s/s "Browick" is due to sail[5] from your city to our port on or about the 10th September and, if possible, please try your best to ship by that steamer.

Should[6] this trial order prove satisfactory to our customers, we can assure you that repeat orders[7] in increased quantity will be placed.

Your close co-operation in this respect will be highly appreciated. In the meantime we await your shipping advice[8] by cable.

Yours faithfully,

Words, Expressions and Notes

1. in connection with 关于、涉及
2. amounting to 合计为，相当于、等于

例句：

Your reply amounts to refusing our request.

你的答复等于拒绝我们的请求。

The weight amounts to 88,000 lbs.

重量合计为 88000 磅。

3. the same 一样、同样，这里指信用证
4. without the least delay 尽量不要延误、延迟
5. due to sail 将在某时起航、开航
6. should 此处的 should 表示一种带有条件从句的虚拟语气倒装句，例如：

Should the buyers be unable to cover insurance in due time owing to the sellers' failure to advise the buyers of the foregoing details by fax, the losses thus sustained shall be borne by the sellers.

由于卖方没能用传真通知买方上述细节导致买方没有及时投保，由此造成的损失应由卖方负责。

7. repeat orders 续订的订单
8. shipping advice 装运通知

注意，装运通知（shipping advice）是卖方完成装货后，发给买方的通知，以方便买方及时办理保险或预先掌握货物到达时间、提前做好进口报关及提货的准备。装运须知（shipping instruction）是货物发运前，买方发给卖方关于货物的装运指示或装运须知，指示卖方应如何装货、发货。

（14）

Gentlemen:

Re: Transshipment of Cotton Piece Goods to West Africa

We acknowledge with thanks, receipt of your letter of the 2nd February. In reply, we have pleasure in providing the following information for your reference:

1. There are 2 to 3 sailings[1] weekly from Shanghai to Hong Kong.

2. Arrangements have been made with the ××× Line, which has one sailing approximately on the 10th every month, from Hong Kong to West Africa ports, such as Lagos, Accra, etc. Shipping space[2] is to be booked through their Shanghai Agents, which communicate with the Line by telegraph. After receipt of the Line's cable reply accepting the booking, their Shanghai Agents will issue a Through Bill of Lading[3]. Therefore, with the exceptions of unusual condition which may happen accidentally[4], the goods will be transshipped from Hong Kong without delay.

3. In general, the freight for transshipment from Hong Kong is higher than that from the UK or Continental port[5], but ××× Line now agree to the same freight, the detailed rates of which are shown on the appendices[6] to this letter. If you wish to have our goods transshipped at Hong Kong, your L/C must reach us well before the shipment month so as to enable us to book space with the Line.

Assuring you of our best attention at all times, we remain.

Yours very truly,

Words, Expressions and Notes

1. sailings 这里指轮船的航班，sail 表示船，航行，航程；作动词指启航，驾驶（船），导航

例句：

The captain safely sailed his ship through the narrow passage.

船长安全地把船驶过了狭窄的航道。

We have our own liner vessels sailing regularly between China and other countries or areas.

我国也有各种班轮，定期航行于中国和其他国家或地区之间。

How many days sail is from Dalian to Hong Kong.

从大连去香港有多少天航程？

He set sail for Shanghai yesterday.

他昨天坐船启程去上海了。

There are no more sailings this month.

本月不再有船了。

If possible, please send us a list of sailings from your port for the next two months.

若可能，请将下两个月从你方港口离港船只的船期表寄给我们。

2. Shipping space 船舶的舱位、船舱

space 作动词（space out）指把…分隔开

例句：

Please telegraph name and approximate sailing date of vessel on which space is booked.

请电告所订舱位的船名与约计启航时间。

If partial shipment is allowed, we will space out consignments over two months.

如果允许分批装运，我方将在两个月内分期装运货物。

3. Through Bill of Lading 联运提单，这种提单适用海陆、海空、海河、海海等联运货物，由第一承运人收取全程运费后并负责代办下程运输手续在装运港签发的全程提单

卖方可凭联运提单在当地银行结汇。各类提单的说法有：

ante-dated B/L 倒签提单

advanced B/L 预借提单

Charter Party B/L 包租船提单

Clean on board B/L 清洁已装船提单

direct B/L 直达提单

foul/unclean/dirty B/L 不清洁提单，有批注的提单

local B/L 近洋提单

ocean B/L 远洋提单

order B/L 指示抬头提单，凭指定提单

received for shipment B/L 备运提单

short form B/L 简式提单

stale B/L 逾期提单

surrendered B/L 电放提单

non-negotiable copy of B/L 提单副本

4. accidentally 偶然的，意外的

5. Continental port 大陆港口

6. appendices 附录、附件，同 appendixes

（15）

Dear Sirs,

We wish to invite your attention to our Order No.5781 covering 500 pieces Blue Woolen Serge, for which we sent to you about 30 days ago an irrevocable L/C expiration[1] date 31st march.

As the season is rapidly approaching, our buyers are badly in need[2] of the goods. We shall be very much obliged if you will effect shipment as soon as possible, thus enabling them to catch the brisk demands[3] at the start of the season.

We would like to emphasize that any delay in shipping our booked order will undoubtedly[4] involve us in no small difficulty.

We thank you in advance for your cooperation.

Yours faithfully,

Words, Expressions and Notes

1. expiration 满期、届期、截止
2. badly in need 非常需要的
3. brisk demands 旺盛的需求
4. undoubtedly 毋庸置疑的，的确

（16）

Dear Sirs,

Thank you for your enquiry of 18th December. The shipping containers[1] we provide are of two sizes, namely 19ft. and 20ft[2]. long and built to take loads up to two and four tons respectively. They

can be opened at both ends[3], thus making it possible to load and unload[4] at the same time. For carrying goods liable to[5] be spoiled[6] by damp or water they have the great advantage of being both watertight and airtight[7]. Containers can be loaded and unloaded at the factory, if necessary. Pilfering is therefore impossible.

There is also a saving[8] in freight charges when separate consignments intended for the same port of destination are carried in one container and an additional saving on insurance because of the lower premiums charges for container-ship goods.

We enclose a copy of our tariff[9] and look forward to receiving your instructions.

Yours faithfully,

Words, Expressions and Notes

1. shipping containers 航运集装箱
2. 19ft. and 20ft. ：19 英尺与 20 英尺
3. at both ends 在集装箱的两端
4. load and unload 装货与卸货

unload 还有抛售、卖掉货物的意思。

例句：

Dealers are trying to unload their holdings.

商人正试图抛售存货。

The ship is unloading.

轮船正在卸货。

5. liable to 易于……的，有……倾向的；liable 还可以表示应负责的，须交纳、接受的

例句：

The insurance company is liable for the indemnity of losses.

保险公司应负责赔偿损失。

Such commodities are liable to customs duties.

这类商品要交纳关税。

We are liable to encounter difficulties in arranging the quantity required.

对于安排所需要数量的商品，我们免不了要遇到困难。

Mr. John is liable to visit Shenyang after attending the Guangzhou Fair.

约翰先生参加广交会后可能来沈阳。

6. spoiled 指货物被损坏

用于人，表示被宠坏、惯坏。

7. watertight and airtight 防水并且密封、不透气的
8. saving 节省、节俭
9. tariff 这里指运费表

（17）

Dear Sirs,

We confirm having received your letter of October 5, for which we thank you.

With respect to the 50000 M/Ts[1] wheat, 5 percent more or less[2] at buyer's option, we would like to say that the loading rate[3] is 5000 M/Ts per weather working day of 24 consecutive hours[4], Sundays and holidays at port of loading included. In case it exceeds this figure, the time will count pro rata[5]. We have to point out that you must submit your final confirmation for laydays[6] to us so that proper arrangements for loading can be made by us as we have other loading commitments[7].

We also agree demurrage and dispatch money[8] shall be settled direct between the sellers and ship-owners and insist that you should advise us of the estimated time of arrival[9] 15 days prior to the arrival of the carrying vessel at the port of loading for firm stem[10]. Please confirm and reply.

Yours faithfully,

Words, Expressions and Notes

1. M/Ts 吨，即 metric tons

2. more or less 溢短装

3. loading rate 装货率

4. per weather working day of 24 consecutive hours 每个连续 24 小时好天气工作日，这是装卸时间的一种计算方法，是指在好天气（能作业）情况下，连续作业 24 小时算为一个装卸工作日，中间因坏天气影响不能装卸的时间要扣除。这种方法适用于昼夜作业的港口，使用较普遍。但是关于星期天、节假日的处理，各国港口规定不一样，主要有 3 种情况；一是“Sundays and holidays excepted”，即明确扣除，不计算装卸时间；二是“Not to count unless used”，不用不算，用了要算；三是“Not to count even used”，不用不算，用了也不算。此外还有其他的计算方法，如：

weather working days of 24 hours，累计 24 小时好天气工作日。其含义是按正常工作日计算，星期天、节假日以及天气恶劣不能装卸作业的时间要扣除。如果港口规定每天作业 8 小时，则一个装卸工作日便跨越几天的时间，这对租船人有利，对船方不利。

running/consecutive days/hours，连续日/小时指 24 小时为一个连续日，连雨天、码头施工时间、不可抗力、星期日、节假日都计为装卸时间，中间没有任何折扣，这对租船人很不利。

5. count pro rata 按比例计算

6. laydays 受载期、装卸时间

lay days 是指允许完成装卸任务的约定时间，常用的规定方法有三种。一是规定装卸货物的定额标准，也即装卸率，每船或每个舱口一个工作日装卸货物的吨数；二是规定固定的装卸天数，不约定每天的装卸率；三是按港口习惯快速装卸 CQD customary quick dispatch ，这是一种笼统规定。

7. loading commitments 此处指装货任务

8. demurrage and dispatch money 滞期费和速遣费。在约定的装卸时间里，若未完成装卸任务，延长了船舶在港停靠时间，就会发生滞期费（demurrage）。一方面，船方要向租船方收取这笔费用，所以滞期费实际就是租船人向船方交纳的罚款；另一方面，租船方在规定时间里提前完成装卸，这会给船方节省船期，从而减少了船舶在港口的费用开支。这时船方应向租船人给付一定的报酬。此项报酬就称为速遣费（dispatch）。依照惯例，速遣费一般是滞期费的一半。滞期费和速遣费常常约定为每天若干金额，不足一天按比例计算。

9. estimated time of arrival 预计到达时间

10. firm stem 是指货方同港务当局联系谈妥迅速装船的事项

Section 3 Supplements 知识补充

Useful Sentences On Packing, Shipping Marks and Shipment

1. The wheat is to be packed in new gunny bags of 100 kgs. and each bag weighs about 1.5kgs.
小麦用新麻袋包装，每袋装 100 千克，每袋重 1.5 千克。

2. Please ship the above order in foam-lined boxes.
上述货物使用内部衬有泡沫塑料的木箱装运。

3. The full details regarding packing and marking must be strictly observed.
有关包装和唛头的详细规定，都要严格执行。

4. The goods are to be marked with our initials in a diamond.
请在货物上刷上菱形，内刷我公司名称缩写。

5. The packing and marking shall be at seller's option.
包装和唛头由卖方决定。

6. Please expedite shipment as soon as possible.
请抓紧时间尽快交货。

7. Please inform us of the approximate date of shipment for contract No.DD23546.
请尽快通知我们 DD23546 号合同项下货物大约交货日期。

8. You must have the goods shipped before August, otherwise, we can not catch the season.
必须在 8 月前交货，否则赶不上季节。

9. Must to our regret, we cannot ship the goods within the time limit of the L/C owing to the unforeseen difficulties on the part of mill.
由于厂方预料不到的困难，在信用证规定的期限内装运货物已不可能，甚歉。

10. Please advise us 30 days before the month of shipment of the contract number, name of commodity, quantity, port of loading and the time when the goods reach the port of loading.
请在交货月份前 30 天将合同号、货名、数量、装运港以及货物到达装运港的时间通知我们。

11. As to destination, we regret to advise the Oslo is unacceptable as direct sailings from our port to that city are few and far between.
关于目的港，很抱歉，奥斯陆不能接受，因为从此地开往那里的航班十分稀少。

12. We have booked freight on s.s. STARS for Order No.97.
97 号订单项下货物，已在“群星”轮上订好舱位。

13. We wish to advise you that your Order No.7779 has been shipped today.
兹通知你方 7779 号订单项下货物今天已装运。

14. The goods under S/C No.25580 went forward on S/S "Yantai" on May 25.
25580 号销售合同项下货物已于 5 月 25 日由“烟台”轮运出。

15. The duplicate shipping documents including bill of lading, invoice, packing list and inspection

certificate were airmailed to you today.

包括提单、发票、装箱单和检验证书在内的装运单证副本今日航寄你处。

16. Could you possibly advance shipment further more?

你方能不能再提前一点交货。

17. Shipment should be made before October, otherwise we are not able to catch the season.

十月底前必须交货，否则我方就赶不上销售季节了。

18. The goods ordered are all in stock and we assure you that the first steamer will make the shipment available in November.

贵公司订购的货物我们均有现货，可保证在十一月份将货物装上第一条便船。

19. Please be informed that the shipment of the cargo was sent yesterday, airway bill No.143.

特此通知这批货物昨天已装运，航空货物的领取号码是 143 号.

20. We ship most of our oil in bulk.

我们装运的油多数是散装的。

21. We can get preferential duty rates when we ship to the U.S.A.

我们能在货物装运到美国时获得优惠税率。

22. Please hold shipment pending our instructions.

请在我们发出通知之前暂停装货。

23. Sometimes, we have to make transshipment because there is no suitable loading port in the producing country or area.

有时因为在生产国或生产地区找不到合适的装货港，我们不得不转船。

24. So far as I know, there are risks of pilferage or damage to the goods during transshipment in Hong Kong.

据我所知，在香港转船期间有货物被盗或损坏的风险。

25. For such a big order, we propose to have the goods dispatched by sea.

数量如此多的货物，我们建议走海运。

26. If the cargo space must be reserved, please send us the necessary application forms.

假如要预订货舱，请将必要的申请表寄给我们。

27. Sometimes, the way of combined transportation has the complicated formalities.

有时联运的手续十分烦琐。

28. Insurance covers both sea and overland transportation.

保险应包括水陆两段的运输。

29. This is one set of the shipping documents covering the consignment.

这是本批货的一套装运单据。

30. When the goods have been loaded, you can get the B/L signed by the master of the vessel.

货装上船后，你可以得到由船长签字的提单。

31. We'll send you two sets of the shipped, clean Bill of Lading.

我们将寄送你方两套已装船清洁提单。

32. The fountain pen is placed in a satin-covered small box, lined with beautiful silk ribbon.
钢笔装在一个锦缎小盒里，外面再系上漂亮的绸带。

33. Shorts are to be packed in plastic-lined water-proof cartons.
短裤应放在内衬塑料并能防水的箱子里。

34. You must reinforce the packing with metal straps.
你们必须用铁箍加固包装。

35. The canned goods are to be packed in cartons with double straps.
罐装货物放在纸箱里，外面加两道箍。

36. Each case is lined with foam plastics in order to protect the goods against press.
每个箱子里垫有泡沫塑料以免货物受压。

37. The eggs are packed in cartons with beehives lined with shake-proof paper board.
鸡蛋要用带蜂房孔，内衬防震纸板的纸板包装。

38. We have especially reinforced our packing in order to minimize the extent of any possible damage to the goods.
我们已经特意加固包装，以使货物遭到的可能损坏减小到最低程度。

39. The packing must be strong enough to withstand rough handling.
包装必须十分坚固，以承受粗鲁的搬运。

40. Our packing will be on a par with that of the Japanese.
我们的包装可以与日本同行相媲美。

41. I think you'll find the packing beautiful and quite well-done.
你们会发现我方产品的包装美观讲究。

42. We have no objection to the stipulations about the packing and shipping mark.
我们同意关于包装和运输唛头的规定。

43. The packing of the machines must be well protected against dampness, moisture, rust and shock.
机器包装必须防湿、防潮、防锈、防震。

44. We use metal angles at each corner of the carton.
每个箱角我们都用金属角加固。

45. Each pill is put into a small box sealed with wax.
每个药丸装入小盒后用蜡封好。

46. These marten overcoats are tastefully packed.
这批貂皮大衣的包装十分精美。

47. The packings are in good order.
包装完好无损。

48. The crux of packing lies in protecting the goods from moisture.
包装的关键是防潮。

49. A packing that catches the eye will help us push the sales.

醒目的包装有助于我们推销产品。

50. Packing has a close bearing on sales.
包装直接关系到产品的销售。

51. The next thing I'd like to bring up for discussion is packing.
下面我想提出包装问题讨论一下。

Terms Used in Shipping

Airway Bill of Lading	空运提单
Ballast	压舱货
Berthage	泊位费
bulk cargo	散装货
cargo plan(stowage plan)	积载图
dangerous cargo	危险货
general cargo	杂货
light cargo	轻泡货
live cargo	鲜货
reefer cargo	冷冻货
return cargo	回运货
through cargo	直达货、联运货
transit cargo	过境货、转载货
charges	费用
shifting charges	移泊费
pilotage	引水费
lighterage	驳船费
surcharges	附加费
tally charges	理货费
waiting charges	待时费
towage	拖船费
trimming charges	平舱费
stevedorage	船内装卸费
dead freight	空船费
dockage(wharfage)	码头费
out of packet expenses	零星杂费
partial shipment	分批装运
loading capacity	装运量
notice of readiness	备装通知
dunnage	衬木

EMP（European main ports）	欧洲主要港口
ETA（estimated time of arrival）	预抵期
FIO（free in and out）	船方不负责装卸费
FI（Free in）	船方管卸不管装
FO（Free out）	船方管装不管卸
Berth terms	船方管装管卸
Liner terms	船方管装管卸
Gross Terms	船方管装管卸
forwarding instructions	装运说明
freighter	货船
general cargo vessel	杂货船
ice-free port	不冻港
indemnity	罚金
itinerary map	航线图
laydays	停泊期
lighter	驳船
tanker	油轮
LASH（Lighter Aboard Ship）	载驳船，字母船
passenger ship	客船
pilot	领航员
seamen's club	海员俱乐部
seasonal port	季节港口
tug	拖船
tonnage dues	吨税

Exercise

Ⅰ. Make sentences with the following words and expressions.

in question	make compensation for
tinned goods	per
in good condition	amount to
shipping company	shipping advice
shipping instructions	freight space
expiry date	obliged to
unloading port	be liable to
be liable for	loading rate
despatch money	demurrage
estimated time of arrival	shipping mark

Ⅱ. Complete the following sentences.

1. Please send us your shipping instructions, ____________.

a. 以便我们备货装船

b. 以便我们立即进行刷唛头

c. 以便我们租订舱位

d. 以便我们办理海关手续

2. According to the contract stipulations,____________.

a. 唛头由买方选定

b. 买方必须在 9 月内完成货物的装运工作

3. We would rather…than…or We prefer…____________.

a. 装直达轮，而不在新加坡转船

b. 货物用木箱包装，箱净重 100 千克，不用双层麻袋包装

c. 采用付款交单方式，而不采用 60 天期汇票支付

4. It is expressly stately that____________________.

a. 货物必须于 10 月底以前装船

b. 500 吨花生应于 9 月装运，其余 500 吨于 10 月装运

c. 1000 吨花生必须一次装船

Ⅲ. Translate the following sentences into English.

1. 我们建议今后将该货改为小包装，如半磅或一磅，以便销售。
2. 这批货物我方建议该用中性包装，请告知可否接受。
3. 为了适应远洋运输，这种货物的包装必须改进。
4. 经过核对库存，我们能设法满足要求将交货期提前到 7 月。
5. 谢谢你方大力合作给我们提前装运 10 台机械。
6. 我们接到当地轮船公司通知。“长风”轮定于本月 5 日左右开往马赛。
7. 要不是你们要求我方在 6 月底装船，我们早就会同你公司成交 5000 吨花生。
8. 使用小箱子轻且牢固，便于商品的储存和销售。
9. 请按提供的图样在箱子上刷唛。
10. 请在装船前 10 天将船名、预计受载量、装船量、合同号和运输代理人通知我们。
11. 买方坚持 8 日交货。
12. 货物每打装 1 纸箱，每 10 纸箱装 1 木箱，箱厚半英寸。
13. 在装船时，请按发票金额开具汇票向我们收款。
14. 请确保按期交货。
15. 谨告知你方须负由于迟装或包装不当而产生的任何损失。
16. 我们要求一下班可订到舱位的轮船装运。
17. 请你方注意，除非在 7 月 11 日前交货，否则撤销订单。
18. 为了顺利过关，请严格按照买方装船须知行事。

19．货物急需，请速发运。

20．请告知订单备妥待装估计所需时间。

Ⅳ.

1. Write to a firm of shipping agents asking them to arrange for consignment to be collected from your factory and make all arrangements for transportation on Dares Slamm. Include imaginary particulars as to nature of consignment, names and addresses of consignors and consignee, and point out who will take delivery of the consignment upon arrival.

2. As secretary of Harding &Co. of Hull, write to Scandinavian Liners Ltd. for details of their sailings to Norway and Sweden and for quotations of their rates for manufactured woolen goods.

Chapter 10

Insurance

Section 1 Business Knowledge 业务知识

在国际贸易中，货物从卖方到达买方，通常要经过长途的运输、装卸和存储等过程。在此过程中，货物常常会遇到许多风险。例如，船舶可能沉没，货物可能在运输途中受损等。为了保障货物遭受损失时能得到一定的补偿，买方或卖方应在货物装船后向保险公司投保货物运输险。

对外贸易的运输保险是指：被保险人（出口人或进口人）对一批或若干批货物向保险人按一定金额投保一定的险别，并交纳保险费；保险人承保后，如果所保货物在运输途中发生约定范围内的损失，应按照它所出具的保险单的规定给予被保险人经济上的补偿。

投保时，通常选择平安险，水渍险或一切险 3 种基本险别的一种。然而，加保其他特殊附加险别在某些情况下也是必要的。

1. 承保责任范围

承保责任范围是指保险公司提供的保险险别，也是承保人责任义务大小及被保险人缴付保费金额的依据。海运货物保险险别分基本险与附加险两大类。

（1）基本险（basic insurance coverage）

基本险也叫主险，是可以独立承保的险别。海洋货运保险的基本险包括 3 种，即平安险、水渍险和一切险。

① 平安险（free from particular average，FPA）

平安险原义为“单独海损不赔偿”，平安险一词是我国保险业的习惯叫法，沿用已久，其承保责任范围包括以下几方面。

a. 被保险货物在运输途中由于恶劣气候、雷电、海啸、地震、洪水等自然灾害造成整批货物的全部损失和推定全损。

b．由于运输工具遭受搁浅、触礁、沉没、互撞、与流冰/其他物体碰撞以及失火、爆炸等意外事故造成的货物全部损失或部分损失。

c．在运输工具已发生搁浅、触礁、沉没、焚毁意外事故情况下，货物在此前后又在海上遭受恶劣气候、雷电、海啸等自然灾害造成的部分损失。

d．在装卸或转运时由于部分或整件货物落海所造成的全部或部分损失。

e. 由于上述事故引起的共同海损的牺牲、分摊和救助费用，以及为抢救遭受危险货物和防止、减少货损而支付的合理费用。

f．运输契约订有“船舶互撞责任”条款，根据该条款规定应由货方偿还船方的损失。

② 水渍险（with particular average，WPA）

水渍险原义是“负责单独海损责任”，这也是我国保险业的习惯称呼。它的承保责任除包括上述平安险各项责任外，还负责被保险货物由于恶劣气候、雷电、海啸、地震、洪水等自然灾害引起的部分损失。

③ 一切险（all risks）

一切险的承保责任除包括平安险和水渍险的责任外，还包括被保险货物在运输途中，由于一般外来原因所导致的全部损失或部分损失。实际上，一切险是平安险、水渍险与一般附加险的总和。

（2）附加险（additional risks）

附加险是指不能单独承保的险别。它必须依附于某项基本险项下，即只有投保一项基本险才能增保附加险，而且并须另外支付一定的保险费。附加险包括 3 种：一般附加险；特别附加险；特殊附加险（详见本章 Terms Used in Insurance）

（3）除外责任（exclusion）

除外责任是由保险公司明确规定不予承保的损失和费用。除外责任中所列的各项致损原因一般都是非意外的、偶然的或比较特殊的风险，由保险公司明确作为一种免责规定。它可以起到防止骗保，划清保险人、被保险人和发货人各自应负责任的作用。除外责任通常规定有：被保险人的故意行为或过失；发货人的责任；保险责任开始前货物已经存在品质不良和数量短缺；保险货物的自然损耗、本质缺陷、货物的市价下跌；运输延迟造成的损失和引发的费用。还有对战争险、罢工险等承保的责任往往在一般货物运输保险里也可作为除外责任。

2. 承保责任起讫期限

平安险、水渍险和一切险的承保责任起讫期限是采用国际保险业务常用的“仓至仓条款（warehouse to warehouse W/W）”。它规定保险责任自被保险货物运离保险单所载明的起运地发货人仓库开始生效（仓库内货损不算），保险责任包括正常运输过程中的海上运输和陆上运输，直到该项货物到达保险单载明的目的地收货人仓库为止（入库后损失不算）。这里的“运离”是指货物一经离开发货人仓库，保险责任即为开始；“到达”一词是指货物一经进入收货人最后仓库，保险责任即告终止，在仓库内发生的损失保险人概不负责。但是货物从海轮卸下后没有运到收货人仓库，而是放在码头仓库、露天场地或海关仓库，那么保险责任继续有效，最长负责至货物卸离海轮 60 天为限。如在上述 60 天内被保险货物需要转运到非保险单所列明的目的地时，则以该项货

物发生转运时保险责任终止。另外，被保险货物在运到保险单载明的目的地或在此以前的某一仓库发生分配、分排等情况，则该仓库就作为被保险人的最后仓库，保险责任也以自货物运抵该仓库时终止。

3. 保险金额与保险费

保险金额（insurance amount）是被保险人向保险公司申报的被保货物的价额，是保险公司承担保险责任的标准；同时也是被保货物发生保险范围内损失时，保险公司赔偿的最高限额，当然还是保险公司计收保险费（premium）的基础。保险金额原则上应该是被保险货物的实际价值，但在国际贸易实践中很难准确核算出货物的真正价值，所以进出口货物运输保险金额一般以发票价值为基础，通常依据发票 CIF 货价金额（从买方进口成本看，除进口商品货物价格外，还包含运费和保险费）。以 CIF 货价作为保险金额，当货物发生损失时，被保险人已经支付的经营费用和本来可以正常获得的预期利润仍无法从保险公司得到赔偿。因此各国保险法规和国际贸易惯例都允许进出口贸易运输的保险金额在 CIF 货价基础上适当加成，一般加成 110%。另外，保险公司与被保险人也可以根据不同货物、不同地区、不同经营管理费用和预期利润水平，约定不同的加成率。但过高的加成一般不会被保险公司接受。

被保险人投保时必须向保险公司交纳一定金额的保险费（premium），双方的保险契约关系才能成立。被保险人缴纳保险费也是保险合同生效的重要条件，保险公司只有在收到保险费后才能承担相应的保险责任。计算保费的主要依据是保险费率。保险费率是保险公司根据一定时期货物的赔付情况来确定的。不同货物、不同险别、不同的目的地的保险费率是不一样的。

4. 保险合同

保险合同（insurance contract）的形式一般以保险单据来表示。保险单据属于一种法律文件，它是保险人与被保险人之间权利与义务关系的书面证明，也是保险公司的承保证明。一旦发生保险责任范围内损失，保险合同或保险单据就是被保险人要求赔偿的依据。海运货物保险合同主要有4种：保险单（insurance policy），保险凭证（insurance certificate），联合凭证（combined certificate），预约保险单（open policy）。

当然，保险公司接受投保的险别、费率及条款内容往往因客观条件的变更而有所变更或修改。因此，要针对货物的性质，运输条件和理赔范围的情况，选择必要的险别投保，这样既可节省开支，又可避免因风险而引起的损失。

Section 2 Specimen Letters 样函

(1)

Dear Sirs,

We refer to the 5,000 cases of Iron Nails under Sales Contract No.324 and are pleased to inform you that we have established with the Bank of Communication, New York Branch the confirmed, irrevocable L/C No.312 in the amount of US$7,876, valid up to[1] May 23.

Please see to it that the above mentioned goods are to be shipped before May 23 and the insurance is covered for 130% of the invoice value against All Risks[2]. As we understand that as per your customary practice[3] you only insure[4] the shipment for 10% above the invoice value, the extra premium for additional coverage shall be for our account[5].

Please arrange insurance according to our request and meanwhile we are expecting your shipping advice.

Yours faithfully,

Words, Expressions and Notes

1. valid up to…指信用证的有效期至……

2. covered for 130% of the invoice value against All Risks 按发票金额的130%投保一切险，cover 在这里是投保、办理保险的意思

3. customary practice 习惯做法、惯例

4. insure 动词，表示投保、保险。具体用法有：

insured amount 保额、保险金额

insured cargo/goods 投保的货物

the insured 被保险人

例句：

Please insure the goods against all risks and war risk.

请将此货投保一切险及战争险。

The insurance company here insures this risk with 5% franchise.

这里的保险公司承保该险种有5%的免赔率。

Please insure against breakage.

请投保破碎险。

5. for our account 由我方承担

（2）

Dear Sirs,

In answering your letter of July 15 in regard to[1] insurance, we would like to inform you of the followings:

- All Risks: Generally we cover insurance WPA[2] & WAR RISK in the absence of[3] definite instructions from our clients. If you desire to cover ALL RISKS, we can provide such coverage[4] at a slightly higher premium[5].
- Breakage: Breakage is a special risk, for which an extra premium will have to be charged. The present rate about…percent. Claims[6] are payable only for that part of the loss which is more than 5%.
- Value to be insured[7]: we note that you wish us to insure shipment to you for 10% above invoice value, which is having our due attention.

We trust the information will serve your purpose and await your further news.

Yours truly,

Words, Expressions and Notes

1. in regard to 关于
2. WPA 水渍险，全称是 with particular average
3. in the absence of 缺乏…时，当…不在时
4. coverage 此处是指保险责任、保险险别
5. premium 保费、保险费，此外还可以表示较高价格

例句：

During Christmas walnuts are selling at a premium.
圣诞节期间，核桃正按高价出售。

This kind of additional risk is covered at a premium of 2%.
此种附加险的保费是 2%。

6. claims 保险索赔
7. value to be insured 保险金额

（3）

Dear Sirs:

We wish to refer you to our order No.113 for 2,000cases Electronic Toys[1], from which you will see that this order was placed on CFR basis.

As we now desire to have the consignment[2] insured at your end, we shall be much pleased if you will kindly arrange to insure the same on our behalf[3] against All Risks at invoice value plus 10%[4], i.e. US$5,500.

We shall of course refund the premium[5] to you upon receipt of your debit note or, if you like, you may draw on us at sight for the same.

We sincerely hope that our request will meet with your approval.

Yours faithfully,

Words, Expressions and Notes

1. Electronic Toys 电子玩具
2. consignment 此处表示所发运的这批货物
3. on our behalf 代表，为……的利益
4. at invoice value plus 10% 按发票金额的 110%
5. refund the premium 付清、退还保费

（4）

Dear Sirs,

When the s.s "Eancastria" arrived at Tripoli on 10th October, it was noticed that one side of Case No.9 containing radio receivers[1] was split. We therefore had the case opened and the contents examined by a local insurance surveyor[2] in the presence of[3] the shipping company's agent. The case was invoiced[4]as containing thirty-six "Panda" receivers, eight of which were badly damaged.

We enclosed the surveyor's report and the shipping agent's statement. As our order was placed on CIF basis and you covered the insurance[5], we should be grateful if you would take the matter up for us with the insurers.

Eight replacement receivers will be required. Please arrange to supply these and charge to our account.

We hope no difficulty will arise[6] in connection with the insurance claim and thank you in advance for your cooperation.

Yours faithfully,

Words, Expressions and Notes

1. radio receivers 收录机

2. local insurance surveyor 当地的保险调查员

3. in the presence of 当……的面，在面前。此处指当着船公司代理的面。

4. be invoiced 这里的意思是，对该货箱所开出发票的产品

5. covered the insurance 办理投保。动词 insure 表示投保、保险；insurance 的常用短语和习惯搭配有：

insurance agent 保险代理人

insurance amount 保额、保险金额

insurance certificate 保险凭证

insurance claim 保险索赔

insurance cover 保险

insurance coverage 保险范围

insurance endorsement/rider 保险批单

insurance premium 保费、保险费

insurance declaration 保险声明书，保险通知书

marine insurance 水险，海上保险

ocean marine cargo insurance 海洋运输货物保险

overland insurance 陆运保险

air transportation insurance 航空运输保险

parcel post insurance 邮包保险

在表示投保，洽办保险时，可以有多种说法：to arrange insurance；to cover insurance；to effect insurance；to provide insurance；to take out insurance

表示投保的货物接 on，如 insurance on the 200 tons of coal

表示保险金额接 for，如 insurance for 110% of the invoice value

表示投保的险别接 against，如 insurance against all risks

表示保险费或保险费率接 at，如 insurance at a slightly higher premium

表示向某保险公司投保接 with，如 insurance with the People' Insurance Company of China

6. arise 出现、发生

（5）

Dear Sirs,

We thank you for your letter of May 10, quoting us 100 metric tons of Wool on CIF terms. We regret, however that we prefer to have your quotations and/or offers on CFR terms.

For your information[1], we have taken out an open policy[2] with the Lloyd Insurance Company, London. All we have to do when a shipment is made is to advise them of the particulars[3]. Furthermore, we are on very good terms with[4] them. We usually receive from our underwriters[5] quite a handsome[6] premium rebate[7] at regular intervals.

In the meantime, we should be obliged if you could supply us with full details regarding the scope of cover[8] handled by the People's Insurance Company of China for our reference.

We look forward to hearing from you at an early date.

Yours faithfully,

Words, Expressions and Notes

1. for your information 兹通知你方
2. open policy 预约保险单
3. particulars 此处是指有关货物装运的详细情况
4. good terms with 与……关系良好
5. underwriters 保险公司、保险业者（主要指专保水险的保险商）
6. handsome 可观的，相当大的
7. premium rebate 保险回扣
8. the scope of cover 指保险责任范围

（6）

Dear Sirs,

We refer to your L/C No. 157 covering Glazed Wall Tiles[1], which we have just received.

Please note for this article we do not cover[2] Breakage. You have to, therefore, delete[3] the word "Breakage" from the insurance clause in the credit.

Furthermore, we wish to point out that for such articles as window glass, porcelains, etc., even if additional Risk of Breakage has been insured, they cover is subject to a franchise[4] of 5%. In other words, if the breakage is surveyed to be less than 5%, no claims for damage will be entertained.

We trust that the position is now clear. Please cable the amendment at once.

Yours faithfully,

Words, Expressions and Notes

1. Glazed Wall Tiles 釉面墙砖，琉璃瓦

2. cover 这里指投保

3. delete 删除，在信用证修改中常会用到 delete，例如：

With reference to your L/C, please delete the word "long" and insert "metric" before "ton".

关于你方信用证，请将“吨”字前面的“长”字删掉，并加上“公”字。

4. franchise 免赔率

此外还有特许、特权的意思。

例句：

This corporation has received a franchise from the Federal Government to deal in this kind of business.

该公司得到了联邦政府关于经营此项业务的特别许可。

This class of goods is sold with a franchise of 5%.

此类商品按免赔率 5%出售。

（7）

Insurance Policy[1]

<u>Policy No. 118765</u>

This is to certify[2] that this Company has insured on behalf[3] of China National Light Industrial Products Import & Export Corp, Shanghai Branch.

The sum of US dollars One Hundred Thousand only[4]

Upon Five Thousand sets "Butterfly" Sewing Machines[5].

At & from Shanghai to New York

Ship or vessel: s.s "Fengching"

Sailing on or about May 20th, 2006

Covering All Risks

In the event[6] of damage, to be surveyed by Johnson Survey Co. and claims payable at Shanghai.

This policy is issued in duplicate at Shanghai on the 7th day of May in the year two thousand and six.

The People's Insurance Company of China

Shanghai Branch

Words, Expressions and Notes

1. Insurance Policy 保险单

各类保险单的说法有：

open policy 预约保单，船名未确定保单

floating policy 流动保单

voyage policy 航程保单

specific policy 单独保单，船名确定保单

time policy 定期保险单

transferable policy 可转让的保单

2. certify 证明，表示证明的词汇还有 attest，witness，vouch

例句：

The accounts were certified correct.

账目被证明正确无误。

While reimbursing, the negotiating bank is required to certify that all the credit terms have been duly complied with.

议付行在索偿时须证明，信用证所有条款已完全照办。

I can attest to the absolute truth of his statement.

我可以证实他的话是千真万确的。

The expert attested to the genuineness of the document.

专家证明此文件是真品。

Heavy enquiries are a witness to the popularity of our product.

大量询盘证明我公司产品深受欢迎。

This gift witnesses to his generosity.

这件礼物证明他的慷慨。

I am ready to vouch for his ability to pay.

我愿保证他的付款能力。

3. on behalf of 代表某人或某公司

4. The sum of US dollars One Hundred Thousand only

sum 在这里是指保险金额；only 表示整

5. Sewing Machines 缝纫机

6. In the event of 假如、如果。event 的相关短语有

in that event 如果是那样的话

in the event 结果，到头来

in either event 两者中无论发生哪件事

例句：

In either event, I'll be there to support you.

无论这样还是那样，我都会支持你。

You could be right, and in that event they'll have to pay you back.

可能是你对，那样的话，他们就得把钱还你。

I was worried about the hotel bill, but in the event I had enough money to pay.

我一直担心旅馆的费用，结果我的钱却足够。

In the event of shipping the goods, please inform us.

倘若装运这批货物，请通知我们。

（8）

Dear Sirs,

This is the reply to your letter of September 4 regarding insurance.

Your customer's request for insurance coverage[1] up to the inland city is acceptable on condition[2] that such extra premium[3] is for his account.

We can not grant you insurance coverage for 150 % of the invoice value, because the contract stipulates that insurance[4] is to be covered for 110% of invoice value.

We trust the above information serves your purpose. Meanwhile we await your reply.

Yours faithfully,

Words, Expressions and Notes

1. insurance coverage 保险责任范围
2. on condition 以…为条件
3. extra premium 额外的保险费
4. insurance 此处是指保险金额

(9)

Dear Sirs,

Our Order No. 4567

When the S.S. "Prince" arrived at Singapore on 16 June, it was noticed that one side of case No. 7 containing the “Fish” Typewriters was split[1]. We therefore had the case opened and the contents examined by a local insurance surveyor in the presence of the shipping company’s agent. The case was invoiced as containing ten typewriters, six of which were badly damaged.

We enclose the surveyor’s report and the shipping agents’ statement. As you hold the insurance policy, we should be grateful if you would take the matter up for[2] us with the insurers.

Six replacement[3] typewriters will be required. Please arrange to supply these and charge to our account[4].

We hope no difficulty will arise in connection with the insurance claim and thank you in advance[5] for your trouble on our behalf.

Yours faithfully,

Words, Expressions and Notes

1. split 裂口、裂开
2. take the matter up for 向某人提出问题进行处理

此处的含义是，为我方将此事提出并向保险人接洽。matter 作名词指事件、事态、事物，动词意为有关系、关系重要。与 matter 有关的短语有：

a matter of ……的问题

a matter of course 当然的事

as a matter of fact 事实上

in the matter of 关于、至于

no matter 无关紧要，不论

the matter 麻烦、毛病

例句：

Does it matter if we substitute 3 tons type 15 for type 30?

如果我们用 3 吨 15 型号替换 30 型号，可以吗?

It does not matter whether you airmail or cable the credit.

用空邮或电报开立信用证均可。

We do not know what the matter with the quality is. Please clarify.

我们不知道质量有什么毛病，请予以澄清。

No matter how large the volume is, we believe we can place it in our market.

不论数量多大，我方相信都能在我们市场销售。

It is no matter from which port the goods are shipped as long as they arrive here in time.

货物从哪个口岸装运无关紧要，只要及时到达这里就行。

To simplify matters, we will draw on you clean draft for the amount short-paid.

为简便起见，所欠金额用光票向你方索款。

These buyers are rather exacting in the matter of quality.

这些买主对质量要求很严。

Our price is quite reasonable; as a matter of fact, we have already done business at this level.

我们的价格十分公道，事实上我们按此价格已有交易。

We took it as a matter of course.

我们视之为理所当然。

It is entirely a matter of views.

这完全是看法的问题。

3. replacement 替换的产品

4. charge to our account 费用记在我方账户上

5. thank you in advance 预先致谢

（10）

Gentlemen:

Endorsement[1] to Our Policy No. 7890

We have received your letter of July 12 asking for an extension of the above policy for a period of 30 days to cover the risk of fire while the goods are laying in[2] Customs Warehouse in Hamburg.

In compliance with[3] your request, we have issued our Endorsement No. AB/201 to this effect[4] together with the relevant debit note[5] for an additional premium of RMB ¥200.00 and are enclosing herewith the same which we hope you will find in order.

Yours faithfully,

Words, Expressions and Notes

1. endorsement 保险批单，指改变保险合同的一种书面证明

在保险合同有效期间，合同双方均可通过协议变更保险合同的内容。对于变更合同的任何协议，保险方都应在原保单或保险凭证上批注或附贴批单，以资证明。此外 endorsement（其动词是 endorse）还表示赞同、背书的意思，如无记名背书（endorsement in blank）；记名背书（endorsement in full）。

例句：

We are sending you herewith the requested endorsement to the policy.

兹寄去你方需要的保险批单。

Bills of Lading are to be written "to order and blank endorsed".

提单要按空白抬头和空白背书（无记名背书）填写。

Please cable us as soon as your application for import licence has been endorsed.

一俟你方进口许可申请得到批准请即电告。

The quality of this product has been widely endorsed.

这种产品的质量已得到广泛的赞许。

2. lay in 储藏，lay in a store/stock of 储备若干

例句：

To lay in a good supply of food for the winter.

贮藏充足的食物以备过冬。

We must lay in a store of good stationery.

我们必须储备若干上等文具产品。

3. in compliance with 与……相一致，满足某种要求

4. to this effect 按照这个意思

5 debit note 借记通知

Section 3 Supplements 知识补充

Useful Sentences On Insurance

1. Insurance is to be covered by the seller for a sum equal to the amount of the invoice.
卖方按发票金额进行保险。

2. We insure the goods for RMB ¥5500 against ALL Risks with PICC.
我们向中国人民保险公司办理投保一切险，保险金额为人民币 5500 元。

3. As usual, the goods have been insured on WPA terms.
按常规做法，货物已保水渍险。

4. Please insure at invoice value plus 10%.
请按发票金额的 110%投保。

5. We have insured your Order No.864 for the invoice cost plus 20% up to the port of destination.
我方的 864 号订单项下货物我们已按发票金额的 120%投保至目的港。

6. Please reply whether we are to insure the above shipment.
请告我方是否要对上述货物投保。

7. We shall provide such insurance (coverage) at your cost.
我们将投保这种险别，费用由你方负担。

8. We thank you for your instructions to arrange the shipment of… . We take it that you wish us to insure this cargo against the usual risks, for the value of the goods plus freight. Unless we hear from you

to the contrary we shall arrange this.

你们有关×××货物装运指示获悉，谢谢。我们推定，你们要我们按货价加运费投保通常险别。除非另有指示，我们要按此办理了。

9. Cover Note (Insurance Certificate) follows as soon as we receive it from the underwriter.

一接到保险人的保险凭证，我们就立即寄给你方。

10. Buyer's request for insurance to be covered up to the inland city can be accepted on condition that such extra premium is for buyer's account.

可以接受买方要求，将货物投保到内陆城市，但其额外保险费须由买方负责。

11. Since the premium varies with the extent of insurance, extra premium is for buyer's account, should additional risks be covered.

保险费率随保险范围而定，如需增保其他险别，额外保险费由买方支付。

12. Regarding insurance, the coverage is for 110% of invoice value up to the port of destination only.

关于保险，按发票金额 110%投保到目的港止。

13. Breakage is a special risk, for which an extra premium will have to be charged.

破碎险是一种特殊险别，要额外收费。

14. We shall of course refund the premium to you upon receipt of your debit note.

收到你借方结账单后，我即将保险费汇付给你们。

15. We have covered insurance on 1,000 cases of beer for 110% of the invoice value against All Risks.

我们已将一千箱啤酒按发票金额的 110%投保一切险。

16. if you desire us to insure against a special risk, an extra premium will have to be charged.

如果你方想投保特殊险别，将向你们收取额外保费。

17. W.P.A. plus Risk of Breakage suit your consignment.

贵方货物适合投保水渍险及破碎险。

18. They will undertake to compensate you for the losses according to the risks insured.

他们将根据所投保的险别，对损失负责赔偿。

19. How long is the period from the commencement to termination of the insurance?

保险责任的起讫期限是多长？

20. We adopt the warehouse-to-warehouse clause that is commonly used in international insurance.

我们采用国际保险业常用的“仓至仓”责任条款。

21. The underwriters are responsible for the claim as far as it is within the scope of cover.

只要在保险责任范围内，保险公司就应负责赔偿。

22. The loss in question was beyond the coverage granted by us.

损失不包括在我方承保的范围里。

23. Please fill in the application form.

请填写投保单。

24. It's important for you to read the "fine print" in any insurance policy so that you know what

kind of coverage you are buying.

阅读保险单上的“细则”对你十分重要，这样就能知道你要买的保险包括哪些项目。

25. The insurance rate for such kind of risk will vary according to the kind.

这类险别的保险费率将根据货物种类而定。

26. WPA coverage is too narrow for a shipment of this nature, please extend the coverage to include TPND.

针对这种性质的货物只保水渍险是不够的，请加保偷窃提货不着险。

Terms Used in Insurance

Aflatoxin Risk	黄曲霉素险
All Risks	综合险（一切险）
Breakage of Packing Risk	包装破碎险
Clash & Breakage Risks	碰损、破碎险
Failure to Deliver Risk	交货不到险
F.P.A.(Free from Particular Average)	平安险
Fresh and/or Rain Water Damage Risk	淡水雨淋险
Hook Damage Risk	钩损险
Import Duty Risk	进口关税险
Intermixture & Contamination Risk	混杂、玷污险
Leakage Risk	渗漏险
On Deck Risk	舱面险
Rejection Risk	拒收险
Rust Risk	锈损险
Shortage Risk	短量险
S.R.C.C.(Strikes, Riots & Civil Commotions)	罢工、暴动及民变险
Survey at Jetty Risk	码头检验险
Survey at Customs	海关检验险
Sweating & Heating Risks	受潮受热险
Taint of Odour Risk	串味险
T.L.O.（Total Loss Only）	全损险
T.P.N.D.(Theft, Pilferage & Non-delivery)	偷盗及提货不着险
W.A.(With Average)=W.P.A.(With Particular Average)	水渍险
War Risk	战争险
perils of the sea	海上风险
extraneous risks	外来风险
total loss	全损
actual total loss	实际全损

constructive total loss	推定全损
absolute total loss	绝对全损
general average	共同海损
particular average	单独海损
combined certificate	联合凭证
contingency insurance	卖方利益险
China Insurance Clause	中国保险条款
Institute Cargo Clause	协会货物条款

Exercises

Ⅰ. Make sentences with the following words and expressions.

Insurance agent	effect insurance
delete	certify
in sum of	in the event of
on condition that	as a matter of fact
lay in	S.R.C.C.

Ⅱ. Translate the following sentences into English.

1. 请将装运给我们的货物投保水渍险和战争险。
2. 请按发票价的 110%投保。
3. 至于第 345 号合约项下的 300 架缝纫机，我们将自行办理保险。
4. 破碎险的保险费率是…%，如你方愿意投保破碎险，我们可以代为办理。
5. 至于索赔，我们的包厢是只接受超过实际损失 5%的部分。
6. 请告我们的价格是否包括偷盗及提货不着险。
7. 如果没有你们的明确指示，我们将按一般惯例投水渍险和战争险。
8. 很遗憾，我们不能接受这一索赔，因为你们的保险没有包括“破碎险”。
9. 根据你们惯的 CIF 价格条件，所保的是哪些险别？
10. 我们常从保险公司那里定期拿到一笔可观的保险费回扣。

Ⅲ. Translate the following letter into English.

关于第号×××3000 桶铁钉的售货合约，兹通知你方，我们已由伦敦中国银行开立了第×××号保兑的、不可撤销的信用证，计金额×××英镑，有效期至 5 月 15 日为止。

请注意(做到)上述货物必须在 5 月 15 日前装出，保险必须按发票价的 150%投保“综合险”。我们知道，按照我们一般惯例，你们只按发票价另加 10%投保，因此额外保险费由我们负责。

请按我们的要求办理保险，同时我们等候你方的装运通知。

Chapter 11

Complaints and Claims

Section 1 Business Knowledge 业务知识

在执行合同的过程中，签约双方都应该严格履行合同义务。任何一方如果不能严格履行合同，就会给另一方带来麻烦，有时还会使另一方遭受损失。在这种情况下，受损失的一方有权根据合同规定要求责任方赔偿损失或采取其他补救措施。受损失一方采取的这种行动称之为“索赔”，而责任方就受损失一方提出的要求进行处理，叫做“理赔”。

在外贸业务中较多见的是买方向卖方提出索赔，如卖方拒不交货，逾期装运，数量短缺，货物的品质规格与合同不符，错发错运，包装不妥，装运单证不全或漏填错发等致使买方遭受损失时，买方可向卖方提出索赔。但在某些情况下，卖方也有向买方提出索赔要求的。如因买方拒绝开或迟开信用证、不按时派船、无理毁约等，致使卖方遭受损失时，就会发生卖方向买方索赔的事情。

在进出口交易中，因涉及多个业务环节，一般来说对索赔应该负责任的对象主要有卖方、买方、承运人、保险公司等。当被保险人的货物遭受承保责任范围内的风险损失时，被保险人可以向保险人提出索赔；由于承运人未履行基本义务而造成货物损失，受害方可向承运人提出索赔。如承运人短卸、误卸造成货物短少；承运人未履行管理义务，如堆积不当、配载不当引起的货物损失，货物运输途中的遗失，船舶不具备适航能力造成的货物损失等；买方和卖方之间的索赔往往是因为一方未能全部或部分履行合同规定的各项义务，致使另一方遭受了损失，受损方就要向违约方提出索赔。

1. 对违约责任的法律规定

索赔是对违约行为的最常用的补救措施。此外，还可以根据违约程度采取其他补救措施，包括延迟履行合同、替代履行合同、减价、修理、换货、退货，甚至解除合同等。按照国际贸

易惯例和一般的法律规则，在采取其他违约补救措施时，不会影响受损害的一方当事人向违约方提出索赔的权利。但是，受害方向违约方提出索赔时是否能同时要求解除合同，则视违约的具体情况而定。在这个问题上，各国的法律规定也不尽相同。

目前，对国际贸易过程中的违约处理，多以《联合国国际货物销售合同公约》的规定为依据或参考。《公约》把违约分为“根本性违约”和“非根本性违约”两类。“根本性违约”是指一方当事人违反合同的结果，如使另一方当事人蒙受损失，以至于实际剥夺了他根据合同规定有权期待得到的东西；“非根本性违约”是指当事人不能预知，而且处于相同情况下的另外一个通情达理的人也不能预知会发生这种结果，那么就构不成根本性违约，即为非根本性违约。只有在违约方的违约行为属于根本性违约时，受损害方才有权利既宣告合同无效，又要求损害赔偿；如果违约行为属于非根本性违约，则受损害方只能要求损害赔偿而不能宣告合同无效。

买卖双方为了在索赔和理赔中有所依据，一般在合同中订有索赔条款。索赔条款主要有两种规定方式，一种是异议与索赔条款，另一种是罚金条款。在一般货物买卖合同中，多数只订立异议与索赔条款。而在大宗商品和机械设备合同中，除了订立异议与索赔条款外，往往还需另外订立罚金条款。

2. 异议与索赔条款（Discrepancy and Claim Clause）

异议与索赔条款一般是针对卖方交货质量、数量和包装等不符合合同规定而订立的，主要适用于商品质量、数量方面的索赔。由于各种商品在质量、数量方面的情况比较复杂，可能发生的损失程度也各有不同，无法在损失发生之前事先确定具体的赔偿金额。因此，异议与索赔条款的内容一般只限于对索赔的依据、索赔的期限、损失赔偿的办法等做出规定。

（1）索赔依据

索赔依据是受损害的一方当事人在提出索赔时必须提供的、证明违约方违约事实真相的书面材料。索赔依据包括法律依据和事实依据两方面。法律依据是指合同和有关国家的法律规定；事实依据是指违约的事实真相及其书面证明，以证实违约的真实性。例如，双方约定：“货到目的港卸货后，若发现品质、数量或重量与合同规定不符，除应由保险公司或船公司负责者外，买方于货到目的港卸货后若干天内凭双方约定的××商检机构出具的检验证明向卖方提出索赔”。索赔时必须按规定提供齐全有效的证据，若证据不全、不清，出证机构不符合要求，都可能遭到对方拒赔。因此，在规定索赔依据时，要与检验条款规定的内容一致。

（2）索赔期限

索赔期限是指受损害方向违约方提出索赔的有效期限。如果受损害方逾期提赔，违约方可不予受理。由买卖双方在合同中明确规定的索赔期限被称为约定索赔期限，其长短要根据交易商品的性质来确定。食品、农副产品及易发生品质变化的商品，索赔期限较短；对于质量比较稳定的商品，如机电商品，其索赔期限相对较长。在合同中未约定索赔期限时，索赔期限可采用法定索赔期限，即根据有关法律，受损害方有权向违约方提出索赔的期限。例如，我国《合同法》中将这一期限规定为四年，至当事人知道或者应当知道其权利受到侵害之日起计算；《公约》中则将这一期限规定为两年。约定索赔期限的效力一般高于法定索赔期限。由于索赔期限实际上就是检验条款中的复验期限，因此有的合同把检验条款和索赔期限结合起来订立，称为“检验

与索赔条款”。

（3）索赔办法

由于签订合同时不能预见违约和损失的具体情况，所以，关于索赔的办法，合同中一般不作具体规定。在处理索赔时，应弄清事实，分清责任，并区别不同情况，有理有据地提出索赔。既要坚持原则，正确运用相关的法律和国际贸易惯例，又要力求在友好的气氛下进行协商，争取公平合理地解决问题。

3. 罚金条款（Penalty Clause）

罚金条款又被称为违约金条款，是指当一方未能履行合同业务时，应向另一方支付一定金额的违约金，以补偿其损失。罚金条款一般适用于卖方延期交货或买方延期接运货物、拖延开立信用证、拖欠货款等情况。在买卖合同中规定罚金或违约金条款，是促使合同当事人履行合同义务的重要措施，能起到避免和减少违约行为的发生。在发生违约行为的情况下，能对违约方起到一定的惩罚作用，对守约方的损失能起到补偿性作用。违约金金额的大小取决于违约事时间的长短，并通常规定罚金的最高限额

例如，在进口合同中可以规定：“如果卖方不能如期交货，除因为人力不可抗拒的原因外，每延误 7 天，买方应收延期交货货物总值 0.5%的罚金，不足 7 天按 7 天计算；延误 10 周，买方有权撤销合同，并要求卖方支付延期交货罚金，罚金数额不得超过货物总额的 5%”。

违约金不以造成损失为前提条件，即使一方违约未给对方造成损失，也不影响对违约方追究违约责任，违约方也应支付约定的违约金。同时，当违约方支付约定的违约金后，并不能解除继续履行合同的义务。如果对方要求继续履行合同，违约方则必须继续履行合同的义务。如果违约方拒不履行其义务，则要承担因此而给对方造成的损失。

应当指出的是，关于合同中的罚金条款，各国法律有不同的解释。例如，德国、法国等大陆法系国家，对罚金条款予以承认和保护；而英美法系国家的法律一般不承认罚金。我国法律承认在合同中规定违约金的做法，但约定的违约金过分高于或低于违反合同造成的实际损失时，当事人可以请求仲裁机构或法院予以适当增加或减少。

草拟索赔信，理赔信应注意哪些事项？它们所涉及的惯用表达又有哪些呢？我们通过本章节例信的学习，相信大家会找到答案的。

Section 2 Specimen Letters 样函

（1）

Dear Sirs,

Our S/C No. 542LK-87E

We have repeatedly requested you by letter and telex to expedite the opening of the relative letter of credit, so as to effect shipment on time. To our disappointment[1], however, we have not received any reply from you so far.

You may be aware that your continuous silence[2] has placed us in an awkward position[3] and have the above S/C left outstanding[4] for too long. Consequently, we shall have no alternative[5] but to cancel the S/C unless your L/C reaches here by May 5. In the meantime, we reserve the right[6] to lodge a claim[7] on you for our loss incurred.

Please give this matter your serious consideration.

Yours faithfully,

Words, Expressions and Notes

1. To our disappointment 令我方失望的是
2. continuous silence 长期默不作声、不加理睬
3. awkward position 为难
4. outstanding 指合同不能够履行，无法执行
5. alternative 选择，可供选择的机会或事物
6. reserve the right 保留权利
7. lodge a claim 提出索赔

（2）

Dear Sirs,

We have just received some information from Messrs. Bombay & Sons in Colombo, the consignees under B/L No.16 dated February 18, that two of the 100 cases shipped from Huangpu to Colombo per S/S "Marria" are missing.

The consignee contacted your agents in Colombo about it and they were advised to get in touch with us directly to inquire into the matter. As matters stand[1], it is legibly[2] indicated in the Bill of Lading: shipped in apparently good order and condition[3]. The same indication appears in our shipping order[4] and your Mate's receipt[5]. It is therefore obvious that the shortage is due to your fault, and we hereby notify you that we reserve the right to claim on you for the shortage, should it be subsequently confirmed.

Your early clarification and settlement of the case will be appreciated.

Yours faithfully,

Words, Expressions and Notes

1. as matters stand 按照目前的情况，事态的发展情况是
2. legibly 容易识别的，清楚的
3. in apparently good order and condition 表面完好，情况正常
4. shipping order 装货单，俗称“下货纸”，又称“关单”，是由船公司或其代理人在接受托运人的托运申请后，向托运人签发的、凭以命令船长收货装运的凭据
5. Mate's receipt 大副收据，是货物装船后，承运船舶的大副签发给托运人的，表明已收到货物并已装船的货物收据。它是托运人向船公司换取正本已装船提单的依据

(3)

Dear Sirs,

We thank you for your letter of April 21, 2010. We have got the information from our agents in Karachi who told us that the two cases referred to were over-carried[1] and landed[2] at that port. We are making immediate arrangements to have the goods returned to Colombo by the first available opportunity[3], and have instructed our agents there to notify your consignees of the returned parcel. Any charges and expenses thus incurred will of course be for our account.

The matter stands that s.s. "Marria" departed from Colombo several hours ahead of schedule to tide over the ebbing[4]. Our tally[5] men hurriedly covered the hatchways[6] under the supervision of the customs officer, leaving the stowage intact[7]. However, had the two cases not been stowed away from the bulk[8], we could have delivered the consignment in good condition.

Please accept our sincere apologies for the mistake in delivery, which may have caused inconvenience to both the consignees and yourselves.

In the future transactions, we assure you of our best services at all times.

Yours truly,

Words, Expressions and Notes

1. over-carried 超载
2. landed 指货物上岸置于港口上
3. first available opportunity 从速、尽快
4. tide over the ebbing 赶潮
5. tally men 理货人员
6. covered the hatchways 盖上舱口
7. stowage intact 未清理货物，stowage 常指堆装物、装载物
8. bulk 货舱

(4)

Dear Sirs,

Your S/C No.775

We have been told by our agents in Beijing that 300 Tea Sets[1] under the above S/C by s.s. "Hongqi" arrived at Port Louis on June 8. Much to our regret, about 15% of the packages were seriously damaged with contents shattered to pieces[2] and the outer bands[3] broken.

We immediately invited qualified surveyors[4] to the spot[5] to look into the case, and their findings show that this was due to careless packing. A detailed survey report will be dispatched to you subsequent to their further study of individual cases.

In accordance with the stipulations of the above Sales Confirmation, we think the tea sets should have been packed in strong seaworthy wooden cases[6] suitable for long distance ocean voyages and in

these circumstances. We are obliged to[7] hold you are responsible for the damage and claim on you for compensation for the loss thus incurred.

Meanwhile our buyers are urging us to settle the case immediately. You are therefore requested to inform us of what you decide to do regarding our losses.

We are awaiting your prompt reply.

Yours faithfully,

Words, Expressions and Notes

1. Tea Sets 茶具
2. shattered to pieces 粉碎
3. outer bands 包装外层箍带
4. qualified surveyors 有资质、有资格的检验员
5. to the spot 到现场
6. strong seaworthy wooden cases 坚固、适合海运的木箱
7. are obliged to 不得不，只能

(5)

Dear Sirs,

Much to our regret, the above shipment arrived at your end with 15% of the packages damaged as mentioned in your letter of June 12, 2009.

You may be aware that our tea sets have been sold in a number of markets abroad for quite a long time, and all our customers have been satisfied with our packing. Each shipment of our exports is strictly inspected by our shipping departments before loading, and each package is subject to a careful examination[1]. The goods under the above Sales Confirmation were in perfect condition when they were shipped, and individual packages were clearly marked with "Handle With Care[2]", "Fragile[3]" and other necessary care marks. The Clean B/L supports these facts.

After going into[4] the matter carefully we estimate that the damage might be due to rough handling[5] in transit or during unloading. We consider it a matter for you to take up with the shipping company or the insurers who have covered you on the said consignment against Risk of Breakage. The responsibility should rest with[6] either of the parties concerned. Consequently we find no grounds to[7] compensate for the loss you claimed for.

Yours faithfully,

Words, Expressions and Notes

1. subject to a careful examination 要经过严格检查
2. Handle With Care 小心轻放、小心搬运
3. fragile 易碎物品
4. going into 此处指调查、着手处理

5. rough handling 粗鲁理货、野蛮装卸

6. rest with 在于，取决于

7. find no grounds to 没有道理，站不住脚

（6）

Dear Sirs,

We regret to inform you that on opening the package of this shipment, we find the color unsatisfactory—most of the material being of amber color[1], a small part even of dark amber. In any case the color can not justifiably[2] be described as Light Amber.

Not meeting the requirements of the users, the goods have been rejected[3] by our customers and thrown upon our hands[4]. We cannot dispose of them at a heavy loss.

Enclosed is a survey report in support of our statement, together with our Debit Note No.231 for £ 600, which is based on our estimate of the smallest amount of the total loss.

We should appreciate a prompt settlement.

Yours faithfully,

Words, Expressions and Notes

1. amber color 琥珀色

2. justifiably 有理由的，证明是正当的

3. rejected 拒绝、拒收货物

4. thrown upon our hands 推给我方处理

（7）

Dear Sirs,

The said goods have been inspected carefully upon arrival in Hamburg and we enclose the Weight Note[1] issued by the sworn inspectors[2].

You will see from the Weight Note that there is a shortage of 42 kgs, or about 911 lbs. in the shipment.

We have noticed lately that several of your shipments have turned out short weight, although this was formerly never the case. Such losses are cutting down[3] our small profits and we think any such shortage will not be allowed to happen again.

We look forward to receiving your suggestion on how you intend to reimburse[4] us for this short weight.

Yours faithfully,

Words, Expressions and Notes

1. Weight Note 重量单

2. sworn inspectors 可靠、可信的检验员

3. cutting down 削弱

4. reimburse 偿还，报销

（8）

Dear Sirs,

Re: Claim on Sewing Machines

The captioned goods you shipped per s.s "Yellow River" on May 14 arrived here yesterday.

On examination, we have found that many of the sewing machines are severely damaged, though the cases themselves show no trace of damage[1].

Considering this damage was due to the rough handling by the steamship company, we claimed[2] on them for recovery of the loss[3], but an investigation made by the surveyor has revealed[4] the fact that the damage is attributable to[5] improper packing. For further particulars, we refer you to the surveyor's report enclosed.

We are, therefore, compelled to[6] claim on you to compensate us for the loss, $27500, which we have sustained[7] by the damage to the goods.

We trust that you will be kind enough to accept this claim and deduct the sum claimed from the amount of your next invoice to us.

Yours truly,

Words, Expressions and Notes

1. trace of damage 损坏的痕迹
2. claim 索赔、索款，此外还有声称、宣称，提出要求的意思

例句：

Only the holder of the B/L may claim to be the owner of the shipment.

只有提单持有人才能要求取得货物的所有权。

We have to claim from you US$ 500 on this shipment for the inferior quality.

这批货由于质量低劣，我方不得不向你方索赔 500 美元。

The firm claims to be well placed for promoting the sales of your product.

对于推销你公司的产品，该公司声称处于有利地位。

表示提出索赔时，与 claim 搭配的动词有很多，例如

lodge a claim; file a claim; enter a claim;

make a claim; raise a claim; put in a claim

3. recovery of the loss 弥补损失
4. revealed 表明、揭示
5. attributable to 归因于，归咎于
6. be compelled to 迫使去做
7. sustain 这里指遭受，此外还有支持、证实的意思；形容词 sustainable 意为可持续的，不破坏生态平衡的

例句：

To sustain our argument, we mention the following facts:

为证实我们的观点，我方举出事实如下：

Sustainable development should be our long-standing state policy.

可持续发展应成为我们的长期国策。

If we comply with your request, we would have to sustain a great deal of trouble.

如果答应你们的请求，我们会遭到很大麻烦。

（9）

Dear Sirs,

We have received your letter of 15th July, informing us that the sewing machines we shipped to you arrived in a damaged condition on account of[1] imperfectness of our packing.

Upon receipt of your letter, we have given this matter our immediate attention. We have studied your surveyor's report very carefully.

We are convinced[2] that the present damage was due to extraordinary circumstances[3] under which they were transported to you. We are therefore not responsible for the damage. But as we do not think that it would be fair to have you bear[4] the loss alone, we suggest that the loss be divided between both of us, to which we hope you will agree.

Yours sincerely,

Words, Expressions and Notes

1. on account of 因为、由于

2. convince 说服、使信服，例如；

Please try to convince them that it is advisable to do so.

请努力说服他们这样做是妥当的。

3. extraordinary circumstances 非正常情况，特殊环境

4. bear 承担，另外还可以表示标明、注明，承受、经得起

例句：

Our product bears tests.

我公司产品经得起检验。

Each package is to bear the shipping mark.

每件货须注有唛头。

Extra expenses are to be borne by you.

额外费用将由你方承担。

（10）

Dear Sirs,

Our Order No. 1487

We duly received the documents and took delivery of the goods on arrival of s.s "Chunlin" at Hamburg.

We are much obliged to you for the prompt execution[1] of this order. Everything appears[2] to be correct and in good condition except in Case No.71.

Unfortunately when we opened this case we found it contained completely different articles, and we can only presume[3] a mistake was made and then contents of this case were for another order.

As we need the articles we ordered to complete deliveries to our new customers, we must ask you to arrange for the dispatch of replacements[4] at once. We attach[5] a list of the contents of case No. 71, and shall be glad if you will check this with our order and the copy of your invoice.

In the meantime we are holding the above mentioned case at your disposal[6]. Please let us know what you wish us to do with[7] it.

Yours faithfully,

Words, Expressions and Notes

1. execution 此处意为履行订单、执行订单

2. appears 似乎，看起来，显得

例句：

As the case is in good shape and does not appear to have been tampered with, we surmise that you must have short-shipped.

由于包装外形良好，且没有被动过的迹象。因此，我们猜测你方一定是少装货了。

Your price does not appear to be reasonable, as the prices we received from sellers in other directions are 5% lower.

你方价格似乎不合理，我们从其他方面卖主所接到的价格比你们低 5%。

3. presume 推测、假定

4. dispatch of replacements 发运替换货物

5. attach 附寄

6. at one's disposal 由某人处理、支配

7. do with 对付、处置

（11）

Dear Sirs,

Claim for Short-land[1] Fertilizers under S/C No. 6543

Further[2] to our cable dated 26th August reading:

CHEMICAL FERTILIZER 36 BAGS BROKEN MATERIAL IRRETRIEVABLE LOST SHORT W/T ESTIMATED 1540 LBS AWAITING SURVEY REPORT[3]

We have just received, the Survey Report from the Dalian Commodity Inspection Bureau evidencing the broken bags being due to improper packing, for which the suppliers are definitely responsible. On the strength of[4] the CCIB's Survey Report, we hereby register[5] our claim with you as follows:

Our claim on short-delivered quantity £357.00

Plus survey charges £25.00

Total amount of claim £382.00

Survey Report No. TE (80)305 is enclosed and we look forward to your settlement at an early date.

Yours faithfully,

Encl.

Words, Expressions and Notes

1. short-land 短卸，指卸下岸的货物数目不足

2. further 继…，进一步的

3. CHEMICAL FERTILIZER 36 BAGS BROKEN MATERIAL IRRETRIEVABLE LOST SHORT W/T ESTIMATED 1540 LBS AWAITING SURVEY REPORT

这句电文的意思是，36 袋化肥破损严重且无法修复。短重数量估计在 1540 磅左右。详情有待检验报告证实。

4. on the strength of 凭借，依靠

例句：

You may draw a clean draft on us on the strength of our written instructions dated the 12th March.

你们可凭我方 3 月 12 日的书面通知向我方开出光票收款。

We shall, on the strength of the Inspection Report by the said Bureau, have the right to reject the goods delivered and file a claim against you.

根据上述商检局的检验报告，我们将有权拒收货物并向你方提出索赔。

5. register 这里指提出索赔，此外还有注册、登记的意思。

（12）

Dear Sirs,

Re: Wolfram Contracts

Nos. 72MSF2431/72MSF2434

You shipped per vessel "Asia Africa" the following lots:

(a) against contract No. 72 MSF 2431—400 bags containing 20 tons of Wolframite

(b) against Contract No. 72MSF 2434—500

According to the analysis on certificates issued by the Guangzhou Commodity Inspection Bureau, the established[1] WO_3 contents are as follows:

(a) 65.64% WO_3 for Contract 2431

(b) 67.19% WO_3 for Contract 2434

After arrival the material was weighed, sampled and assayed[2] by Messrs. Alfred H. Knight Ltd., Wallasey, Cheshire as per[3] certificates attached. You will observe that the variance[4] in the outturn[5] WO_3 figures as established by Messrs. Alfred H. Knight Ltd., are well in excess of the 0.50% tolerated[6] under the terms of contract.

For the record[7], the figures are as follows:

GCIB	Alfred H. Knight Assay	Difference
65.64%	on average 64.49%	0.70%
67.19%	66.25%	0.94%

We would emphasize that for these two shipments we did not receive the GCIB samples as stipulated in the contract and we were, therefore, unable to make cross assay[8] on these samples to establish whether the GCIB figures were correct. We are, on the other hand, sending you, under separate cover, three samples drawn out by Alfred H. Knight Ltd. To cover the lots in question, and we would kindly ask you to arrange for these to be assayed by your laboratories, and advise us of their results.

In the meantime, we hope that we shall be able to iron out[9] this unfortunate discrepancy, as the transaction, as it stands at the moment, shows a considerable loss to us.

We look forward to your reply, we remain,

Yours faithfully,

Words, Expressions and Notes

1. established 已证实的，既定的，如 established fact 既定事实

例句：

It is established beyond controversy that the shipping company is reasonable for the damage of the goods in transit.

确定无可争议的是，船公司对货物运输途中受损负有责任。

Established customs are difficult to change.

公认的习惯很难改变。

It is our established policy to trade with the people of all countries in the world on the basis of equality and mutual benefit.

在平等互利的基础上与世界各国人民进行贸易是我们的既定政策。

2. sampled and assayed 抽样并进行化验

3. as per 依照、根据

4. variance 差异、不一致，分歧

5. outturn 货物到达时的情况，产量，常见的短语有：

outturn sample 货物到达时所取的样品

outturn report 卸货报告

outturn weight 到货重量

例句：

The outturn of the shipment is satisfactory.

到货情况令人满意。

The outturn of wheat this year is declined very much due to serious flood.

因为有严重的洪水，今年的小麦产量下滑很多。

6. tolerate 容忍、宽恕

tolerance 表示公差，如：

manufacturing tolerance 制造公差

location tolerance 安装公差

tolerance unit 公差单位

7. for the record 记录在案，为准确起见

8. cross assay 交叉化验

对外贸易中，卖方从货物中抽取货样，将此一部分进行检验或化验，称为“初验”；将此货样中另一部分寄交买方，买方对其进行检验或化验，称为“交叉检验（化验）。买方从所运到的货物抽取货样进行检验属于“复验”。

9. iron out 消除

（13）

Messrs, Beauty Clothing Co., Ltd.
234 Min Cheng Rd.
Kao Hsiung, Taiwan

Dear Sirs,

After carefully examining the dress materials[1] supplied to our order of 15th April, we must surprise and be disappointed at their quality. They certainly do not match[2] the samples you sent us. Some of them are so poor that we can not help[3] feeling there must have been some mistakes in making up[4] the order.

The materials are quite unsuited to the needs of our customers and we have no choice but to ask you to take them back and replace[5] them by materials of quality ordered. If this is not possible, then I am afraid we shall have to ask you to cancel our order.

We have no wish to embarrass[6] and if you can replace the materials we are prepared to allow the stated time for delivery to run from the date you confirm that you can supply the material we need.

Yours faithfully,

THOMSON TRADING CO.

C.D.Badey

Manager

Words, Expressions and Notes

1. dress materials 布料
2. match 匹配、相配
3. can not help doing 不禁，不得不
4. making up 此处指履行订单
5. take them back and replace 将货物取回并替换
6. embarrass 使窘迫、为难

(14)

Messrs, Thomson Trading Co.

105 West 35th Street

New York, N.Y. 1001

Dear Sirs,

We very much regret to learn from your letter of 2nd May that you are not satisfied with the dress materials supplied to your order No. 87.

From what you say it seems possible that some mistakes has been made in our selection of the materials meant for[1] you and we are arranging for our Mr. F. Cheng to call on[2] you later this week to compare[3] the materials supplied with the samples from…you ordered them.

If it is found that our selection faulty, then you can most certainly rely on us to replace the materials. In any case[4], we are willing to take the materials back and, if we can not supply what you want, to cancel your order, though do this reluctantly since we have no wish to lose your custom.

Yours faithfully,

T. L. Wang

manager

Words, Expressions and Notes

1. be meant for 预定给，命中注定

例句：

These materials were meant for you.

这些料子是预定给你们的。

I'm meant for such kind of job.

我命中注定要干这样的工作。

2. call on 拜访某人
3. compare with 与……比较
4. in any case 无论如何，不管怎样

Section 3 Supplements 知识补充

Useful Sentences On Complaints and Claims

1. The goods under our Order No.1234 should have reached us a week ago.

1234 号订单项下货物本应当在一周前到达我处。

2. Five cases of the shipment were badly damaged when delivered on 8th.

8 日送达时有五箱货物严重损坏。

3. We have to sell the desk fans at greatly reduced prices.

我们不得不降价出售台扇。

4. After reinspection we found that the quality of the goods was not in conformity with the contract stipulations.

复验后发现，质量与合同规定不符。

5. We have received many complaints from the customers concerning the tooth brushes under our Order No.1176.

我们收到了许多客户对你们供应 1176 号订单牙刷的投诉。

6. After checking the goods against your invoice, we discovered a considerable shortage in number.

经对照发票查对之后，发现数量少了很多。

7. The buyers have filed a claim on the shipment for RMB ¥1200.

买方对货物提出索赔人民币 1200 元。

8. We have already lodged a claim against the underwriter for Stg.560 for damage in transit.

由于货物在运输途中受损，我们已经向保险商提出索赔 560 英镑。

9. We claim US $2050 for short shipment on the 50 tons peanuts ex s.s. "Daqing".

由"大庆"轮运来的 50 吨花生，由于短运，我方提出索赔 2050 美元。

10. We request to extend the time limit for claim on the above shipment to the middle of March.

我们要求对上述货物的索赔时间期限延长到 3 月中旬。

11. Your claim should be supported by sufficient evidence.

你方索赔须有充分的证据。

12. The survey report issued by The China Commodity Inspection Bureau will be taken as final and binding upon both parties.

由中国商品检验局出具的检验报告将作为最后依据，对双方都有约束力。

13. Our cheque for US $3000 was airmailed to you today in settlement of your claim for short-weight of 500lbs.

今天航空邮出 3000 美元支票一张，以支付你方 500 英镑短重索赔。

14. In the spirit of goodwill and friendship we agree to accept all your claims.

本着友好的精神，同意接受你方的全部索赔。

15. Please make immediate remittance so as to close account.

请立即汇款，以便结账。

16. Claims for incorrect material must be made within 60 days after arrival of the goods.

有关不合格材料的索赔问题必须在货到后 60 天内予以解决。

17. We want to settle our claim on you for the 100 tons of bleached cotton waste, as per Sales Confirmation No. 3426E.

我们想处理一下关于销售确认书第 3426E 号 100 吨漂白废棉的索赔问题。

18. The Japanese company agreed to compensate us for the defective watches by 5% of the total value.

日本公司同意就手表不精确问题向我方赔偿货物总值的 5%。

19. We shall lodge a claim for all the losses incurred as a consequence of your failure to ship our

order in time.

由于你方未能及时交货，我方将向你们索赔由此遭受的全部损失。

20. Any complaint about the quality of the products should be lodged within 15 days after their arrival.

任何有关该产品质量问题的申诉应该在货物到达后 15 天内提出。

21. Our investigation shows that improper packing caused damage. Therefore we have to refer this matter to you.

我方检验证明，货物受损是由于包装不当造成的。因此，我们不得不将此事提交你方解决。

22. As the goods are inferior in quality, we are returning the whole of the 20 cases and must ask you to replace them.

由于这些产品质量低劣，所以我方把 20 箱全数退回，并务请你方更换这些产品。

23. We very much regret the mistake in article number, which resulted in your receiving the wrong goods.

因货号有误，致使到货错误。对此，我们深表歉意。

24. The goods we've received do not tally with the sample on which we ordered.

我们收到的货物与订货样品不符。

25. In view of the long business relations between us, we wish to meet you half way to settle the claim.

考虑到我们长期的业务关系，我们愿意各让一半解决这项索赔。

26. Here's a survey report by a well-known lab in Houston, whose testimony is absolutely reliable.

这是由休斯顿的一个著名实验室提供的一份检验报告，证据绝对可靠。

Terms Used in Making Complaints

a justified claim	有充分理由的索赔
an equitable settlement	公平解决
an impartial judgment	公正判断
bags torn	袋子撕破
blown cans	膨听（罐头）
bundles burst	捆带松散
conciliation	和解调停
conglomeration	结块
contingency	意外事故
crushed	压碎
dented	碰凹
evidence of damage	残损证明
fermentation	发酵
hoops off	掉了箍

mildew	发霉
lid off	没有盖子
rust stains, spots	锈斑
spotty	有污点
to leak, to seep into	渗漏
to reinforce	加固
to be soaked	浸透
to be soiled	弄脏
to be cracked	破裂
to compensate partly	部分赔偿
to help one get out of the mess	帮助排除纠纷
to offset the difference	抵消差额
to raise an objection	提出抗议
to resort to arbitration	诉诸仲裁
to resort to litigation	打官司
to settle the case amicably	友好解决
to stretch a point	通融让步
to tackle the problem properly	适宜地处理问题
to view the matter in a proper light	正当地对待问题
to withhold business	找出解决办法
vermin bitten	虫咬
water stain	水渍

Exercise

Ⅰ. Translate the following words and phrases and then make sentences.

discharge one's duty	discharging port
compel sb. to do sth.	in urgency
claim upon sb.	lodge a claim against sb.
attribute to	be convinced of
due to	hold sb responsible of
bear the loss	at one's disposal
do with	on the strength of
at variance with	can not help
have no choice but	compare with

Ⅱ. Complete the following sentences.

1. When unpacking the bale, we find that______________________.

a. 颜色不能令人满意

b．货物与原先式样不符

c．包内货物与你方通知单不完全一致

d．一些货物在运输途中受到损坏

2. We have to ask you to cancel our order,________________________________.

a．由于这类货物的需求已终止

b．由于这类货物是为春季订购

c．除非货物能立即发运

d．考虑你方毁约是我们支付了不应有的费用

3. We receive a CCIB's survey report,________________________________.

a．证明短重 500 千克

b．证明短交 50 袋化肥

c．证明破包 36 袋

d．证明化肥品质次于合同规定

4. In view of the long business relations between us ,________________________________.

a．我们愿意友好解决这次争端

b．我们愿意各让一半解决这项索赔

c．我们准备接受 D/P 付款方式

5. We consider that the suppliers are responsible for the short-weight,________________________.

a．因为卸货时发现破包 50 只

b．因为上海商检局检验证明短重 500 千克

c．因为破包是包装不妥的缘故

6. Further to our cable of 26 August, ____.

a．我们坚持短重应由供应商负责

b．我方要求你方早日解决这次索赔

c．我们提出索赔 500 美元，并附寄上海商检局检验报告一份

Ⅲ. Translate the following sentences into English.

1．鉴于原料价格近日上涨，我们不得不调整部分价格。

2．很遗憾地通知你方，3 号箱及 6 号箱破损，箱内货物因包装不良严重损坏。

3．如果你们退回机器，我们将进行必要的修理，并以最完整的运转情况送还你方。

4．对于所遭受的损失，我们不得不要你方负责。

5．无论如何，我们要求你方采取措施以防止类似事件再次发生。

6．我们已彻底查询，但所得到的唯一解释是标签混乱了。

7．货号有误，导致你方收到错货，我们对此深表歉意。

8．请完全按照我们所订的货物立即补发一批。

9．发错货物是由于我方包装人员的错误造成的。

10．已和买主按以下条款取得一项解决方法。

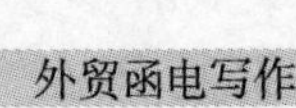

11．我们将在卸货完毕后检查此货。

12．我方订单 1361 号来货发现短重 2500 千克，为此特向你方提出索赔。

13．我方强烈要求你方遵守这一条件，否则今后将被迫拒绝供货。

14．兹寄去中国商品检验局检验报告一纸，作为我方索赔的依据。

15．兹歉告你方，第 45 号箱货物在存放仓库期间被窃。

Ⅳ. Write to your suppliers explaining that in the delivery of metal wastepaper bins twenty-seven were either slightly dented or badly scratched and that you have had to sell them at a price considerably below the recommended retail selling price. Submit a claim for the difference between the recommended retail price and the price at which the damaged bins were actually sold.

Chapter 12

Eleven Agency

Section 1 Business Knowledge 业务知识

代理是国际贸易中经常采用的贸易方式。代理是指出口商（即委托人）授权进口商（即代理人）代表委托人向其他中间商或用户销售其产品的一种贸易方式。

在我国进出口业务中，对具有某些特点的商品，如订单多，批量少的某些商品，为了扩大出口，在一些国家和地区选择适当的客户建立代理关系。由我进出口公司给予代理商，在特定地区和一定期限内，享有代销指定商品的权利，双方属于一种委托和被委托的代销关系。

1. 代理的种类

根据委托人授予代理人权限的不同，可分为总代理、一般代理和独家代理。

（1）总代理

总代理（General Agent）是指代理商在指定地区和一定期限内不仅享有专营权，除了有权代表委托人从事代理协议中规定的一般商务活动外，还有权进行某些非商业性活动。实际上，总代理是委托人在指定地区的全权代表。

（2）一般代理

一般代理（Agent）是指不享有独家代理专营权的代理，即委托人在同一地区和期限内，对同一商品可同时委托几个代理人代表委托人的行为。一般代理人根据推销商品的实际金额和根据协议规定的办法和百分率向委托人计收佣金，所以又称佣金代理。

（3）独家代理

独家代理（Sole Agent or Exclusive Agent）是指代理人在协议规定的地区和期限内，对指定商品享有专营权，即委托人不得在规定范围内自行或通过其他代理人进行销售。

2. 代理的特点

（1）代理人与委托人之间是一种委托代理的契约关系，而不是买卖关系

在代理方式下，代理人作为委托人的代表，是为委托人在当地销售货物提供服务的。代理人的行为有招揽客户、招揽订单、代表委托人签订买卖合同、处理委托人的货物、收受货款等。因此在代理业务中，两个基本当事人的关系不是买卖关系，而是通过代理协议或合同的订立所建立的委托代理关系。

（2）代理人通常运用委托的资金进行业务活动

代理人是委托人的代表，其本身并不参加交易，其进行业务活动所使用的资金为委托人的资金，而并非自筹资金。

（3）代理一般不以自己的名义与第三者签订合同

代理人是在授权范围内以委托人的名义行事，委托人与代理人不发生货物所有权的转移，货物所有权转移在委托人与第三方之间完成。

（4）代理人赚取的报酬即为佣金

代理人在委托人授权范围内所作的行为、所产生的权利和义务，直接对委托人发生效力，代理人不承担销售风险和费用，也不必垫付资金。交易结束后，委托人按达成交易的数额向代理商支付约定比例的代理佣金。

3. 代理协议

代理协议是明确规定委托人和代理人之间权利与义务的法律文件。内容主要包括以下几方面。

- 订约双方的基本情况。包括双方的名称、地址及订约的时间、地点。
- 定义条款。包括代理的商品种类、地区范围及商标等和代理期限。委托人对代理人的授权中，应明确说明代理销售商品的类别和型号，独家代理则必须明确其业务的地理范围，并约定代理协议的有效期限，或者规定中止条款。
- 代理的委任、受任及法律关系。
- 委托人与代理人的权利与义务。
- 佣金条款。代理协议中必须规定佣金率、支付佣金的时间和方法。佣金率可与成交金额或数量相联系。
- 不可抗力和仲裁。

另外，在独家代理下，为了约束代理人，一般还会订有非竞争条款。为维护出口企业的利益，一般规定最低代销额条款。若代理人未能达到或超过最低代销额，委托人对代理人的报酬可作相应的调整。一般规定若委托人直接与代理区域内的客户签订买卖合同，代理人仍可获得佣金。

4. 独家经销与独家代理的区别

独家经销与独家代理的做法，虽均能在一定程度上起到扩大销售渠道、减少自相竞争的作用，但存在着以下主要区别。

第一，独家经销的当事人出口商与经销商之间是买卖关系；而独家代理的委托人与代理人之

间的关系是委托代理关系。

第二，独家经销商自担风险，自负盈亏；而独家代理人则不承担市场经营风险。

第三，独家经销商自购自销，自行承担履行合同规定的义务；而独家代理人招揽客户、介绍业务、收取佣金，合同的内容和条款则由实际卖主和买主负责履行。

Section 2 Specimen Letters 样函

（1）

Dear Sirs,

Because of the steady increase in demand for our china ornaments we have decided to appoint[1] an agent to handle our export trade with your country. When we last met, you mentioned that you might be interested in an agency and we can perhaps come to some arrangements[2].

There are signs of promising market[3] for our particular type of product and there is little doubt that a really active agent[4] could bring about a big increase in our sales. Being aware of your wide experiences of the China trade and of your connections with the principal buyers[5] in your country, we feel that your firm is the right one to do this and we have pleasure in offering you a sole agency.

Should you not be able to accept it, perhaps you could recommend some other reliable and well-established[6] firms whom we might approach. We hope, however, that you yourself will accept. If you decide to do so, please state the terms on which you would be willing to represent[7] us.

Yours faithfully,

Words, Expressions and Notes

1. appoint 任命、委派

2. arrangements 办法，计划，准备，商定的办法

例句：

We have reached an arrangement with them.

我方已和他们商量妥当。

We have to come to an arrangement with you on the question of agency.

关于代理问题，我们希望能和你方商定一个办法。

As soon as your L/C arrives, we will make arrangement to ship the goods.

你方信用证一到，我们就准备装货。

3. promising market 有销路的市场，前景看好的市场

lose one's market 失去市场，失去买卖机会

market uncertain 市况不定（指市场行情涨落）

market glutted 市场货物充斥

overrun one's market 不肯脱手以致失去出售机会

4. agent 代理人、代理商；agency 指代理业务、代理处

agency agreement 代理协议

agency commission 代理佣金

sole/exclusive agency 独家代理

general agency 总代理

例句：

If you would appoint us as your agent, we could give you a reasonable guarantee to sell $100,000 a month, because yours is a line we can handle well.

假如你们委任我方为代理，我们保证每月销售 10 万美元，因为你方的产品领域是我们所善于经营的。

Your application for sole agency for a period of one year is now under our careful consideration.

你们担任我方代理为期一年的申请，我们正在仔细考虑。

The volume of business done does not warrant entrusting you with exclusive agency at present.

已达成的营业额还不足以让我们在目前委任你方独家代理。

5. principal buyers 主要买主。principal 还表示资本金；校长；委托人

6. well-established 生根的、根深蒂固；信誉卓著

7. represent 代表，这里指做我方代理。此外，represent 还可表示声称、说明；指出，使明白；再提示，再提交

例句：

You need to represent a cheque at the bank.

你需要再向银行提示、兑付支票。

We must represent to you our buyer's urgent need of these goods.

我方必须向你方着重指出买主急需此货。

We are willing to represent you for the sales of Chinese Men's Shirts in our country.

我们愿意代理你方在我国销售中国男式衬衫。

The user represented that he has received offers from various sources and that yours was not so competitive.

用户说他已收到各方面报价，并称你方报价缺乏竞争力。

（2）

Dear Sirs,

We wish to thank you for your cooperation and assistance[1] over these past years in the sales of our embroideries[2].

You may recall[3] that Mr. John Nathan, when he was in Beijing, brought up the question of our representation as your sole agent for Chinese embroideries in Sweden. It was agreed upon at that time that we were to postpone[4] an agreement until the total sales have reached Stg. 100,000.

Now, we should like to discuss again this question of acting as your sole agent in Sweden. Such an agreement would not only facilitate[5] our sales promotion, but would also eliminate[6] unnecessary discrepancies[7] between your offers when quoting through different channels. We would like to have your comments on this matter.

We shall continue our efforts to canvass[8] the Swedish market for more orders of Chinese embroideries so as to further expand the market.

We await your favorable reply.

Yours faithfully,

Words, Expressions and Notes

1. cooperation and assistance 合作和帮助

2. sales of our embroideries 刺绣产品的销售

关于 sale 的短语有：

for sale 待售

on sale 上市，出售

push the sales of sth. 推销、销售某产品

例句：

We will make every effort to push the sales of your tea sets in our market.

我们将尽一切努力在我方市场上销售你们的茶具。

Grapes from many directions are on sale.

来自各地的葡萄正在出售。

This house is for sale.

这所房子待售。

3. recall 回忆、记起。此外还有召回、唤回的意思。例如，

The factory began recalling its product under the pressure of public opinions.

在舆论的压力下，厂家开始召回产品。

4. postpone 延缓、推迟

含此意思的词汇还有，defer，intermit，suspend，stay；但是它们在用法上略有差异，请看以下例句：

I shall defer replying till I hear form him.

我将等到收到他的信息后再进行答复。

Ship's departure was deferred for 10 hours by the captain because of tornado.

由于飓风，船长推迟 10 个小时启航。

In our opinion, we had better postpone the decision until a more appropriate time.

在我们看来，最好等到一个较适当的时候再做决定。

Shall I suspend final decision until I have further evidence?

在我未得到进一步证据之前是否暂不做出结论？

She has to intermit her effort due to the effect of climate.

受气候的影响，她不得不暂停努力。

The court has decided to stay the proceeding.

法庭已决定暂缓进行这个诉讼程序。

5. facilitate 促进，有利于

6. eliminate 消除、清除

7. discrepancies 差异、不同、不一致

8. canvass 游说，此处是指兜揽生意、推销

canvas 是指帆布、油画。

例句：

Please canvass your market for orders.

请向你方市场兜揽订货。

Many shipping companies find it difficult to canvass for freight at this time of year.

每年这个时候，许多船公司感到兜揽货运有困难。

Turner's canvases are still attractive today.

今天特纳的油画仍有吸引力。

The goods should be packed into a canvas bag.

货物应该被装进帆布袋里。

（3）

Dear Sirs,

Re: Sole Agency for Embroideries in Sweden

We have received your letter of the 15th and are favorably impressed[1] by the proposal you make. You are kindly informed that we have decided to entrust[2] you with the sole agency for our Embroideries in the territory[3] of Sweden.

The agency agreement has been drawn up[4] for duration of one year, automatically renewable[5] on expiration for a similar period unless a written notice is given to the contrary[6]. Enclosed you will find a copy of the draft. Please go over[7] the provisions[8] and advise us whether they meet with your approval.

We shall do all in our power to assist you in establishing a mutually beneficial trade.

Yours faithfully,

Words, Expressions and Notes

1. favorably impressed 这里是指对你方建议反应积极，或被你方建议打动了

2. entrust 委托、托付、信托

3. territory 地域，指代理产品的地区限制

4. draw up 草拟

5. automatically renewable 自动展期、自动的续约

renewal 是名词可用于合同续订，有效期延长；renewable 还表示可再生的。

例句：

We regret being unable to accept your request for a renewal of our offer of June 12.

抱歉，你方要求延长我 6 月 12 日盘有效期一事，我方无法接受。

Renewable resource is the effective solution to cope with energy crisis.

可再生资源是应付能源危机的有效方法。

6. unless a written notice is given to the contrary 除非另有反面的书面通知

contrary 表示相反，对立面。

on the contrary 正好相反，另一方面恰好

to the contrary（意思）相反的

例句：

Unless you advise to the contrary we will continue selling this article at this price.

如果没有相反的通知，我方将继续按这个价格销售此批货物。

Cash zinc closed $30 upon the weekend; cash lead, on the contrary, closed $6 down.

现货锌（收盘价）周末上升了 30 美元；而现货铅（收盘价）恰好下降了 6 美元。

7. go over 浏览、查阅

8. provisions 条款、规定，准备

例句：

We are making provision for the busy season ahead.

我们正在为即将来临的旺季做准备。

There is no provision in the contract that sets a limitation of the percentage of small size.

合同里没有规定小尺寸百分百的限度。

（4）

Dear Sirs,

This is to inform you that[1] we are acting as agents on a sole agency commission basis. We specialize[2] in the trade of household and decorative wares[3], such as porcelain wares, lacquer[4] wares and crystals.

We have been working with the Ceramics[5] Department of your Shanghai Office and our relations have proved mutually satisfactory. You may refer to[6] them for any information concerning our firm.

We are very much interested in an exclusive arrangement with your corporation for the promotion of sales of your products in Cairo.

We await your news with keen interest.

Yours faithfully,

Words, Expressions and Notes

1. This is to inform you that…兹通知你方……

类似的句型还有：

This is to acknowledge …兹收到……

This is to advise that… 兹通知……

This is to announce that 兹宣布……

例句：

This is to announce that, in consequence of the rapid rise in cost of raw materials from which our products are manufactured, from and after October 15, our previous price list will be canceled and replaced by the new one which is enclosed.

兹宣布，由于我们产品原料价格急剧上涨，从10月15日起，我们过去的价目单作废，由随函附寄的新价目单代替。

2. specialize 专门经营、专门从事，也可写成specialise；specialization 表示专门化，分工

3. household and decorative wares 家用装饰品

4. lacquer 漆，发蜡、定型剂。动词表示涂漆于……上

5. Ceramics 陶瓷、陶器，制陶工艺、制陶术

6. refer to 参考，查阅

（5）

Dear Sirs,

We thank you for your letter of 14th September.

As we are now only at the get-acquainted stage[1], we deem[2] it rather premature[3] to take into consideration the matter of sole agency. In our opinion, it would be better for both of us to try out[4] a period of cooperation to see how things prove[5]. Also, it would be necessary for you to test the marketability[6] of our product at your end and continue your efforts in building a large turnover[7] to justify[8] the sole agency arrangement.

We enclose two copies of our latest pricelist covering all the products we handle within the framework of[9] your specialized lines.

We shall be pleased to hear from you again.

Yours faithfully,

Words, Expressions and Notes

1. get-acquainted stage 指在了解、熟悉阶段

2. deem 认为、相信

3. premature 不成熟的，过早的

4. try out 试用、试验，选拔

例句：

We would like to express our opinion on the plan until it has been tried out.

我们想计划试行后再发表意见。

Please try out this new product free for one year.

请免费试用一年这种新产品。

5. how things prove 看事态进展如何

6. marketability 可销售性，适销性

7. turnover 营业额；turnover rate 周转率；turnover tax 周转税

8. justify 证明……的合理性

9. within the framework of 在……范围内

(6)

Dear Sirs,

Through the courtesy of[1] our Commercial Counselor's Office in your country we have obtained your name. They recommended you as a possible agent for our products at your end[2]. Recently, we have produced a new kind of electric toys and would like to have an agent in your area to sell our newly produced products.

From your Commercial Counselor's Office we have learned that your company has a very good reputation and credit[3] on pushing the sale of electric goods. We, therefore, write to approach you to discuss the matter of agency. We expect an annual turnover[4] of not less than US$600,000 and on all order executed. You will be allowed a commission of 5% to be calculated on CFR basis.

We would be grateful if you let us know at an early date whether you are interested in representing us and the volume of business you can do would warrant[5] our granting you the sole agency. We feel confident that with your help we are sure to build up a good market in your country very soon.

On receipt of your affirmative answer[6], we will prepare a draft agreement and send it to you for your final confirmation without any delay.

Yours faithfully,

Words, Expressions and Notes

1. through the courtesy of 通过……获悉，了解到
2. at your end 在你处
3. reputation and credit 声誉和信誉
4. annual turnover 年营业额
5. warrant 保证，指派，授权
6. affirmative answer 肯定的答复

(7)

Dear Sirs,

We have obtained your name from the Chamber of Commerce in your country that you are handling the export business of Cotton Printed Sheets[1]. They told us that these goods are not directly represented in New York, so we are writing you today to offer you our services as your sole agent.

We have a well-developed sales organization and are represented by a large staff all over the country. When we study the reports by them, we have confidence that there will be promising prospects[2] of a very profitable market for your products, because nowadays there is a growing demand for such goods.

In view of the wide connections and experience in pushing the sales of this line, we think we can work up a very satisfactory business[3] with you in the future. If you think a 6% commission on net sales is reasonable and other terms satisfactory, we are prepared to guarantee payment of all accounts, but we would like to have Del Credere commission[4] of 2%.

We would refer you to the Bank of China, London as our credit reference[5] if you want to get some information about our financial and credit standing[6].

We are waiting for your favorable reply and feel sure that we could come to an agreement as to terms.

Yours faithfully,

Words, Expressions and Notes

1. Cotton Printed Sheets 印花棉布床单
2. promising prospects 前景看好的
3. work up a very satisfactory business 建立起令人满意的业务关系
4. Del Credere commission 保付佣金（保证收取货款佣金）
5. credit reference 信用备询，信用备询人
6. financial and credit standing 财务与信用情况

（8）

Dear Sirs,

We are pleased to confirm the agreement about agency reached between us after so many discussions. We wish this would be a very good beginning of the business relationship between our two companies and look forward to a happy and successful working relationship with you. Before drawing up the formal contract for signature we would like to confirm the main points on which we have reached as the followings:

- The agency you will operate would begin from January 1st next[1] for a period of two years, subject to renewal.
- The commission we can grant on your sales of our products is 5%.
- You will undertake not to sell the competing products[2] of other manufacturers either on your account or on that of other suppliers.
- All customers' orders should be transmitted to us immediately for supply direct.
- Credit terms[3] not to be given or promised to any customer without our consents.
- A special del credere commission of 2% will be added.
- A commission of 5% on CFR will be granted with goods shipped to Torquay, England.
- All questions of difference arising under our agreement will be referred to arbitration[4].

Upon receipt of your confirmation for the above points we will arrange for the contract to be drawn up and sent to you for your signature.

Yours faithfully,

Words, Expressions and Notes

1. January 1st next 自 1 月 1 日起接下来

2. competing products 竞争性产品

3. Credit terms 指赊销付款条件

4. referred to arbitration 交付仲裁解决

（9）

Sole Agency Agreement

This agreement is entered into between the parties concerned on the basis of equality and mutual benefit to develop business on terms and conditions agreed upon as follows:

1. The Parties Concerned

Supplier: China National × × × Import and Export Corporation(here in afer called Party A)

Agent: × × × Company(hereinafter called Party B)

2. Commodity and Quantity

Party A hereby appoints Party B as its sole agebt for the sales of…Party B shall undertake to achive the sales of the aforesaid commodity not less than…in the duration of this Agreement.

3. Territory

In…only.

4. Confirmation of Orders

The quantities, prices and dates of shipment concerning the commodity stated in this Agreement shall be confirmed in each transaction, the particulars of which will be shown in Party A's S/C.

5. Payment

After confirmation of an order, Party B shall arrange to open 100% irrevocable L/C available by draft at sight in favor of Party A within the time stipulated in the relevant S/C. Party B shall also notify Party A immediately after the L/C is opened, so that Party A may make preparations for shipment.

6. Commission

A …percent (…%) commission on invoice value against each shipment will be remitted to Party B by Party A after receipt of the payment.

7. Report on Market Conditions

Party B shall have the obligation to forward once every three months to Party A detailed s on current market conditions and on consumers' comments. For Party A's reference, Party Bshall, from time to time, forward to Party A samples of similar commodity offered by other suppliers, together with their prices, sales position and advertising materials.

8. Advertising & Publicity Expenses

Party B shall bear all expenses for advertising and publicity within the aforementioned territory in the duration of this Agreement and submit to Party A all drafts and/or drawings intended for such purposes for prior approval.

9. Validity of Agreement

This Agreement, when duly signed by the parties concerned, shall remain in force for…to be effective from…to….if a renewal of this Agreement is desired, notice in writing should be given by either party one month prior to its expiry. Should one of the parties fail to comply with the terms and conditions of this Agreement, the either party is entitled to terminate this Agreement.

10. Arbitration

All disputes arising from the execution of this Agreement shall be settled through negotiation between both parties. In the event that no settlement can be reached, the case in dispute shall then be submitted for arbitration to the China International Economic and Tade Arbitration Commission, Beijing, China, in accordance with its Rules of Procedure of Arbitration. The decision made by this commission shall be regarded as final and is binding both parties.

11. Other Terms & Conditions

1) Party A shall not supply the contracted commodity to other buyers in the above-mentioned territory. Direct enquiries, if any, will be referred to Party B. however, should any other buyers insist on dealing directly with Party A, Party A have the right to do so. In the latter case, Party A shall send Party B a copy of relevant S/C and reserve …percent (…%) commission for Party B on the net invoice value of the transaction concluded.

2) Should Party B fail to send their orders to Party A for a minimum of …for a period of …months, Party A shall not be bound to this Agreement.

3) For any business transacted between governments of both Parties, Party A shall have full right to handle direct dealings as authorized by Party A's government without binding themselves to this Agreement. Party B shall not interfere with such direct dealings, nor shall Party B bring forward any demand for compensation or commission thereof.

4) Other terms and conditions shall be subject to those specified in the S/C signed by both parties.

This Agreement is made out in quadruplicate, each party holding two copies.

Party A (Supplier) Party B (Agent)

(10)

Sole Distributorship Agreement

No. LITP098

Guangzhou, April2, 2010

This Agreement is made and entered into by and between the China National Light Industrial Products Import & Export Corporation Guangdong Branch (hereinafter called Supplier) and ABC Company (hereinafter called Distributor) whereby Supplier agrees to grant Distributor the exclusive right to sell the Products in the Territory on the terms and conditions stipulated as follows:

Article 1. Appointment

During the effective period of this Agreement, Supplier hereby grants to Distributor the exclusive right to sell Products in Territory and Distributor accepts and assumes such appointment for the sale and Distribution of Products in Territory.

Article 2. Privity

The relationship hereby established between Supplier and Distributor, during the effective period of this Agreement, shall be solely that of Seller and Buyer, and Distributor shall under no circumstances be considered to be the agent or legal representative of Supplier for any purpose whatsoever and shall have no right or authority to create or assume any obligation or responsibility of any kind, expressed or implied, in the name of or on behalf of Supplier.

Article 3. Products

The products covered under this Agreement shall expressly be confined to Television Sets sold and exported by Supplier with its registered trademark "ZHUJIANG" (hereinafter referred to as Products).

Article 4. Territory

The territory covered under this Agreement shall be confined to the United States of America (hereinafter referred to as Territory)

Article 5. Prohibition of Competitive Transaction

In consideration of the exclusive right herein granted, Supplier shall in no way directly or indirectly sell or export Products to Territory through any other channel than Distributor and Distributor shall in no way sell or promote the sales in territory, directly or indirectly, of any products which are of the same kind as, similar to or competitive with Products and shall in no way make any purchase of such products without the prior written consent of Supplier during the effective period of this Agreement.

Article 6. Prohibition of Re-export

Distributor shall sell Products only in Territory and shall not, directly or indirectly , resell or re-export Products to any place or country outside Territory, nor shall resell Products to any other person, firm or corporation in Territory, whom Distributor, to the best of his knowledge and belief, knows and has reason to believe to have the intent to resell or re-export Products to any place or country outside Territory.

Article 7. Minimum Purchase

Distributor shall guarantee the annual purchase of Products from Supplier not less than US $ 1,000,000 during the effective period of this Agreement. For this purpose, Products shall be deemed to have been purchased when the payment for Products has actually received by Supplier.

Article 8. Information and Report

During the effective period of this Agreement, both Supplier and Distributor shall from time to time and/or on the request of either party furnish each other with information and market reports to promote the sales of Products as much as possible. Distributor shall give Supplier quarterly such reports as inventory, or on market conditions and other activities of Distributor.

Article 9. Sales Promotion

Distributor shall exert his best efforts with diligence in advertising and promoting the sales of Products throughout Territory in an effective manner on his own account and Supplier shall provide Distributor free of charge with a reasonable quantity of advertising or sales promotion material such as advertising literature, catalogues, leaflets and other material, which Supplier deems useful to Distributor in his activities under this Agreement.

Article 10. Trademark

Distributor may use the trademark of Supplier during the effective period of this Agreement only in connection with the sale of Products, and after the termination of the Agreement, Distributor may use the trademark in connection with the sale of Products held by him in stock at the time of termination. Any and all rights granted herein by Supplier to Distributor shall terminate upon termination of this Agreement, and Distributor shall hence force cease to exercise any right or rights granted under this Agreement. In case Distributor has found that Supplier's trademarks, patents, copyrights or other industrial property rights are infringed upon by any third party, Distributor shall promptly inform Supplier of such infringement and assist Supplier in taking necessary steps to protect his rights effectively. In case any dispute and/or claim arises in connection with the above rights, Supplier shall have the right to cancel this Agreement at his own discretion and hold himself free from any liability arising therefrom.

Article 11. Duration

This Agreement shall be valid and remain in force for a period of three years commencing from the date appearing first above written signing by both Supplier and Distributor and can be extended for another period of three years on the same terms and conditions unless either of the parties hereto give the other party at least thirty days written notice to terminate the Agreement prior to the expiration of the original term.

Article 12. Cancellation or Termination

1) In case there is any breach of the provisions under this Agreement by either party during the effective period of this Agreement, the parties hereto shall first of all try to settle the matter in question as soon and amicable as possible to mutual satisfaction. Unless settlement is reached within thirty days after the notification in writing of the other party, such other party shall have the right to cancel this Agreement and the loss and damage sustained thereby shall be indemnified by the party responsible for such breach.
2) Further, in the event of bankruptcy, insolvency, dissolution, modification, consolidation, receivership proceedings affecting the operation of business or discontinuation of business for any reason and/or reorganization by the third party, either of the parties hereto shall have the absolute right to terminate this Agreement forthwith.

Article 13. Secrecy

All information made available under this Agreement shall be kept in strict confidence from any third party without prior consent in writing of the other party. The only exception, however, shall be the disclosures force by the laws, orders or regulations of Governments or Organizations having the necessary authorities and such disclosures shall not be deemed to constitute a violation of this Article under this Agreement.

Article 14. Entire Agreement

This Agreement constitutes the entire and only agreement between the parties hereto supersedes all previous negotiations and agreements relating to the sale of Products, shall not be modified or changed in any manner except by mutual consent in writing of a subsequent date signed by a duly authorized officer or representative of each of the parties hereto.

This Agreement is drawn up in both Chinese and English languages, each in two originals and one original of each is t be held by Supplier and Distributor. Both versions are equally effective.

SUPPLIER DISTRIBUTOR

Section 3 Supplements 知识补充

Useful Sentences On Agency

1. We should be glad if you would consider our application to act as your agency for the sale of your shoes.

如能考虑我们担任贵公司鞋子销售代理的申请，我们会很高兴。

2. We have already represented several other manufactures and trust you will allow us to give you similar services.

我们已是其他几家厂商的代理，深信也能为贵公司效力。

3. Please let us be notified whether you now represent any suppliers in the same line.

请告你方是否是其他同类产品供应商的代理。

4. We would like to know your plan for promoting the sales and the annual turnover you may realize in your market.

请把你们的推销计划和在你地市场可能达到的年营业额通知我公司。

5. Thank you for your offering us the selling agency in Japan for your manufactures.

谢谢你方授权我公司作为你们的产品在日本的销售代理。

6. After investigation and due consideration, we have decided to appoint you our agent in the district you defined, subject to the following terms and conditions.

经过调查和适当考虑，我们决定按照下列条件，在你们提出的地区内由你们担任我方代理。

7. We shall be glad to offer you a sole agency for the sale of our products in England.

我们很高兴由你们担任我方产品在英国的独家销售代理。

8. The question of agency is still under consideration.

代理问题仍在考虑中。

9. We accept your terms and conditions set out in the draft agency agreement and look forward to a happy and successful working relationship with you.

我们接受代理协议草案中提出的条件，并盼望同贵公司令人愉快的关系顺利发展。

10. While appreciating your inquiry for Leather Shoes, we wish to inform you that this term is under the exclusivity of ABC Co. In you district. We regret being unable to make you an offer direct at present. You may contact them for your requirements.

感谢你们对皮鞋的调查，但由于该项商品在贵地已由 ABC 公司独家代理，目前不能直接报盘，请同他们联系订货。

11. We would suggest that we leave aside the problem of agency until circumstances necessitate doing so.

我们建议，暂把代理问题搁置一下，等有此需要时再谈。

12. As regards the question of sole agency, in our opinion, we both had better leave it in abeyance pending the development of business.

关于独家代理问题，我们的意见是，双方最好暂且不谈，留待交易发展后再说。

13. We suggest a trial period of one year. If everything turns out satisfactory, we can renew the agreement on its expiry.

我们建议试行一年。倘全都同意，可在协议期满时续订。

14. We have already appointed Messrs…as our agent in your territory.

我们已委托……公司为你地区的代理。

15. We have noticed that in canvassing for orders, you have more than once exceeded the limit of your district. We wish that it wouldn’t happen again as it is against the stipulations in our agreement.

我们注意到，在招揽订单中你方曾不止一次超越你代理的地区范围，希望不再发生这类违反协议规定的事情。

16. We should be interested in acting as your sole agen’t. We would be doing better if we developed some kind of sales network there.

我们很乐意做贵公司的独家代理人。如果我们在那里打开一些销售网络，我方可以做得更好。

17. I propose a sole agency agreement for bicycles for period of 3 years.

我建议订一个专销自行车的为期三年的独家代理协议。

18. How can we appoint you as our sole agent for such a small quantity?

订货量如此少，我们怎能请你方做独家代理呢?

19. When opportunity matures, we will consider making you our exclusive agent for the U.K.

当机会成熟时，我们将考虑委托你方为我公司在英国的独家代理。

20. Don’t you think the annual turnover for a sole agent is rather conservative?

对独家代理来讲，这样的年营业额，你不认为太保守吗?

21. I have come again to renew our sole agency agreement for another 3 years.

我这次再访是想把我们的独家代理协议延长 3 年。

22. I hope you'll spare no efforts to promote the sale of our products so as to pave the way for renewing the agency agreement when it expires at the end of this year.

希望贵公司能尽力促进销售，为协议在今年年底期满后续订铺平道路。

23. Our agency agreement calls for a timely market report.

我们的代理协议要求你方及时递交一份市场报告。

24. If you appoint us as your agent, we can work up a big demand for your products at our end.

如果你们指定我方做代理，我方可以在本地为贵公司产品创造很大的需求。

25. I hope we can see eye to eye about the other terms of the agency then.

希望到那时我们能在代理协议的其他条款上取得一致意见。

26. According to the power the principal has delegated to a selling agent, the agent may just introduce the potential customer to the principal or actually negotiate and conclude the contract between the two parties. They have the following characteristics:

按照委托人授予代理人的权利，销售代理可能只负责向委托人介绍潜在客户或者实际谈判、签订双方之间的合同。代理人有以下几个特点：

27. We inform you that, as our agreement with Messrs.B. & S. will come to an end on the 4th April, they will cease to represent us after date, and we appointed as their successor Mr. A.G., who will take up the agency from 5th April.

我公司与 B.S 公司的协议将于 4 月 4 日期满，自即日起该公司不再是我方代理。为此特任命 AG 先生为下任代理商，并从 4 月 5 日起开始代理业务。

28. You will be pleased to notice that this consignment will consist of an assortment of fancy goods.

你方定会发现，此寄售商品花色搭配令人炫目。

29. The goods will be shipped by the s.s. "Tokai", sailing on the 7 December we enclose herewith a consignment invoice, and the B/L will follow by the next mail.

该货物将于 12 月 7 日由 “东海号” 货轮运往你地。兹寄上寄售发票一份，提单下次寄出。

30. Our friends inform us that you have a good connection in this trade, and that you import largely from this country, acting entirely upon their advice, we are sending you a consignment as a trial.

据本公司的客户告知，贵公司对此项生意有很好的关系，并且从我国大量进口。因此按照他们的建议，我方准备将产品寄给贵公司，请代为销售。

Exercises

Ⅰ. Make sentences with the following words and expressions.

appoint sb. Fo	give assistance to sb.
above-mentioned	for sale
exclusive agent	on sale
push the sales of sth.	draw up
to the contrary	on the contrary
act as	specialize in

at the get-acquainted stage	take sth into consideration
try out	annual turnover
valid	null and void

Ⅱ. Translate the following sentences into English.

1. 我们愿意担任你们现行出口商品的代理，因为我们拥有一个广阔的国内市场。

2. 我们深信，担任你们海外贸易的进口代理，能起重要作用。

3. 代理问题尚在考虑中，希望在现阶段继续努力推销我们的产品。

4. 我们认为讨论代理问题的时机尚未成熟。

5. 我们已委托 ABC 公司为你地区的代理。

6. 得知你方推销瓷器很有经验，非常荣幸能和你们打交道。

7. 对你们想担任独家代理的请求，我们正在仔细考虑。同时，我们很想了解你方推销我们产品的计划。

8. 在产品的广告方面我们尽了很大努力，营业额仍不能令人满意。

9. 我们所有做这类商品的代理都只拿 5%的佣金。

10. 如果情况令双方满意，协议有效期可以延长。

Ⅲ. Translate the following letter into English.

我们仔细研究了你方 9 月 10 日函，现愿与你方进一步商谈你方要求在苏格兰建立代理处的建议。你方为詹姆士·内尔公司工作的情况，我们不了解，但鉴于你方在苏格兰的贸易关系，我们认为你方在该地发展我们的业务是可以大有作为的。

我们的最后决定取决于条款是否合适。因你公司史密斯先生将于下月访问我地，我们愿与史密斯先生面谈而不愿进行旷日持久的通讯往来。为此，请告史密斯先生何时来面谈。

Chapter 13

International Trade Forms

Section 1 Business Knowledge 业务知识

在国际市场上，交易的方式多种多样，除了前一章讲的代理业务之外，对外贸易在交易方式上还有许多其他的选择。本章将继续介绍几种主要的贸易方式。

1. 寄售（Consignment）

这是一种有别于通常的代理销售的贸易方式。它是指由寄售人（委托人或货主）先将准备销售的货物运往国外寄售地，委托当地的代销人（受托人）按照寄售协议的条件，由代销人代替寄售人在当地市场上进行销售。货物售出后，再由代销人按协议规定的方式与寄售人结算货款的一种贸易方式。

同一般的进出口业务相比，寄售方式具有以下特点。

- 在寄售方式下，双方当事人是委托代销关系而不是买卖关系。代销人只为寄售人提供服务并收取佣金，其责任只限于在货物抵达后照管货物，尽力推销，并依照寄售人的指示处置货物；他不拥有货物的所有权，不承担寄售货物的任何风险与费用。
- 在寄售方式下，卖方出运货物在先，与买主成交在后。
- 寄售属于现货交易，一般是在货到目的地后由买主看货成交，并可以立即提货，很受买方的欢迎。
- 在寄售方式下，由于寄售货物在出售前的所有权属于寄售人，因此寄售人要承担货物在出售前的一切风险和费用；只有当货物出售后，风险及此后发生的费用才转由买主负担。可见，这是一种有利于买方的贸易方式。

2. 招投标（Invitation for Bids and Bid）

招标（Invitation to Tender）是指招标人（可以是买方，也可以是卖方）发出招标通告，提

出拟购或拟销商品的具体交易条件，邀请投标人（交易的另一方）在规定的时间、地点，按照一定的程序进行投标的行为。然后招标人择优选出中标人，与其达成商品交易的一种方式。投标（Submission of Tender）是指投标人应招标人的邀请，根据招标的要求和条件，在规定的时间向招标人发盘，争取中标并与其签约的行为。可见，招标与投标是一笔交易中缺一不可的两个方面。招标与投标业务的基本程序一般包括招标、投标、开标、签约 4 个环节。

招投标是一种常见的贸易方式，经常用于国际工程承包和大宗物资的采购业务。它与一般进出口贸易不同，其特点主要表现以下三个方面。

- 招标投标属于竞卖方式，即一个买方面对多个卖方

卖方之间激烈竞争使得买方在价格及其他条件上有较多的比较和选择，从而在一定程度上保证了采购商品的最佳质量及服务水平。

- 交易达成不经过一般的交易洽商程序

招标与投标一般不经过磋商，只按照招标人发出的招标通告所规定的条件由多家卖主投标，最后由招标人从中选择出对其最有利的条件进行购买。

- 投标人只能做一次性投标，没有讨价还价的余地

招标与投标是由招标人邀请递价，投标人应邀递价，中标与否、是否具有竞争性、能否被招标人所接受，取决于投标人所报的条件，一般没有讨价还价的余地。

3. 加工贸易（Processing Trade）

来料加工贸易指通常所讲的“三来一补”中的“三来”，即来料加工、来样制作和来件装配的总称，也称对外加工装配。这种贸易方式的具体做法是，委托方（外商）提供原材料、样品和零部件，由受托方（承接方或加工方）按其要求进行加工生产或装配成制成品、半制成品，然后交由委托方自行处置，受托方按照约定收取一定的加工费作为报酬。这种贸易本质上是一种委托加工，从原材料或配件的提供，到产品销售和利润的赚取，均属委托方所有。受托方仅负责加工装配，其得到的只是劳动力费用补偿。

4. 补偿贸易（Compensation Trade）

补偿贸易是在信贷的基础上进行的，又称产品返销，指交易的一方在对方提供信用的基础上进口设备、技术等，然后以该技术设备所产生的产品或其他产品或者提供劳务来分期抵付进口设备技术的价款及利息。根据补偿产品的不同可以将补偿贸易分为直接产品补偿、间接产品补偿和劳务补偿 3 种。直接产品补偿是补偿贸易中最基本的做法，指设备与技术的进口方以设备与技术生产出的直接产品来偿还设备与技术价款的本息。但由于在实际业务中，设备与技术的出口方往往并不需要这些直接产品，因此这种做法实际上比较少。间接产品补偿是补偿贸易中较常见的做法，被用来偿还进口设备与技术价款本息的不是直接产品，而是交易双方商定的其他商品。这实际上是互购方式中的一种情况，特别适用于进口设备与技术不生产有形的物质产品，或设备与技术的出口方不经销直接产品的情况。劳务补偿常见于与来料加工或来件装配业务相结合的补偿贸易业务，由承接对外加工、装配业务的单位分期以加工费偿还其进口设备、技术价款的本息。

5. 租赁贸易（Rental Trade）

租赁贸易是以商品在一定期间内的使用权作为贸易对象的交易方式，出租人（租赁方）与承租人（用户）在订立租赁契约的基础上，出租人以收取一定数量的租金为条件，将商品租给承租人在一定时期内使用，但设备仍归出租人所有。这种贸易方式，又称"租赁信贷"。

租赁贸易往往是三边贸易，即有 3 个当事人：一是物质供应方，即出售物质的厂商；二是出租方，即购买物质出租者；三是用户，即承租人，通常为生产或服务企业。

租赁贸易的一般做法是：出租人根据承租人的要求和愿望，购进有关设备，再将这些设备租给承租人使用。出租人负责将设备运至承租人指定的地点，并负责安装，交付使用。在租赁设备使用合约期限内，双方不得随意中止合同，出租人拥有设备所有权，并按合同向用户收取租金。承租人拥有充分的使用权，但对该物品有责任进行妥善保管和合理使用。

租期届满后，有 3 种处置方式：一是承租人将设备退还给租赁公司；二是用户可要求按原租约以少量租金继续租用；三是由承租人按双方商定的较低价格将租赁设备购为己有（称为购留，有时也可无偿取得）。

Section 2　Specimen Letters 样函

（1）

Dear Sirs,

Work Gloves[1]

We have the pleasure of informing you that we are airmailing you today 5 pieces of Grey Split Leather[2] and would ask you to arrange for us from this sample delivery, the following gloves:

Item P97242-as per sample enclosed.

This particular glove is required for the largest company in Australia, B.H.P., who is a mining company and also produces steel in their Port Kemble Steel Works. They require a glove to be made to the Australia Standards with certain specifications.

The leather palm[3] is to measure 205 mm[4] from the tip of the middle finger to the wrist[5].

We would appreciate it if you would make for us 10 pairs of Work Gloves to this style against the material which we are sending to you. However an important point to be remembered is that the size of the hand should be 125 mm wide so we can conserve[6] some leather. This of course also refers to the back of the hand. Please point[7] this out to the manufacturer.

We have a possibility of obtaining an order for this particular glove for 30,000 dozen and we would ship the leather to you from Japan. We are very keen to promote the supply of leather to you and as advised to the writer, you have the capacity[8] in your new factory to supply gloves.

Please be kind enough to rush the samples[9] made by you to us so they can be submitted to our customers here in Australia. Of this type of glove, we will require at least 20,000dozen, and we are quite sure your factory would be much interested to make these gloves for us.

Please also advise us of the manufacturing costs after completing the sample products.

We look forward to your earliest reply.

Yours truly,

Words, Expressions and Notes

1. Work Gloves 劳动手套
2. Grey Split Leather 灰色二层革
3. palm 手掌
4. mm 毫米，即 millimeter
5. from the tip of the middle finger to the wrist 从中指尖到手腕
6. conserve 节省，保存
7. point sth. out 指出
8. capacity 此处指生产能力
9. rush the samples 赶制样品

（2）

Dear Sirs,

Re: Compensation Trade[1] of Window Glass

This letter is regard to the Window Glass business between us. Our two sides sincerely worked in the past and the Window Glass has already been done successfully.

However, the quantity of products doesn't meet our requirements. This company wants to develop the trade and business further in this line. We now expect to begin working with you on the same basis of compensation trade.

For the USA market, we require very large quantities of Window Glass. We are certain that with your prompt cooperation, our purchases of Chinese Window Glass for sales in the USA market will very quickly increase to a large and substantial volume[2].

For your information, we are doing everything possible to cooperate in achieving our mutual goal of making the Window Glass Business a very large one. We have offered to purchase various equipment for your factory which will increase its products, improve quality and raise its efficiency[3]. We have offered to accept with your factory in making suggestion for better efficient packing and containerization[4]. The factory has been very cooperative and receptive[5] to our ideas.

During our next visit to China, we will discuss the appointment of our firm as the exclusive agent for Chinese Window Glass in the USA. Market. Since we have the question in the past, we expect the official appointment[6] of our firm as the exclusive agent will be made during our next trip.

Thank you for your prompt attention to the above.

Best regards.

Sincerely yours,

Words, Expressions and Notes

1. Compensation Trade 补偿贸易
2. to a large and substantial volume 大量的
3. efficiency 效率，效能
4. containerization 集装箱化，集装箱运输
5. cooperative and receptive 易合作的且容易接受的
6. official appointment 正式任命，正式指派

（3）

Dear Sirs,

We are interested in setting up a fruit processing line[1] in this city with equipment and technology to be leased[2] from you.

We are prepared to sign an agreement with you on the Maintenance Lease[3] basis, i.e. you will take care of serving, maintenance, replacement of spare parts[4], insurance and other expenses during the contracted term of the lease.

Besides, after expiration of the lease[5], we will have the option either to extend the lease or to purchase the equipment at a price to be fixed by experts jointly by both parties, which price shall not be higher than 10% of its original value[6].

We are looking forward to receiving your detailed information and favorable quotations.

Yours faithfully,

Words, Expressions and Notes

1. fruit processing line 水果加工生产线
2. lease 租赁、出租（既是动词也可做名词）
3. Maintenance Lease 维修租赁
4. spare parts 备用零件，散件
5. expiration of the lease 租期届满
6. original value 原值

（4）

Dear Sirs,

Our good friends Messrs Smith Co. of this city, with whom, we understand, you have extensive dealings , has suggested your name to us as being in a position to handle our consignment[1] of thirty cases Cotton Towels[2] as under, which please dispose of[3] as advantageously as possible[4].

Nos.1-11 1,000 dozen Cotton Towels, White;

Nos.11-21 1,000 dozen Cotton Towels, Cream;

Nos.21-3o 1,500 dozen Cotton Towels, Mixed.

These goods have been shipped to you by s.s "Xingyun", sailing from here today direct to your port. Enclosed we hand you copies of Consignment invoice[5] and B/L. please cover these goods by insurance till sold, as we do not wish to run any risk[6].

We should like to know something of the conditions governing[7] the sale of the goods in your city, so kindly give us all information you can when the goods reach you.

Very truly yours,

Words, Expressions and Notes

1. consignment 寄售，代销货物
2. cotton towels 棉布毛巾
3. dispose of 出售，处理
4. as advantageously as possible 尽可能使其有利
5. consignment invoice 寄售发票
6. run a risk 冒险
7. the conditions governing the sale of the goods 有关这种货物的销售情况

（5）

Dear Sirs,

We have received your letter of October 21 from which we learn that you are interested in establishing an Auto Parts[1] Factory in China in the form of a joint venture[2] and enquire about its feasibility[3].

You are probably aware that China has always persisted in an open policy[4] and taken a positive stand[5] with regard to introducing foreign investment, with a view to expanding economic cooperation and technical exchange with other countries on the basis of equality and mutual benefit. China permits foreign firms, enterprises and other economic organizations. At present, there are two types of joint ventures in operation[6] i.e. Equity Joint Venture[7] and Contractual Joint Venture[8]. Besides, joint exploration of China's offshore oil[9] is also in existence[10]. The main features of this form of business are joint investment, joint management and joint share in profits and losses, being beneficial to both parties in that they will enhance[11] business relations and cooperation.

On July 8, 2007, our government promulgated[12] "The Law of the People's Republic of China on Joint Venture Using Chinese and Foreign Investment[13]". Later on April 4, 2009, the third Session of the Seventh National People's Congress[14] made amendments to the law. In order to help you get fully acquainted[15] with the various provisions in connection with the joint venture, we take pleasure in enclosing a copy of the Law for your perusal and hope to have your comments.

Should you be interested in forming a joint venture with us, please let us know your tentative[16] idea as to the type of commodity, quantity of production, material procurement[17], sales channels and principal machinery and equipment, so that we can make a thorough study of your plan and go further into the matter.

We look forward to your reply with interest.

Yours faithfully,

Words, Expressions and Notes

1. Auto Parts 汽车零件
2. joint venture 合资企业、合营企业
3. feasibility 可行性
4. open policy 开放政策
5. positive stand 积极的态度
6. in operation 在实施中，生效
7. Equity Joint Venture 股权式合资企业
8. Contractual Joint Venture 契约式合资企业（即合作企业）
9. offshore oil 海洋石油，近海石油
10. in existence 存在
11. enhance 增强
12. promulgated 公布、颁布
13. The Law of the People's Republic of China on Joint Venture Using Chinese and Foreign Investment 《中华人民共和国中外合资经营企业法》
14. the third Session of the Seventh National People's Congress 七届人大三次会议
15. acquainted 使熟悉、了解
16. tentative 尝试性的，试验性的
17. procurement 采购，获得

（6）

Dear Sirs,

We thank you for your comments and proposals on our draft contract for the construction of the car assembly plant[1].

We are glad to tell you that having studied your amendments, we accept them on the whole[2] and are ready to introduce them into our contract.

At the same time we would like to restate[3] that in accordance with our contract for the construction of the car assembly plant on a "turn-key"[4] basis, the contractor[5] assumes full responsibility for the organization and execution of all civil works[6].

The civil works shall be carried out by both Chinese specialists and local firms engaged as subcontractors[7]. The works to be executed by your local firms shall be supervised by competent[8] Chinese specialists; the cost of their service is included in the contract price. We have already made enquiries about the firms and believe that they have sufficient experience, competence[9] and facilities[10] to execute the works we intend to entrust to them.

In view of the above we ask you to consider the present letter and if the contract is of interest to you, please let us know by cable when you are ready to sign it.

We look forward to your prompt reply.

Yours faithfully,

Words, Expressions and Notes

1. car assembly plant 汽车装配厂
2. on the whole 基本上、大体上
3. restate 重申，再次说明
4. "turn-key" 交钥匙工程

交钥匙工程指跨国公司为东道国造工厂或其他工程项目，一旦设计与建造工程完成，包括设备安装、试车及初步操作顺利运转后，即将该工厂或项目所有权和管理权的"钥匙"依合同完整地"交"给对方，由对方开始经营。因而，交钥匙工程也可以看成是一种特殊形式的管理合同。要完成交钥匙工程，不等于组织大而全的集团公司， 而是按市场经济规律，本着互惠互利、相互促进及相互支持的原则。要承担交钥匙工程，服务单位没有一定经济实力是不行的。

5. contractor 承包人
6. civil works 民用工程
7. subcontractor 分包者，分包合同承包人
8. competent 能胜任的、有能力的
9. competence 能力、技能
10. facilities 设备、设施

(7)

CHINA PETRO-CHEMICAL INTERNATIONAL COMPANY (SINOPEC INTL) INVITATION FOR BIDS FOR ANQING ACRYLIC FIBRE EQUIPMENT

BID NO. SINOPEC 03305

LOAN NO. PRC-1114

In accordance with the Loan Agreement between Chinese Government and Asian Development Bank(ADB) for ANQING Acrylic Fiber Project[1], Sinopec Int'L now invites bids[2] from eligible[3] suppliers from members of ADB for the supply of the following Goods to be financed with the proceeds[4] of ADB:

DCS Systems for Acrylonitrile and Acrylic Fiber Units[5] (Package No.11)

Refrigeration Equipment [6](Package N0. 20)

Stretch-breaking Machines[7](Package N0. 21)

Primary Gill Box[8], Balling Gill Box [9](Package No. 22)

(for Package No.11,only the eligible bidders[10] who have signed the secrecy[11] agreement with BP Chemicals America, Inc., can obtain the bidding documents[12] and are entitled to bid.)

Interested eligible bidders who are willing to participate in the bidding may obtain detailed information from the address below and inspect the bidding documents. A set of bidding documents may be purchased in the 4th floor at the address below between 9:00 am and 11:00 am (Sundays and holidays accepted) from February 16, 2008 or be promptly dispatched by express mail upon receipt of nonrefundable[13] payment of (RMB) 1800 Yuan (or US $300) plus US $50 postage fee.

The bids[14] should reach the address below before 16:00 on March 23, 2008 and will be opened publicly[15] by Sinopec Int'L at 9:00 am on March 24, 2008. Each bid package must be submitted in separate sealed envelope and be accompanied by a bid bond[16]. Those bids which are not accompanied by a bid bond will not be accepted.

Bids will be opened in Rm[17]. B0401 at the address below

The 3rd Petro-Chemical Department

China Petro-Chemical International Company

Hui Jin Office Building, No. 9 Beichenlong St.,

Chaoyang District, Beijing, China

P. O. Box: 9804

Post code: 100101

Telex: 22655 CPCCI CN

Tel: 4926647, 4926651

Fax: 4216621

Homepage:

E-mail:

Words, Expressions and Notes

1. ANQING Acrylic Fiber Project 安庆腈纶项目
2. invites bids 招标
3. eligible 有资格的，合适的
4. proceeds 此处是指收益、款项
5. DCS Systems for Acrylonitrile and Acrylic Fiber Units 丙烯腈、腈纶集散控制装置
6. Refrigeration Equipment 制冷设备
7. Stretch-breaking Machines 多区拉断直接成条机
8. Primary Gill Box 头道针梳机
9. Balling Gill Box 成球针梳机
10. bidders 投标人
11. secrecy 秘密、保密
12. bidding documents 投标文件
13. nonrefundable 不可退还的、不可归还的
14. bids 投标标书
15. be opened publicly 指公开开标
16. bid bond 投标保证金
17. Rm 房间，即 room

（8）招标通知

ABC Oil Tools & Service Ltd.

ABC Petroleum Supply Base

Shenzhen, P. R. C

Attn: Li Jiang

Dear Sirs,

INVITATION TO TENDER-TENDER No.HB-407

TENDER TITLE-SUPPLY OF DRILLING TOOLS[1]

You are hereby invited by GALL Petroleum Development (Purchaser) to submit a Tender for the above Goods and Services, in accordance with this Letter of Invitation[2] and the Invitation to tender Document[3] transmitted herewith. It is understood that if you Tender is accepted, Purchaser will issue a Purchase Order on the terms and Conditions contained in this Invitation to Tender and your offer, for the provision of DRILLING TOOLS and associated equipment and services[4]. One copy of the Invitation to Tender Documents is enclosed herewith and comprises:

Section A　Instructions to Tender

Section B　form of Tender

Section C　Conditions of Purchase

Summary of work

The goods and services, described in this Invitation to Tender Agreement is to provide drilling tools and ancillary[5] equipment/services in supply of Purchasers drilling activities in contract area[6] 15/24 offshore People's Republic of China in the South China Sea. The firm Scope of supply will be for the provision of drilling tools and ancillary equipment/services with an option for standby tools at a later date. The intended date for spudding[7] the firm well is early November 2008.

Provisions are listed briefly:

— provision of fishing tools[8]

— provision of back up fishing tools[9]

— provision of standby tools and running tools[10]

— provision of service engineer[11] (optionally)

If you can not or do not wish to submit a Tender for the services described in this Invitation to Tender then please return the documentation to us in accordance with the requirements of the Instructions to Tenders stating that you do not wish to submit an offer.

Tendering Details

You are requested to check the contents of the Invitation to Tender package for completeness when you receive it and then return the enclosed Tender Acknowledgment[12].

Tenders shall be submitted in accordance with the Instructions to Tenders and Form of Tender. Any

deviation from the requirements of these Instructions may render your Tender invalid[13].

Your Tender must be received no later than 12:00 o'clock on Friday, 3rd July, 2007(closing date[14]) at the office of the Purchaser in Shenzhen, People's Republic of China.

Tenders shall be forwarded by courier service or delivered safe-hand[15], sealed and clearly addressed and marked on the outside in accordance with the Instructions to Tenders.

Please note that uninvited visits to our offices to discuss the Invitation to Tender are not acceptable and that all contacts shall be in writing (by letter or fax) as set out in the Instructions to Tenders.

The Tenderer shall consider this Letter of Invitation and the enclosed Invitation to Tender documents to be confidential, and the contents shall not be divulged[16] to any person or persons not directly concerned with the preparation of the tender.

This Invitation to Tender is subject to your signing and returning to the Purchaser the Tender Acknowledgment contained within Section A.

Words, Expressions and Notes

1. DRILLING TOOLS 钻探工具
2. Letter of Invitation 邀请函
3. Invitation to tender Document 招标文件
4. associated equipment and services 关联设备与服务
5. ancillary 辅助的
6. contract area 合同区域
7. spud 挖掘，铲锄
8. fishing tools 打捞工具、捕鱼工具
9. back up fishing tools 辅助打捞工具
10. standby tools and running tools 备用工具和常用工具
11. service engineer 维护工程师
12. Tender Acknowledgment 投标确认书
13. render your Tender invalid 将你方投标视为无效
14. closing date 截止日期
15. safe-hand 安全可靠的人士
16. divulged 泄露（秘密）

（9）回复——同意投标

To: CALL Petroleum Development

Attn: Mr. Tammy Hutchinson/Head of Contract and Supply

From: Shenzhen ABC Oil Tools Ltd.

Li Jiang/General Manager

Re: INVITATION TO TENDER – TENDER NO. HB-403

Tender Title: SUPPLY OF DRILLING TOOLS

Dear Sirs,

We acknowledged receipt of your Invitation to Tender Documents for the above and we agree to maintain confidentiality[1] in regard to the Invitation to Tender and the contents thereof.

We confirm we intend to submit a bona fide[2] tender in accordance with all your requirements by the date and time stated in your letter of Invitation to Tender.

Our details are given below:

Name: Shenzhen ABC Oil Tools Ltd.

Address: ABC Petroleum Supply Base D3—4

ABC Shenzhen 518068 PRC

Tel No: (0755)6694302, (0755)6851356

Fax No:(0755)6694008

Contact person: Li Jiang/General Manager

Please accept our best wishes for quick and successful completion to your planned program.

Li Jiang

General Manager

Words, Expressions and Notes

1. maintain confidentiality 保密
2. bona fide 真实的、真诚的，合法的

（10）投标书（abridged）

Proposal No. FAS20020008

Submitted to

Gall Petroleum Development

12—16 Floors, Offshore Petroleum Building

No.1, Industrial Road, Shekou

Shenzhen, PRC

For

Tender No. HB—403

By

Shenzhen ABC Oil Tools Ltd.

Address: Chiwan Petroleum Supply Base D3—4

Chiwan, Shenzhen 518068 PRC

Tel No: (0755)6694302

(0755)6694529

Fax No: (0755)6694008

Web Site: http://www.shenzhen ABC.com

E-mail: fetool @ szptt.net.cn

Contents

DATE: Jun. 30.2008

GALL PETROLEUM DEVELOPMENT

12 –16 Floors, Offshore Petroleum Building

No.1, Industrial Road, Shekou

Shenzhen, Guangdong Province

P. R. of China

Attention: Mr. TAMMY HUTCHINSON/ Head of Contract and Supply

Subject: Tender HB-403

For Drilling Tools/Equipment and Services

Gentlemen:

We appreciate the opportunity to put in bid[1] for providing drilling tools/equipment & services to your company. In the past years we have enjoyed working with all groups[2] in China drilling area and are very hopeful that your new operation in the South China Sea will be very profitable.

We have carefully examined your invitation letters to tender "Tender HB-403 Supply of Drilling Tools" and form of contract entitled "Contractor Service Contract[3]" and related documents. We hereby submit our proposal[4] No FAS020008 to bid Tender HB-403 for drilling tools/equipment and service in accordance with the terms of Tender document.

Shenzhen ABC Oil Tools is also looking forward to a long term profitable future in service of the oil industry in this area and therefore invested heavily in setting up a fully capable tool rental service[5] as drilling operation expand. Most of our drilling tools are available[6] in our ABC Base. Our offshore operation supervisors are very experienced. We also have complete machine shop service[7] in ABC Base and it is easily and quickly to maintain and repair for all related equipment.

Enclosed please find 3 copies of our price list prepared for drilling tools/equipment and services tender No.HB-403 including also our explanation and support documents. If any points that are not clear, we will be glad to explain in more details at any time.

Our company's information is given below:

Company Name: Shenzhen ABC Oil Tools Ltd.

Address: ABC Petroleum Supply Base D3—4

ABC, Shenzhen, PRC

Tel No: (0755)669432, (0755)6694529

Fax No.: (0755)6694008

Website: http:// www. Fetool. Com.cn

e-mail: fetool @ public. Szptt. net.cn

Contact persons: Li Jiang/General Manager

Wang Xing/Engineer

Liu Guo/ Assistant to General Manager

Welcome you to our warehouse in ABC Base for visiting and inspecting of the equipment.

Yours sincerely,

Li Jiang

Words, Expressions and Notes

1. put in bid 指投标
2. groups 这里是指公司
3. Contractor Service Contract 劳务承包合同
4. proposal 方案，意向书
5. tool rental service 工具租赁服务
6. available 有现货可以供给
7. machine shop service 设备维修服务站

Section 3 Supplements 知识补充

Useful Sentences On Invitation for Bids and Bid

1. The date , hour and place for latest delivery of bids by the bidder, and of the bid opening, should be announced in the invitation to bid, and all bids should be opened at the stipulated time.

投标人投标截止的日期、时间和地点，以及开标的日期、时间和地点都要在招标时公布。

2. The time allowed for preparation of bids should depend on the magnitude and complexity for the contract.

投标所需准备时间需视合同的规模和难易程度而定。

3. Extension of validity of bids should normally not be requested; if , in exceptional circumstances, an extension is required, it should be requested of all bidders before the expiration date and Bank should be notified.

一般来说，不应延长投标有效期限。如果在特殊情况下，需要延长投标期限，就要在终止日期之前向所有投标人提出要求，并通知银行。

4. Bidders are expected to read carefully all the provisions set forth in the ITC bid document including the Technical Specifications.

希望投标者仔细阅读 ITC 标书中包括技术指标在内的所有条款。

5. Catalog sheets submitted with the bid must be "originals" and not copies; drawings, schematics and/or circuit diagrams and printed circuit board diagrams must be legible; operation manuals and maintenance instructions must be complete; application references should be as comprehensive as possible.

投标提供的产品样本必须是原件而不是复印件；图纸、略图、电路图、印制电路板必须清楚易读；操作手册和维修细则应当完整；应用参考资料应尽可能全面。

6. For items requiring installation, calibration, initial operation test running and domestic or abroad training, the respective Technical Specifications will state such requirements.

对于那些要求安装、校验、试运转和国内、国外培训的品目，将在标书中加以说明。

7. The seller means the firm or entity supplying the goods and services under the contract.

"卖方"系指根据合同提供货物和服务的公司或实体。

8. The seller shall guarantee that the goods are brand new, unused, fully tested and made of the best adequate materials, with first class workmanship, and complies in all respects with quality, specification and performance stipulated in the contract.

卖方应保证货物是崭新的未使用过的，并且是第一流的工艺以最优良的合适的材料制造成的，并完全符合合同规定的质量、规格和性能的要求。

9. In case the seller is liable for the discrepancies and a claim is lodged by the buyer within the time limit of inspection and quality guarantee period as stipulated in Articles 12 and 13 the seller shall settle the claims upon the agreement of the buyer in one or combination of the following ways.

如卖方对这些差错负有责任，买方根据合同第 12 条和第 13 条规定的在检验期限内和质量保证期内提出赔偿，卖方应在征得买方同意后采用下列一种或多种方式解决索赔。

10. The bidding documents should state clearly whether contracts will be awarded on the basis of unit prices for work performed or goods supplied or of a lump sum of the contract, according to the nature of goods or works to be provided.

招标文件应清楚说明，根据所提供的货物或工程建筑的性质，合同是以分项价格（完成的建筑或提供担任货物），还是以总价格为基础制定的。

11. The organization form of Joint Venture Company is a limited liability company.

合营公司的组织形式是有限责任公司。

12. If you agree to our proposal of a barter trade, we'll give you paper in exchange for your timber.

如果你方同意我们进行易货贸易的建议， 我们将用纸与你们交换木材。

13. Shall we sign a triangle trade agreement?

我们订一个三角贸易协议好吗？

14. Compensation trade is, in fact, a kind of loan.

补偿贸易实际上是一种信贷。

15. We may agree to do processing trade with you.

我们同意与你们进行来料加工贸易。

16. We wonder whether you do counter-trade.

我们不知道你们是否做抵偿（对销）贸易。

17. I came about the possibility of undertaking compensation trade with you. To be frank with you, compensation trade is considered preferable by our side to save foreign exchange.

我研究了和你们做补偿贸易的事。坦白说，由于你节省外汇，我方青睐补偿贸易。

Exercises

Ⅰ. Translate the following into English.

寻找贸易伙伴是开展国际贸易的前提。在传统贸易方式下，无论是买方还是卖方，为了寻找合适的贸易伙伴，必须通过咨询公司、银行、行业组织或亲自到国外考察等方式进行，费用高、耗时长、收集到的信息量有限。以互联网及其技术为核心的电子商务不同于以往传统的方式，如企业可以通过互联网向全球市场发布信息和产品广告；可以通过建立自己的网站或借助有关国际贸易电子商务平台，向全球范围内的潜在客户提供有关产品和服务信息和在线目录，吸引相关客户咨询洽商贸易；企业可以主动上网搜索各种经贸信息，在全球范围内寻找理想的贸易伙伴和更多的商机。

电子商务方便快捷及低成本的宣传、促销、物色贸易伙伴的功能，在一定程度上削弱了传统展览会、博览会的作用。各国的进出口企业足不出户就可以找到理想的贸易伙伴。

Ⅱ. Translate the following into Chinese.

The prevailing mode of building large or complex civil works or turnkey project adopted internationally is through invitation of international bidding.

Conditions of a contract for construction project vary with different natures of projects. For example, some contracts are drawn up for civil works only such as the construction of highway, bridge, reservoir, stadium, etc., some not only for the construction of a plant but also for the erection of machinery even including technical training. Different contracts require different conditions. Generally speaking, a contract for construction of a plant including erection of machinery and technical training usually consists of the following articles:

1. Visa
2. Performance bond
3. Prepayment
4. Progress payment
5. Penalties
6. Warranties, maintenance period
7. Inspection taking-over test
8. Suspension of work

9. Variations in the work
10. Transfer of know-how
11. Training
12. Insurance
13. Completion of works
14. Governing law
15. Force majeure
16. Settlement of disputes

Ⅲ. Translate the following sentences into English.

1. 本公司合同经双方签字后 7 天内，由乙方按工程总费用的 10%交付履约保证金，或提供即期的不可撤销的银行担保，工程结束后由甲方无息退还乙方。

2. 承包的工程项目全部完成并经验收后，由乙方书面通知甲方之日起 14 天内，甲方除扣下工程总费用的 5%作为总保留金将于工程交付后一个月支付给乙方外，其余工程总费用，一次性结清付给乙方。

3. 在整个施工过程中，乙方须服从甲方工程顾问的决定，乙方对工程顾问在施工现场的检查、监督与校核应提供方便。但工程顾问的上述工作并不减轻乙方对于施工应负的责任。

4. 若甲方拖延支付乙方工程款项时，应根据拖欠的金额和天数按月息 15%支付利息，工程顺延。由于未按时支付工程款而造成的停工损失，由甲方负责。

5. 乙方应在本合同规定的期限内完成本工程，如有延误则须向甲方支付罚款，每日的罚款为剩余工程费用的 1%，但罚款的总额不得超过合同总金额的 5%。

6. 甲方应在合同签署后 15 天内付给乙方 15%的预付款，预付款的偿还，按其所占合同金额的相同比例从甲方对乙方的已完成的部分工程应付款额中扣除。

7. 乙方安排的施工进度和顺序，事前应征得甲方工程顾问的同意方为有效，工程顾问必要时可以在该工程项目施工前 5 天修改图纸，乙方应相应调整工程施工计划，如因修改图纸引起工程量的增加其费用超过合同总价的 5%时，则可相应增加工程费用。

8. 乙方如发生下列任何一点时，应及时采取补救措施，否则甲方有权随时取消本合同，为此而使甲方遭受的经济损失，由乙方负责赔偿：

A. 甲方如发现乙方所承包的工程存在严重的质量问题时；

B. 工程不能于合同规定时间内完成，逾期达 30 天时；

C. 如果甲方发现乙方使用的材料中有不符合图纸要求，而乙方又强行擅自采用时；

如乙方违背上述条款，而又阻碍新的承包人工作时，甲方将依法起诉。

9. 工程验收后半个月，乙方须负责指定时间内将其所用的一切机械设备，材料等搬出甲方工地，否则甲方有权代为搬走，一切费用由乙方负担。

参考文献

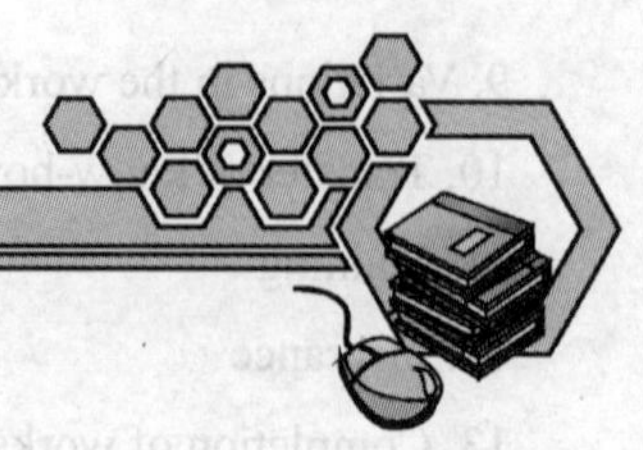

[1] 易露霞，王娜娜，陈原. 外贸英语函电. 北京：清华大学出版社，2008.

[2] 兰天. 外贸英语函电. 大连：东北财经大学出版社，2007.

[3] 程同春. 新编国际商务英语函电. 南京：东南大学出版社，2002.

[4] 陆墨珠. 国际商务英语函电. 北京：中国对外经济贸易出版社，2002.

[5] 徐美荣. 外贸英语函电. 北京：对外经济贸易大学出版社，2007.

[6] 尹小莹，等. 外贸英语函电. 西安：西安交通大学出版社，2007.

[7] 冯祥春，刘卓林. 外贸英语函电句型 150 例. 南京：南京大学出版社，1993.

[8] 江澄. 外贸英语用法词典. 北京：北京科学技术出版社，1989.

[9] 诸葛霖. 外贸英文书信. 北京：对外经济贸易大学出版社，2000.

[10] 曹元寿. 外贸英语函电读写译. 北京：北京理工大学出版社，2000.

[11] 简新亚. 英文合同协议“快易通”. 北京：清华大学出版社，2003.

[12] 林泽拯. 对外贸易出口单证实务. 北京：中国对外经济贸易出版社，1994.

[13] 徐良霞. 实用英语教你写合同. 北京：北京航空航天大学出版社，2004.

[14] 修露. 外贸英语函电. 大连：大连理工大学出版社，1996.

[15] 董宏祥. 外贸跟单实务. 上海：上海财经大学出版社，2007.

[16] 曲得清. 外贸英语函电. 大连：东北财经大学出版社，1998.